Success in a Low-Return World

Michael J. Oyster

Success in a Low-Return World

Using Risk Management and Behavioral Finance to Achieve Market Outperformance

palgrave
macmillan

Michael J. Oyster
Chief Investment Strategist
Cincinnati, OH, USA

ISBN 978-3-319-99854-1   ISBN 978-3-319-99855-8   (eBook)
https://doi.org/10.1007/978-3-319-99855-8

Library of Congress Control Number: 2018960925

Cover image © anyaberkut/ iStock/ Getty Images Plus
Cover design by Akihiro Nakayama
Edited by Catherine Lennon
Author portrait: Peggy Joseph Photography

This Palgrave Macmillan imprint is published by the registered company Springer Nature Switzerland AG
The registered company address is: Gewerbestrasse 11, 6330 Cham, Switzerland

For Catherine

Preface

In 1999, I was a brash, 29-year-old know-it-all investment analyst. I remember remarking to my CIO, at the time Chris Meyer, that it was interesting to think that never again in our lifetimes would we see the index value of the Dow Jones Industrial Average (DJIA) below 10,000. The stock market was on a tear and I was caught up in the excitement of the dot-com boom. Chris, who had then, and retains today, a galvanized understanding of investment history, knew such bravado was foolhardy and tamped down my enthusiasm. I brushed it off as a guy just being a Debbie downer (he is anything but). Not only was Chris correct in his skepticism, he was doubly so. Within three years, the DJIA had dropped to below 7300. Then after moving back above 10,000 and pressing close to 15,000 a few years later, it crashed again falling to the unimaginably low level of 6547 on March 9, 2009.

Boy was I wrong. The best lessons are those hardest learned. From that experience and others like it, I learned that human emotion and natural cognitive biases can inhibit the quality of investment decisions. To this day, my friend Chris brings up my late 1990s misplaced optimism about once every three times we get together. He probably thinks about it every time but mercifully keeps it to himself 67 percent of the time. I owe him a debt of gratitude.

For 19 years, I was part of an organization known as FEG Investment Advisors, serving as an investment consultant and provider of outsourced investment solutions. I studied markets and the economy and met with/conducted in-depth research on hundreds of different investment managers. Prior to FEG, I spent five years with options-advisory firm Schaeffer's Investment Research, where I conducted quantitative analysis on options and volatility metrics while managing a number of proprietary investment products. The combination of those experiences provides me with a unique vantage point from which to view the world of investing. I've seen a lot of investment strategies that work well, some that are truly unique and differentiated. I've seen others that provide nothing worth paying for. I've seen some investment strategies blow up in spectacular fashion and I've even seen a few frauds. Covering the entire spectrum of the investment universe, studying the history of markets and economies, and doing so with a background in derivatives gives me a distinct perspective on the past, present, and likely future of investing.

I don't have all the answers, but I do know that if events were to unfold in a way that provided investors with the same US stock market returns in the future that had been enjoyed in the near decade following the end of the *Great Financial Crisis* (GFC), it would be truly monumental and highly unexpected. Far more likely is a lower-return world, maybe not like the lost decade following the end of the dot-com bubble where the US stock market failed to break even, but perhaps positive returns that don't keep up with the long-term averages of 11 percent or so. With an objective view, we should expect 5 to 7 percent.

We start out with a treatment of what actually makes up a stock market's performance number. Looking at the components that sum to total return, a healthy dose of skepticism is necessary. We then spend time looking at stock pickers, the common philosophy shared by many, and the vast challenges they face. This is not meant to suggest that stock-picking active managers are mistaken in what they do, rather to shed light on how challenging their world has become in recent years. And it is becoming even more so.

Most of the discussion in this book is localized to the large capitalization subset of the US stock market. I will grant that stock picking and security selection in general stands a better chance of adding value in less efficient marketplaces such as micro caps and frontier markets. But considering the astronomical amount of money that remains in large-cap US stock-picking funds, despite the surge of assets flowing out of them into passive index funds, it's a discussion worth having.

Interspersed throughout this work is the concept of *behavioral finance*, the idea that psychology can help identify how and when ingrained human instincts can inhibit decision-making. Chapter 6 takes a deep dive into cognitive biases featuring a really smart categorization scheme from Buster Benson.

You will also notice that I frequently cite academic research to support a point. I am a person who needs evidence and can be more comfortable entering the dark unknown that follows an investment decision when I am holding the hand of a demonstrated bit of statistical significance. This is why Chap. 9: Intuition (of Part II: Solutions) is so important and will provide somewhat of an interlude in financial theory between the first and second half of the book. The chapter includes a discussion of intuition, more specifically, the use of *practical intuition* and how gut feel can help with decision-making written by my wife, Catherine Lennon. Intuition can provide guidance beyond that which can be found in the data alone. Investors who are able to draw upon it in a positive way give themselves an additional tool and improve their chances of outperforming.

While fees and regulations make the stock picker's job all the more difficult, I wouldn't simply suggest that your only recourse as an investor is to buy an index fund and cheerfully accept the market's return less a fee. We can do better than that. That's not to say indexing is a bad idea; it has shown to outperform the average active manager. We will spend some time on that. Additionally, outperforming the stock market isn't the only way to add value in a low-return world. There are some interesting big picture asset allocation ideas worth discussing as well as how applying the concept of momentum can help with subcategory asset-allocation decisions.

And there are others. Opportunities to outperform are available and are perhaps more numerous than you think. Private equity, high active share stock picking, and smart beta, all offer the potential for outperformance. We will spend some time with each.

Among the concluding points is a statement to which I assign a staunch belief—the Volatility Risk Premium, the persistent overpricing of options, stands as the most significant, untapped investment resource available today. What that is and how it can be monetized are a big part of later chapters, with a conclusion focused on portable alpha—a terrific strategy shunned by many investors who were burned by its misuse, but one worthy of our attention in the future as we seek opportunities to outperform in what stands to be a low-return world.

Thank you for reading. I hope the time doing so is productive and enjoyable.

Michael

Acknowledgments

I feel tremendously grateful for the opportunity to acknowledge the people who mean so much to me and have meant so much to this project.

First and foremost, my wife Catherine. Your love, support, and encouragement to write this book helped make it happen and your contributions to it are co-author worthy. You stepped in and applied your attention to detail and expert editing skill, significantly improving the quality of the work. The insight you provided for Chap. 9 on intuition added tremendous value and differentiation while contributing meaningfully to the investment narrative.

I would also like to thank my mentor and friend, Chris Meyer. Your stalwart commitment to the established fundamentals of investing continues to inspire. Thank you also to Price Headley and Bernie Schaeffer who opened the world of options and derivatives for me, as well as the Cboe's wealth of knowledge, Matt Moran.

A big thank you to the many smart and dedicated professionals at FEG Investment Advisors including but certainly not limited to Greg Dowling, Alan Lenahan, Greg Houser, Mike O'Connor, Dan Regan, Gary Price, Andy Boedecker, Nolan Bean, Tony Festa, Keith Berlin, Christian Busken, Devinne Kelly, Matt Schwier, Mark Koenig, Phil Scherrer, Mike Aluise, Brian Hooper, Jere Whiteley, Brad Derflinger, and Scott Stumpf.

Thank you to the many educators and researchers for your insight and work having either guided me, inspired me, or both including Eugene Fama, Ken French, Myron Scholes, Burton Malkiel, Mark Carhart, Rob Arnott, Cliff Asness, Roni Israelov, Toby Moskowitz, Robert Shiller, Jeremy Siegel, Daniel Kahneman, Richard Thaler, and last but certainly not least, my high school math teacher, Fred Feichter, who taught me the importance of critical thinking.

To my children and stepchildren, Zach, Nick, Lucas, and Makena, thank you for being the amazing individuals each of you are! To my parents, Jim and Betty Oyster, thank you for love and guidance in both word and deed. Thank you to my siblings, Brian Oyster, Greg Oyster, and Erin Keller and their families and to my many friends including Charles Conour, Mike Muse, and most notably Clint Hines, thank you for your sage advice and can-do attitude.

Contents

List of Figures

List of Tables

Part I

Challenges in Investing

1

The Future Isn't What It Used to Be

Why do we invest? Why do we deploy capital into a marketplace with the risk of loss? In most cases, the main reason is to have more money than we have today at some future date. There have been times when bonds have been great for generating regular income, but most people who need their money to grow rely on stocks. For many years, investors seeking asset growth have placed their trust in large cap stocks and, assuming they remained invested long enough, these investors have usually been rewarded.

At the most fundamental level, stocks are ownership shares in companies. Stock prices generally ascend through time as the economy grows, with companies reaping the benefits of improved efficiency and technology. Barring worldwide economic collapse and a termination of all technological advancement, the economy should continue to grow (save the occasional recession), and stock prices will continue to rise. An investment in stocks will not grow *all* the time, but we can expect that it will grow *over* time.

Disregarding the specific stock investment for the moment, let's focus on the market in general; in this case, the US market of large cap stocks. An investment in the stock market, regardless of how and where it is made, will be impacted by factors that affect the market as a whole. In fact, most of the feast or famine an investor actually experiences is caused by movements of the stock market, while only a fraction of their total return is due to the unique characteristics of the investment itself. Therefore, we need to know a few things about the US stock market before we invest there. The amount of wealth we will see at some future date depends highly on what happens to the market in general.

© The Author(s) 2018
M. J. Oyster, *Success in a Low-Return World*,
https://doi.org/10.1007/978-3-319-99855-8_1

Even if you include the bear market in stocks surrounding the Great Financial Crisis (GFC), many of today's investors have enjoyed one of the healthiest bull markets in history. Nevertheless, past performance may be giving investors a false sense of optimism. In the same way that those who don't understand history are doomed to repeat it, investors (as well as the professionals who advise them) must understand that the recent past has been far better than the long-term past, and quite possibly, better than the future will be as well. Although tempting, projecting the short-term past into forecasts of the future may result in a painful bear market in expectations, in that what you ultimately earn is far less than what you expected.

Stock Market Performance Building Blocks

No one can consistently and accurately predict the future movements of the stock market, but we can look at the building blocks that produce its performance. As complex as stock markets are, the total return of the major indexes can be boiled down to just three things:

1. Earnings growth (including inflation)
2. Dividend yields
3. Changes in price (price-earnings or P/E ratio)

Some investors break out earnings growth into real growth and inflation and/or consider the market impact of share buybacks separately, but for our purposes, we will focus on these three building blocks. A value for each exists for every stock in a market, so when looking at the total market, we can add all three for all of the stocks in that particular market. The sum of the three building blocks represents the market's total return. Certainly the global investment universe is comprised of multiple marketplaces, but for the purpose of discussion here, the term "market" is large cap stocks in the United States, generally represented by the Standard & Poor's 500 Index (S&P 500). The approximate relative contribution from each of the three building blocks for the S&P 500 (the market) from 1880 through 2017 has been as follows (Fig. 1.1).

Notice how earnings, the largest contributor, represented over half of the long-term return.

The influence of the same three building blocks is shown below, only this time they represent their respective contributions to the market's total return during a period of exceptionally strong performance, 2008 through 2017 (Fig. 1.2).

1880-2017

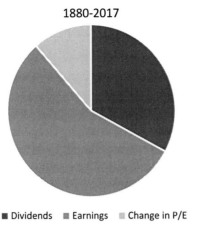

■ Dividends   ■ Earnings   ▨ Change in P/E

Fig. 1.1 Approximate Contributions to US Stock Market Total Return, 1880–2017. Data source: Robert Shiller, Stock Market Data Used in *Irrational Exuberance*, Princeton University Press, updated 2000, 2005, 2015

2008-2017

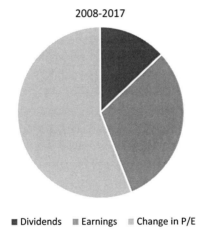

■ Dividends   ■ Earnings   ▨ Change in P/E

Fig. 1.2 Approximate Contributions to US Stock Market Total Return, 2008–2017. Data source: Robert Shiller, Stock Market Data Used in *Irrational Exuberance*, Princeton University Press, updated 2000, 2005, 2015

Although change in price, P/E expansion, was the least important contributor to the stock market's total return since 1880, it was the most important one from 2008 through 2017. Dividends and earnings were relatively stable, while an expanding P/E ratio drove returns. So not only can we boil stock market returns down to three data points, we only need one of them, P/E expansion, to explain the nearly decade-long bull market through 2017. If P/E expansion coincided with tremendous stock market returns, how might a contraction affect performance and how might that come about? Before answering those questions, let's first look back at the building and then the bursting of the technology and telecom stock bubble of the late-1990s.

P/E Ratios and the Bull Market of the 1990s

In May 1982, the S&P 500 Index was priced barely more than seven times earnings. At this level stocks were selling at fire sale prices. By the time the technology-driving bull market of the late 1990s was coming to an end, the P/E ratio had risen to over 30, its highest level ever.

Why did stocks become so pricey? Demographics certainly played a role. From 1976 through 1996, the number of Americans in the workforce between the ages of 35 and 54 (prime saving and stock-buying years) rose by more than 80 percent.[1] Just as in any auction, the greater the demand for something, the higher the price people will be willing to pay for it.

The US government also played a role. Fearing future problems with Social Security, the government created investment programs such as 401(k) savings plans and Roth IRAs, which gave average Americans an incentive not only to invest in the markets but to remain invested, even when times got tough. Continued stock buying, as a result of steady inflows from retirement savings vehicles and sharp penalties for selling, played a major role in the stock market's late twentieth-century ascent.

Both demographics and government incentives led to increased demand, which pushed P/E ratios higher during the 1980s and 1990s, but another important (albeit less quantifiable) reason stocks rose to unprecedented heights had to do with the burning desire of investors. Behavior and preferences, if strong enough, can heavily influence demand and ultimately, price.

The late-1990s represented a period in which fundamental truths—the ideas that investors had relied on for decades to help them make decisions—were being pitched out the window. For a time, it really didn't seem to matter whether a company was actually profitable or not, or if it was priced fairly relative to earnings. But ultimately the fundamentals won out. From the stratospheric P/E multiples that peaked during the tech bubble at all-time highs, the stock market posted a negative total return for the next decade—a very rare event.

We can learn a lot from the tech bubble, its bursting and ultimately the poor returns that followed. Professional investors fell prey to behavioral errors as they discarded tried and true fundamentals believing that in the new economy the only thing that mattered was growth potential. Many hard lessons were learned. Fundamentals matter, especially fundamentals such as the price of an investment relative to its value can provide great insight into future performance.

There is a powerful connection between the prevailing P/E multiple and subsequent long-term returns that follow thereafter. It is, in fact, a better predictor of future returns than just about anything else we might scrutinize. Vanguard produced an interesting study[2] that looked at the proportion of the variance of future real stock returns that was explained by a variety of different metrics. In other words, they explored to what extent the current value of a particular metric explained the variability of future stock market performance. The study looked at a variety of things that people commonly consider when projecting future returns, such as valuation ratios, dividend yield, earnings growth, and economic factors including GDP growth trend, government debt-to-GDP, and corporate profits.

What they found, as illustrated in Fig. 1.3, is that the P/E 10, or the price to trailing ten-year earnings ratio, explained 43 percent of the variability of future stock market variability, better than any of the others. The P/E 10 is also known as the Shiller P/E ratio named for its creator Robert Shiller, or the cyclically adjusted P/E ratio (CAPE). Though not perfect, the study showed that the CAPE ratio has potential as a predictive tool. Notice also that Vanguard dropped in rainfall as one of the potentially predictive metrics. Although obviously not a viable stock market predicting tool, rainfall showed more explanatory power than some of the commonly used ones.

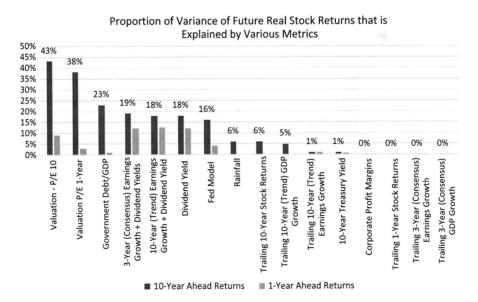

Fig. 1.3 Proportion of Variance of Future Real Stock Returns, 1926–2011. Data source: Vanguard

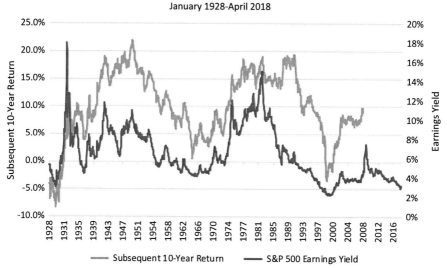

Fig. 1.4 Earnings Yield vs. Subsequent Stock Market Return. Data source: Robert Shiller, Stock Market Data Used in *Irrational Exuberance*, Princeton University Press, updated 2000, 2005, 2015

Figure 1.4 is another powerful visual supporting the long-term viability of the CAPE ratio. The data shows the inverse of the CAPE ratio, or earnings yield, which in this case is the ten-year normalized earnings divided by price versus the subsequent ten-year total return on the S&P 500. Notice not only the correlation between the lines but how low the earnings yield was as of April 2018. At just 3.1 percent, the earnings yield was lower than just 5 percent of all readings since the beginning of 1928. Similar lows were followed by a decade where the S&P 500 failed to produce a positive absolute return.

The next graph, Fig. 1.5, details historical data of valuations from 1881 to the end of 2017. In April 2018, the S&P 500's price was 31.2 times trailing ten-year normalized earnings. That placed it in the top 96th percentile of all readings back to the late 1800s, which was almost exactly on par with the peak preceding the stock market crash of 1929, well above pre-2008 levels, and was bested only by the stratospheric heights reached during the tech bubble.

So valuations as measured by CAPE suggest that the ten-year return for the S&P 500 Index following 2018 could be challenged. It is worth mentioning here that reasonable criticisms of the CAPE have been levied. In a 2016 paper titled "The Shiller CAPE Ratio: A New Look" published in the May/June

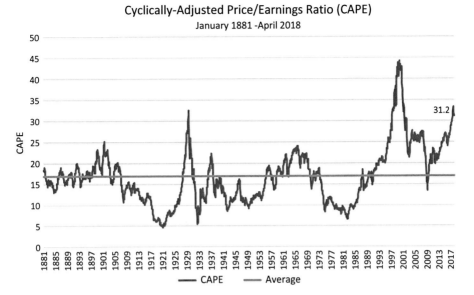

Fig. 1.5   CAPE January 1881—April 2018. Data source: Robert Shiller, Stock Market Data Used in *Irrational Exuberance,* Princeton University Press, updated 2000, 2005, 2015

Financial Analyst Journal, Jeremy Siegel wrote about the impact of accounting changes on earnings, specifically mark to market rules, and the differences between the use of operating and as-reported earnings in the denominator of a P/E ratio. CAPE uses reported earnings in its calculation methodology. According to Siegel, operating is more appropriate and if used in place of reported, the ratio would not be as high and predictions of future returns would not be as dire. Although a reduction is seen if operating earnings is substituted for reported, the drop in the CAPE is not terribly dramatic falling from 32.1 times to 28.2 times (end of 2017), a reading still well above the long-term average around 15 times.[3]

Another common criticism of CAPE is that part of its history is overstated given the catastrophic plunge in earnings during the global financial crisis (GFC). As of the end of 2017, the ten-year trailing earnings average used in the CAPE's denominator still included the GFC's earnings collapse and without it, the CAPE reading would not have been so high and again, less pessimistic of future stock market returns. But even if that recession had not happened and earnings remained elevated throughout, the CAPE ratio would have only been reduced to 29.8 times relative to its actual reading of 32.1 times at the end of 2017.[4]

Seigel's 2016 paper also includes the following statistic (updated through 2017):[5] In 426 of the 432 months from 1981 through 2017 (98.6 percent of the time), the actual ten-year real returns in the market exceeded forecasts using the CAPE model.

The CAPE isn't perfect, but an expectation that above-average long-term stock market returns will follow exceptionally high valuation levels is optimistic at best and foolhardy at worst. Regardless, there may be something even more important to consider here. Look back at that last statistic from Seigel— the period in question starts in 1981. I don't know why Professor Seigel chose 1981 as the start date for that analysis, but I do know that year marked the peak in interest rates and rates fell almost unabated for the next three-and-one-half decades thereafter.

Culminating with a peak in June 1981, interest rates had risen steadily for approximately 35 years, and did so with a vengeance in the final years as then-Federal Reserve chairman Paul Volcker slammed the economy into recession intending to stamp out inflation. Over the 35 years that followed, interest rates declined from their stratospheric heights. Declining interest rates support bond price ascension all else equal, but falling rates can also help stocks.

At the most fundamental level, interest rates wield great influence over stock prices. A higher rate of interest means companies pay more in debt servicing costs, which cuts into profits. Rising rates will prompt individuals and businesses to cut back on spending. But perhaps most significantly for investors, interest rate movements can affect P/E ratios and as such, directly impact stock market performance.

The dividend discount model (DDM)[6] is a method of valuing a company's stock price where the company is worth the sum of all its future dividend payments discounted back to their present value. The discount rate in the formula is the constant cost of equity capital for the company and that rate is in the denominator. So, all other things being equal, the price of a company's stock goes down as its cost of equity (interest rate) goes up. This is important because taken in aggregate across the entire stock market, interest rate values and movements have a direct, inverse relationship with stock prices.

Here is another way to think about the connection between stock prices and interest rates. Some investment analysts seek to determine the relative attractiveness of stocks versus bonds with a methodology known as the Fed model. It is often used to determine whether stocks are overvalued or undervalued; but, in the previously mentioned Vanguard study, the Fed model explains very little of future stock market variability. It might not be a good predictor of future stock market returns but that's OK. We just want to show another connection between interest rates and stock prices. Here's how:

Start by flipping the P/E ratio upside-down so you have E/P, also known as the earnings yield on stocks. Compare this number to the ten-year treasury yield (a proxy for interest rates given a ten-year time horizon). If the ratios are nearly the same, stocks (some believe) are fairly valued.

An argument can be made, however, that when the ratios are the same, stocks are actually undervalued, because an investor would be paying the same effective price for stocks as for bonds. Stocks, at least according to perception, are riskier than treasury bonds, so if they can be had for essentially the same price, an investor should buy stocks expecting a higher return—compensation for holding a riskier investment. The greater return of stocks over bonds due to the higher risk associated with stocks is known as the equity risk premium (ERP).

Now flip both ratios, so we have P/E again and the inverse of the treasury yield. If the current yield on the T-bonds is low, its inverse will be high. Therefore, the lower bond yields go, the higher P/E ratios can go and stocks will still be "fairly valued." Although the Fed model has encountered harsh criticism as a valuation technique, it illustrates the connection between declining interest rates and expanding P/E ratios, which we know have had a substantial positive impact on stock market returns. More to the point, a declining interest rate environment provides fuel for a bull market, and rising rates a potential headwind.

Seigel is correct that CAPE underestimated future stock market performance for many years after 1981 but that may not necessarily represent a problem with CAPE. Perhaps that understatement of future returns was the result of a healthy boost from a declining interest rate environment. So what happens when interest rates stop falling or even start moving up? Investors in the late 2010s and into the 2020s may find out.

Future Returns

From the June 1981 high of 19.1 percent, the Fed funds rate declined to essentially zero in 2011 where it stayed until beginning to move back up starting in late 2015. No one can accurately predict long-term monetary policy, but the protracted decline in interest rates appears to have ended, meaning that the favorable environment for P/E expansion is over. This eliminates one of the most significant positive factors that drove the general upward trend in stocks since the early 1980s. P/E ratios started low in 1981 and moved higher over the ensuing 35 years as interest rates declined. At the end of 2017, P/E ratios were high and interest rates low and rising. The stock market performance in the decade following the GFC was stellar, the decade thereafter almost certainly will be less so. The future isn't what it used to be. Unfortunately, many investors may fail to recognize this turning point, choosing instead to follow their behavioral instincts and project forward the returns of the recent past. Such investors will feel the most pain from the bear market in expectations.

Demographics won't offer much help either. The baby boomers formed an abnormal block of buying demand, which helped along P/E expansion, but that demand will soon be diminished. Baby boomers are generally considered to be those Americans born between 1946 and 1964, meaning that many boomers have been and will be taking more money out of the stock market than they are putting in. Their demand that pushed prices higher will begin to slow and even reverse as this huge population block continues to age.

The point is that mid-teen returns from stock markets are abnormal, and when they occurred since 1981 they were generally supported by declining interest rates then turbo-boosted by the Fed's bond-buying quantitative-easing program that squashed rates to zero. Rather than mid-teens' returns from large cap US equities, middle single-digit returns represent a more prudent projection.

Although any prediction of the future is ultimately a matter of opinion, market returns represent the sum of the three building blocks that comprise a market's total return (earnings growth, dividends, and P/E expansion). Earnings growth has provided just under 2 percent in real returns to large cap stocks since 1926, and only slightly above 2 percent since 1950. Over time, earnings growth cannot be higher than overall gross domestic product growth. Even if you add a 2.5 percent expectation for inflation, a reasonably optimistic contribution from nominal earnings growth would be 5 percent. Dividends have declined since the 1950s and have settled in at 2 percent, so that represents a reasonable expected contribution.

That leaves changes in P/E ratios, which ended 2017 at relatively high levels and will not be boosted by future interest rate declines. Will P/E ratios go down? Perhaps, but no one knows for sure. A reasonable assumption might be some contraction from historically high levels that would then detract from stock market performance over time. Even if you assume no changes in P/E in either direction, the returns you can expect from stocks would come from just earnings growth and dividends, which we can expect to be at or slightly below 7 percent. That leaves only 4.5 percent real growth net of inflation if we assume inflation will eat away returns at a 2.5 percent pace.

What does that mean in real dollars? Let's say an IRA or some other retirement account has $50,000 in it, has 20 years until it will be needed, and an additional $10,000 is added to the account at the end of each year. If all the money is placed in a stock fund, which returns 12 percent per year on average and experiences 16 percent standard deviation (which approximates the actual variability experienced by the S&P 500 since 1950), the total investment will grow to $1.2 million in 20 years. This figure is derived from a Monte Carlo study that simulated 500 examples of 20-year periods of stock returns averaging 12 percent return with 16 percent standard deviation.

But what if past performance really isn't indicative of future results and stock returns fall short of long-term averages? If stocks return 7 percent per year, even if standard deviation is moderately lower at, say, 11 percent, the same $50,000 portfolio with new investments of $10,000 per year would grow to only $605,730 over the 20-year time horizon—about half of what would have been expected using long-term average returns as the assumption for stock market performance. That bear market in expectations would come as quite a shock.

It seems almost ludicrous to place expectations on something like stock market returns when nearly infinite variables influence the outcome. Companies, in response to more favorable tax treatments, could increase dividends and stock buybacks. The economy might grow faster than expected, and P/E ratios could push higher due to unforeseen demand. Any number of factors could lead to more average-like returns from stocks, but the possibility of below-average returns is significant enough that investors should be wary as they conduct their investment planning.

If the performance of the market drives most of the return we experience, and those returns are below average, our specific investments will be required to make up the difference. Unfortunately, most mutual funds have historically not been able to add value. Many of the problems with traditional funds were glossed over by the tremendous returns over the past 35 years or so. After all, who really cares if your fund lagged the S&P 500 by a couple of percentage points if the fund was up 25 percent? Future returns in line with long-term averages might keep investors looking the other way, but what if returns are below average? Funds that fail to outperform will do so far more conspicuously if the market advances only 7 percent or so. Such is a very real possibility for traditional investments, so many of the old ways of thinking may need to be discarded.

Notes

1. Robert I. Lerman and Stefanie R. Schmidt, *An Overview of Economic, Social, and Demographic Trends Affecting the U.S. Labor Market*, final report (Washington, D.C.: The Urban Institute, August 1999).
2. Vanguard Research, "Forecasting stock returns: What signals matter, and what do they say now?" October 2012. https://personal.vanguard.com/pdf/s338.pdf.
3. Data source: Robert Shiller; Analysis: Greg Houser, FEG Investment Advisors.
4. Data source: Robert Shiller; Analysis: Greg Houser, FEG Investment Advisors.
5. Jeremy J. Siegel presentation, "Stocks, Bonds and Future Returns," Matthew McCormick Cincinnati Investment Symposium, January 23, 2018.
6. John Burr Williams, *The Theory of Investment Value*, Harvard University Press, 1938.

2

An Obsolete Fundamental Philosophy

At the end of 2006, registered investment companies—mutual funds, exchange-traded funds, closed-end funds, and unit investment trusts—managed a record $11.2 trillion of our money (compared with less than $200 billion under management before 1980)[1] and all seemed right in the world. But something happened on our collective way to the bank. Within a few short months, the real estate market began to buckle, structured products built around mortgages and other loans began to fail, and on September 15, 2008, Lehman Brothers filed for bankruptcy—an event that still remains (as of print) the largest bankruptcy of assets (over $639 billion) in US history. Surrounding it all was the deepest recession since the Great Depression and the most significant stock market decline that most people alive then had ever observed. By March 2009 when the stock market had lost about 50 percent of its value relative to its all-time high, the foregone conclusion held by a generation of investors—that buying into stock funds would ultimately guarantee handsome returns—was being abandoned in droves. So where did that leave the typical investor, other than extremely frustrated?

The recovery in stock prices that followed in the decade thereafter was supported by highly accommodative monetary policy as the US Federal Reserve embarked upon an unprecedented bond-buying program (quantitative easing or QE) that ballooned its balance sheet from $886 billion in 2007 to a peak of $4.5 trillion in 2015, which was over 23 percent as large as the entirety of the US economy.[2] In addition to the direct connection between rates and P/E expansion mentioned previously, the downward pressure QE placed on rates nudged investors into riskier investments than they might have otherwise preferred, that is, equities. The aggregate demand for stocks, combined with

© The Author(s) 2018   15
M. J. Oyster, *Success in a Low-Return World*,
https://doi.org/10.1007/978-3-319-99855-8_2

improving corporate fundamentals, led to a full recovery in stock prices and beyond as the major indexes blew past the prior peaks achieved in 2007 well into new-high territory. That was the good news. The bad news was that most well-compensated, actively managed mutual funds didn't keep up.

Mutual Funds Have Disappointed

Despite the monstrous amount of fees they charge, most mutual funds have failed in their single, most important mission—they haven't outperformed the market in which they invest. All investors are entitled to at least market returns, so a fund manager who earns money and invests differently from the market should be expected to outperform it. In the same way that a doctor should do no bodily harm to a patient, a fund manager should do no financial harm to an investor relative to the market's return, but nearly all of them do. And it's not because they lack ability or don't work hard enough. The problem is an obsolete philosophy.

Although growth in assets allocated to passive/index funds has been substantial in recent years, most stock market investments in the United States are managed in a general style known as *active management* in which fund managers seek out and buy stocks that they believe will, as a group, outperform the market. If asked, many people may say that stock selection is the *only* way to beat the market. This simply is not true, but the mutual fund industry desperately needs to promote this misperception. And it works for them. Ninety-five million individuals own mutual funds;[3] and about two-thirds of these are actively managed[4] yet are highly unlikely to provide the outperformance they promise. According to a report from Standard and Poor's, 92.15 percent of all actively managed large cap funds trailed their appropriate benchmark (S&P 500 Index) over the 15-year period ending December 2016.[5]

Much of my professional career has been dedicated to researching fund managers for large institutional investors, and I've heard every cheesy cliché that fund managers use to differentiate their products. The vast majority, however, are almost exactly alike, and their storyline is some variation of the following: "You see, we don't try to hit home runs; we shoot for singles and doubles. Our team does all the heavy lifting, meeting with management, kicking the tires, and at the end of the day, we don't buy stocks, we buy companies." Translation: "I can't offer you anything different than anyone else, so I'm going to try to make you feel good about what I'm saying and divert your attention from the fact that you should realistically expect nothing more than mediocre performance from my product."

This isn't to say that the folks working for fund companies are bad people, quite the contrary. Most are kind, honest, hard working, and really smart. They are just faced with the unenviable task of differentiating themselves in a sea of commonality.

Professional investing has been relegated to a commodity because the competitive advantage it previously enjoyed no longer exists. Gone are the days when a smart, skillful investment professional could guide your investments to relative outperformance and actually earn the fees they charge. Smith Barney may have made money the old-fashioned way by earning it, but that message implies today's money is not earned. If you could find someone in the industry who would actually tell you the truth on the subject, they would probably agree. Unfortunately, so much money and way too many careers are designed to keep the mutual fund machine moving that the average investor may never hear the painful truth. Today's markets offer few, if any, readily known opportunities for outperformance relative to investing in a broad-based index designed to track the overall market. The future, by contrast, will be ruled by those who can add value without betting on individual stocks. Not only do opportunities exist for investors to outperform the average mutual fund and the market but neither stock selection nor market timing is required to do so.

Equity Mutual Funds

Whether you are an individual investor, a fiduciary for institutional capital, or both, chances are you invest in the stock market. The bulk of this discussion will be focused on equity (stock) fund managers and, most specifically, large cap domestic equity managers. Most investors have at least a portion of their holdings in stock funds—usually a large portion, which is good unless the mandate requires a low-risk, consistent return, such as retirement income or assets being held for a near-term cash need.

Equity funds are almost always comprised of a pool of individual stocks. Shares of this pool are then sold to investors who mutually believe these selections will be more profitable than a passive investment in the market as a whole, after the fees the investor pays to be a part of the fund.

Every mutual fund is run by a manager or committee, who is normally a single point person or small group making most, if not all, of the buy and sell decisions for the fund. At the most fundamental level of an actively managed mutual fund's philosophy is the belief that the manager can find and invest in stocks that will, on average, outperform the pool of stocks from which they choose (the market) and avoid those that will lag the market. This strategy is known as *active management* because the fund manager makes active buy and sell decisions in an attempt to add value over the market.

The first rule of investing is to buy low and sell high. Although it may not be the first thing a manager looks at, valuation almost always plays a role in the stock-buying process. As budding investors, we're taught that the way to invest in stocks is to buy good companies for the long term but not to pay more than they're worth. If the stock is cheap relative to what the company is worth, then it should be purchased. If not, it should be sold.

Simple, right? Well, maybe, but certainly not distinctive. The problem with this most basic of stock buying philosophies is not that it doesn't work or that the people implementing it don't know what they're doing. One of the main reasons fund managers fail to add value over the market this way is because practically everyone else is doing the exact same thing.

Stock Picking

The most influential investor of all time is Benjamin Graham. Argue all you like about the best baseball player or the tastiest toppings for pizza, but when it comes to who has made stock picking what it is today, the debate begins and ends with Graham.

Benjamin Graham is the father of *fundamental analysis*, meaning detailed analysis of the fundamental factors that make up the intrinsic value of a company by examining economic, financial, as well as qualitative and other quantitative factors. By Graham's measure, a company should be purchased if its fundamental analysis shows that it is actually more valuable than the total value of its stock. Eventually, the stock price will wake up to the fact that the company is actually more valuable and rise as more and more investors buy it.

The term *fundamental analysis*, which describes how Graham analyzed companies, is appropriate because it defines the fundamental basis for any stock selector. Everyone who buys stocks wants to do so as cheaply as possible. Most mutual funds utilize some form of fundamental analysis, but the strategy has encountered great difficulty in recent years.

Since the 1930s, investors have followed the Benjamin Graham philosophy of seeking good businesses at an attractive value. Graham's revolutionary work, *The Intelligent Investor*, is one of the most revered books on investing, and it serves as the jumping off point for many a new stock-selecting analyst.[6] Legendary investors Warren Buffett and Peter Lynch followed that philosophy with great success. Buffett, in fact, called that book "By far the best book on investing ever written."[7] That's strong praise from one who enjoys near godlike status in some investment circles.

The fatal flaw of the Benjamin Graham philosophy of buying good companies at attractive values is that it's too good. Buffett and Lynch are smart people, as are most of those who follow their lead. Although, as a group, investment managers play in what's worse than a zero-sum game; somebody wins, somebody loses, but they all charge fees. As a result, the likelihood of actually outperforming is lower than a 50–50 proposition.

Years ago, a stock picker's job wasn't necessarily easier than it was today, but there was more fruit. Prior to the mid-1970s, professional investors could add value by ferreting out the great companies that were selling at prices well below their true value, á la Benjamin Graham. Often, a competitive advantage could be had just by talking with the company's managers, employees, suppliers, and customers, because information was not disseminated as quickly and widely as it is today. In those days, company executives weren't required to disclose information to the whole world as they are today.

Before the advent of computers, the true value of a company's worth was much more a matter of opinion. Mining for uncovered data in a sea of confusing accounting statements often yielded a treasure trove of useful information. If you worked hard enough, you could actually learn something no one else knew and profit from it.

But starting in the mid to late 1970s, computers made this process much easier for everyone. One reason is that complex calculations, which previously had required a prohibitive amount of time to do by hand, could be run in a flash.

The dividend discount model (DDM) mentioned earlier was one such calculation. The DDM is what many believe to be the truest means of valuing a company. In a nutshell, the DDM gives a value for the company based upon the current worth of future earnings or cash flow. John Burr Williams, in his doctorate dissertation that was later published as *The Theory of Investment Value*, first proposed the basis for the DDM in the mid-1930s.[8] Where Graham focused on valuation, Williams considered a potential investment in a stock based upon the cash flows that stock's company could be expected to provide. Although his feelings on valuation were slightly different than many who use the DDM today, Williams said, referring to the dividend a stock pays to its shareholders, "A stock is worth only what you can get out of it." Williams didn't want to count on the stock price actually going up in value because the stock market at the time was swinging wildly about.

In a review of Williams' book published in *The Journal of Political Economy*, Benjamin Graham alluded to the speculative atmosphere pervasive on Wall Street at the time when in that same review he said, "One of the disastrous consequences of the New Era madness in Wall Street has been the disappearance of the former clean-cut distinctions between investment and speculation in common stocks … Present-day 'investment,' as practiced by investment trusts and everyone else, is not much more than an undisciplined wagering upon the future and as such logically indistinguishable from speculation."[9] In the review, Graham took issue with parts but offered praise to Williams for his approach describing how dividends could guide stock picking when he said, "A vast amount of original thought, comprehensive research, and laborious mathematical study has gone into this impressive work."

Although the DDM had been around for a long time by the 1970s, the computer allowed it to be used on a far wider scale than ever before. Investment managers who harnessed computing power to determine the valuation of stocks tended to profit from their efforts.

But the golden egg-laying goose didn't live long. By the mid-1980s, every investment manager worth their salt was using a computer to determine the price of a stock based on the DDM. What had once been a beautiful tool for stock valuation, based on rock-solid fundamentals, had suddenly been reduced to no better than throwing darts. It's not as though the DDM was wrong; rather its usefulness diminished because it had been far too right. When everyone uses the same valuation technique, it benefits no one, because new information immediately moves the stock price to a new level, more reflective of the new information.

Some managers tried to find a way to front-run the DDM, believing that if they had a good idea that a stock would become more profitable, they could get one step ahead of everyone else. Enter earnings estimates. The Institutional Brokers' Estimate System or I/B/E/S began collecting and compiling earnings estimates for US companies around 1976, which allowed investment managers to see what analysts were saying about a company's future prospects. What a concept! Managers didn't have to wait until earnings were announced to value the company using the DDM. Instead, they could plug earnings estimates into their computer models and see what the stock price should be in the future. Alas, this advantage would also be diminished due to its popularity. Again, the concept didn't go bad; it just lost its effectiveness because everyone was using it. Even today, analysts' estimates are widely viewed by fund managers, because studies show an advantage to watching what they say, but active stock selection faces a variety of additional challenges.

So the computer no longer gave managers as much of an advantage. They had been able to front-run earnings by using analysts' estimates, but that approach no longer helped as much as it once had. Professional investors needed a way to front-run the analysts' estimates. The next big thing was factor analysis.

With a little help from a firm called BARRA, which was founded in 1975 and began factor analysis in their first year, managers began trying to not just predict the future earnings of a company but to determine which fundamental factor would have the greatest impact on earnings. Drilling down a level deeper into the company would allow a hard-working professional investor to gain a much-needed competitive advantage.

Factor models provided great insight to those who used them in the beginning, but their effectiveness in the modern marketplace is arguably diluted. Today, even minor details of most publicly traded companies are picked over in incredible detail. Additionally, changes in key factors affect the stock instantaneously. Don't even bother trading on recently released information. By the time you hear about it, it's already too late.

The Bottom Line: Market Efficiency

This account is certainly not a comprehensive review of all the tools stock investors have used over the years in an attempt to gain a competitive advantage, but it does show how a good idea remains so only until its effect is diluted by popularity. More to the point, markets are highly efficient, and the opportunities to profit from an unused method or tool are rare. Stock prices may not always reflect perfectly rational indications of a company's worth, but the ability to profit from such mispricing is another matter completely.

So why do so many managers still rely on a once great philosophy that now is obsolete? Many professional investors suffer from the behavioral error of overconfidence, believing that they have a better mousetrap and can beat the system, but more likely, this strategy's persistence has to do with the system's need to perpetuate itself. So many companies, careers, news organizations, information providers, and educational programs have been built around the concept of outperformance through security selection that very few investment professionals stop to question its viability.

The issue of market efficiency is perhaps the greatest challenge mutual fund managers face today, and it's getting worse. Computers can process more data. Information is becoming more detailed, and companies no longer bury important information deep in their books and will be less likely to give preferential treatment to an analyst whose firm will underwrite a new stock offering. Combine these factors with what many believe will be a lower total return from the stock market in general, and traditional fund managers are looking at a future where they may have to start answering some very tough questions about their viability.

People love to wax philosophical about how Benjamin Graham might invest today. Some publications even come up with a list of stocks in which they believe Graham would be invested.[10] The modern investment landscape, however, looks very different than it did before World War II when Graham developed his ideas, and the future will likely look nothing like today. Graham's basic philosophy of buying quality companies at an attractive value is timeless and will always serve as the fundamental basis of stock selection, but I'm certain he would agree that attempting to implement that philosophy today would be far more difficult than it was in his time.

Notes

1. Investment Company Institute, *2007 Investment Company Fact Book: A Review of Trends and Activity in the Investment Company Industry*, 47th edition (Washington, D.C.: Investment Company Institute, 2007), 4.
2. Federal Reserve Bank of St. Louis, Economic Research, fred.stlouisfed.org.
3. Investment Company Institute, 2017 *Investment Company Fact Book, A Review of Trends and Activities in the Investment Company Industry*, 57th edition, 2017.
4. Charles Stein, "Active vs. Passive Investing," Bloomberg.com, December 4, 2017.
5. Aye M. Soe, CFA, Ryan Poirier, FRM, S&P Dow Jones, A Division of S&P Global, "SPIVA® U.S. Scorecard," Year End 2016.
6. Benjamin Graham, *The Intelligent Investor*, revised edition (New York: Harper Business Essentials, 2003).
7. Patrick Morris, "3 Books That Changed Warren Buffett's Life," The Motley Fool, December 25, 2013.
8. John Burr Williams, *The Theory of Investment Value*, Harvard University Press, 1938.
9. Benjamin Graham, *The Journal of Political Economy*, Volume XLVII, April 1939, Number 2, 276.
10. Begintoinvest.com, "What Stocks Would Ben Graham Buy Today? Q1 2018," January 4, 2018.

3

As a Group, Professional Investors Are the Market

Despite years of proven effectiveness, the most basic fundamental strategy of buying low and selling high was called into question during the late 1990s, when internet and technology stocks were trading at astronomical values. At the time, this practice of paying any price for companies with no earnings was actually considered appropriate by many who claimed the old ways had become obsolete in the new economy. Fund managers, who had previously touted their stalwart commitment to only buying stocks at attractive values, bent over backward trying to explain why the stocks they were buying were actually trading at a fair price. They needed a way to get into the tech game; competing funds were posting stratospheric returns and bringing in new assets at a breakneck pace. The new investment money was allocated quickly to the same high-flying stocks, which kept advancing, boosted by ever-growing demand. The snowball effect of everyone buying at virtually any price was a self-fulfilling prophecy that fed on itself right up to the point where everyone was buying in. Then the tech stocks crashed. Some were able to survive, like eBay and Amazon.com, but not without an initial decline in value. The few tech stocks that were to survive recovered quickly.

People blamed runaway optimism, the media, greed, and blatant disregard of traditional valuation measures after tech stocks crashed, but the real culprit was competition. Sure, valuations were off the charts relative to historical norms, but no valuation is too high as long as someone is willing to buy. Some money managers were making big bucks by owning internet stocks, so their competitors had to do the same. Pretty soon, even some of the most stoic value managers had internet exposure—a lot of them managing to get in right at the top.

© The Author(s) 2018   **23**
M. J. Oyster, *Success in a Low-Return World*,
https://doi.org/10.1007/978-3-319-99855-8_3

At the end of 2017, an air of speculation surrounded the markets that seemed reminiscent of the wild days of the technology bubble. Stock market volatility was grinded to historic lows and investors eschewed the protection of put option protection. The so-called FAANG stocks (Facebook, Apple, Amazon, Netflix, and Alphabet's Google) were the darlings of the market and stock index P/E multiples had pushed to levels on par with that seen prior to the 1929 market crash. The FAANGs were exceeded only by the stratospheric levels reached during the tech bubble. Some highly speculative investors were finding success with leveraged bets that volatility would remain low into perpetuity. Such strategies proved profitable for a time, became an excitingly hot fad that compounded the trend, but then many exploded in spectacular fashion. Volatility returned in early February 2018, and although the stock market didn't fall as much as it did after the tech bubble burst or the financial crisis of 2008, the strikingly fast resurgence of volatility served as a reminder that markets are cyclical, trends don't last forever, and it tends to be the early adopters who find success while the later movers accelerate the trend until it breaks. This represents the behavioral bias known as the *bandwagon effect*; by the time an investment concept reaches mass adoption and approval, it could be past its prime. Betting on a fad is dangerous. Investing in line with long-standing fundamental truths is better.

Just Because Everybody Else Is Doing It

Yet again, a good idea remains so only until everyone is using it. Competition in the mutual fund world won't diminish any time soon, so the best way to gain an advantage is to get in on the front end of a good idea and get out when its popularity peaks. Unfortunately, doing so is not as easy as it seems. Not only do you have to find the idea before everyone else, you have to stop using it just as it is being praised everywhere by everyone. The time between the discovery of the next new market-beating technique and when it becomes diluted by overuse is painfully short. Many strategies do not survive discovery. You may build a better mousetrap but beware: the world will soon beat a path to your door.

Today's investment industry is as competitive as it has ever been, which means that finding and using the next big idea is increasingly difficult. The asset-management business today, at time of printing, supports a staggering number of investment managers who chase a limited number of ideas, are armed with essentially the same philosophy, and fight like crazy to gain a competitive advantage. As a group, these investment managers are the market, but their performance lags the market.

In 1965, households accounted for 83.3 percent of stock ownership in the United States with institutions owning 16.2 percent,[1] but in 2016, household ownership of stocks had dropped to 40.4 percent and institutional ownership had risen to 59.6 percent.[2] Actual mom and pop household ownership was even lower because that household percentage statistic includes nonprofit organizations, many of which hold massive professionally managed equity portfolios. When individuals accounted for most of the transactions, the market was less efficient and provided the professional an opportunity to outperform. Individuals, on average, don't have the same knowledge, information, and dedication as professionals. In the past, professionals might have been able to outperform at the expense of less informed individual investors, but now, the markets are comprised of virtually nothing but professionals, all with the same information.

As professional ownership of stocks has risen, "errors" in pricing have become fewer and smaller, yielding fewer opportunities to gain a competitive advantage. If professional investors are the market, it's easy to see why the average mutual fund (after fees) lags the market over time.

According to the mutual fund industry trade group, Investment Company Institute, there were 4752 equity (stock) mutual funds managed in the United States at the end of 2016, 3234 of which held US equities while the others were classified as world equities. The number of US stock funds has contracted somewhat in recent years from a peak in 2006 of 3748 but still remains vast. In 1997 there were only 2183 domestic equity mutual funds and in 1987, just 743.[3]

The Wilshire 5000, which is said to include all equity securities of companies headquartered in the United States with readily available price data, held 3485 stocks as of March 2018,[4] meaning that publicly traded stocks outnumbered US equity mutual funds, but just barely. Most equity fund managers couldn't invest in many of those stocks because they were so thinly traded. The total market capitalization of the Wilshire 5000 was about $28 trillion in March 2018[5] while the market capitalization of the S&P 500, an index comprised of about 500 of the largest stocks in the United States by market capitalization, was about $23 trillion[6] representing over 80 percent of the total US stock market. Clearly, the large names dominate the market, and that's where most mutual fund managers do their bidding. As a result, we see thousands of mutual funds chasing only hundreds of stocks.

Most mutual fund managers focus on large cap stocks because, quite frankly, that's where the liquidity is. Funds can buy and sell virtually at will in the large cap space, because large cap stocks are more heavily traded than small cap stocks. Far fewer mutual funds operate in the small cap space. Why?

Because savvy shareholders force the fund companies to close these funds to any new investors when assets grow too large. Moving a massive amount of assets through the small cap asset class would adversely affect prices and hurt performance. However, a large cap fund can grow its assets under management virtually without limit, and the fund's asset-based fee can grow right along with it.

But even large cap funds can grow so large that they run into liquidity issues. Massive stock-picking funds are like the 800-pound gorilla that can't sit wherever they want because when they get into and out of positions they affect the stock price. Causing the price to go up when you buy and go down when you sell hurts performance.

The same can be said for the asset-management business as a whole. Professional fund managers, who are charged with investing massive amounts of money, use essentially the same methodology and chase a limited number of stocks. They compete with each other, exploiting the other's good idea until it doesn't work anymore.

Years ago, a hard-working fund manager had more opportunities to beat the market because competition wasn't as fierce as it is today. The finer details of each and every publicly traded firm weren't voraciously devoured by an army of investment analysts bent on finding any crumb of data that could give them even a slight competitive advantage. But, that's the way it is today. Who is the big loser? The consumer, not the manger.

Mutual Fund Industry Growth Hurts Investors

The important point here is that competition in the mutual fund business can have an adverse effect on the performance investors receive. It's easy to disregard the growth in professional investing as simply something that makes fund selection more difficult or even a positive, in that we have more selections from which to choose. In reality, the growth hurts all investors. In a very real way, competition between one smart, hard-working investor and another inhibits the returns we all are able to achieve. An example can show how this works.

Let's look at a mutual fund in 1982, one of only 340 equity funds in business at that time. It invests in 100 stocks with an equal allocation to each. Keep in mind that no investment manager has 100 percent confidence in all the stocks they invest in, which is why they invest in so many. If they knew without question that one stock would go up, why would they invest in anything else?

In 1982, the markets were made up of mostly individual investors and information was harder to come by than it is today. Let's say that of the 100 holdings in the 1982 fund, the manager may realistically expect 25 to beat the market by 2 percent, 25 to outperform by 1 percent, 25 to have market-like returns, and 25 to lag by 1 percent. If this happens, the fund will outperform the market by 0.5 percent. Over time, most funds haven't been able to outperform, so the 0.5 percent added over the market would be considered a sterling return.

Continuing with a different example, a modern-day mutual fund has fewer stocks from which to choose. There were approximately 5000 stocks in the Wilshire 5000 in 1982 but just 3485 in March 2018.[7] That combined with the greater competition and market efficiency serves to limit the number of outperformers. In today's tougher investment environment, the best fund shouldn't be expected to outperform by as much as funds years ago because competition has eaten away the opportunities that the 1982 fund could have expected. Stock prices reflect current economic knowledge far more quickly today than they did years ago, partly because of the speed with which information is disseminated but also because far more players are in the game.

If competition limits the amount and quality of the winning names in the portfolio, fund managers' performance will suffer. If today's fund has fewer winners, and those winners will not outperform by as much, how will performance be affected? Let's say that in today's fund, the top 25 names can only be expected to outperform by 1 percent, 50 will post market-like returns, and 25 will lag the benchmark by 1 percent. Such a fund would experience market-like returns before fees and lag after fees are assessed, which is representative of the mutual fund industry today.

Although this simple example fails to consider the transaction costs that mutual fund managers incur and the complex expectations associated with each position, it does illustrate how competition inhibits performance and hurts the shareholders. In most areas of a capitalistic society, competition helps the consumer. Not so with the mutual fund industry, at least not the way it is today. If four new gas stations opened in a town that previously had only one, the town's residents would not expect the quality of gas to go down and the price to go up. But that's what has happened in the mutual fund industry and why the search for alternate solutions has become so important.

Consider the Fidelity Magellan Fund. Magellan outperformed the S&P 500 by more than three percentage points annualized over the ten years ending December 1992. Recall that in 1982, there were only 340 stock funds, but that number grew nearly fourfold by 1992. Over the following ten years ending December 2002, Magellan failed to outperform the S&P 500, and its performance has been no better since then.

Is it possible that from 1992 through 2002, Magellan lacked the investment-management skill it enjoyed in the prior decade? Perhaps, but the outperformance may have been due to luck rather than skill as well as a far less competitive environment. The value style that Magellan has practiced was in favor relative to the market in general over the ten years ending 1992. This good fortune helped the fund's performance and had nothing to do with security selection decisions. But perhaps, more importantly, the lack of competition in the marketplace between other professionals provided an opportunity to add value through stock picking that diminished in the years that followed.

At this point you may be saying, "Yeah sure, intense competition between stock pickers limits opportunities for everyone, but actively-managed funds are going away and being replaced by index funds. If everyone is indexing, wouldn't there be greater opportunities for active management?" Possibly, but we are still a long way away from that. According to a report from Credit Suisse, assets under management for US equity index funds were only $3 billion in 1989, or about 1 percent of the industry. By 2016, they reached nearly $2 trillion, or just under 30 percent of assets under management.

The growth in indexing has been particularly pronounced following the financial crisis in 2008. Poor market returns and the rise of exchange-traded funds as a financial innovation were large drivers. In recent years, active managers have lost substantial market share to passive vehicles. For US equities, active funds had an outflow of $331 billion while passive funds had an inflow of $272 billion in the 11 months that ended in November 2016.[8] Basically, passive investing had become more popular, but the greater majority of assets deployed in the US stock market was still being done so by active managers. If the day ever comes when most US equity investment dollars are held in passive vehicles, one of the many structural inhibitors to active management that exist today will have become less so. From a behavioral standpoint, human beings suffer from the bias of overconfidence where a person's subjective confidence in his or her judgments is greater than the accuracy of those judgments.[9] I suspect there will always be an enormous number of people who believe they can outperform the market by picking stocks, as well as an enormous number of people willing to allocate investment funds to them with the hope that they can. I wish them luck.

As we will discuss in Chap. 8, returns alone cannot tell us whether outperformance is due to luck or skill, but clearly a more competitive marketplace will inhibit the opportunities to add value through security selection. Unfortunately for stock-selecting fund managers, the environment is becoming more difficult all the time.

Notes

1. Grace Toto and George Monahan, eds., *2002 Securities Industry Fact Book* (New York: Securities Industry Association, 2002), 66.
2. The Securities Industry and Financial Markets Association, Produced by SIFMA Research Department, *2017 Fact Book*, 82.
3. Investment Company Institute, *2017 Investment Company Fact Book, A Review of Trends and Activities in the Investment Company Industry*, 174.
4. Wilshire Associates Incorporated, Wilshire 5000 Total Market Index^{SM}, March 31, 2018 Fact Sheet.
5. Ibid.
6. YCharts.com.
7. Robert J. Waid, Managing Director, Wilshire Associates Incorporated, "Wilshire 5000®: Myths and Misconceptions," November 2014, 2.
8. Michael J. Mauboussin, Dan Callahan, CFA, Darius Jajd, Credit Suisse Global Financial Strategies, "Looking for Easy Games, How Passive Investing Shapes Active Management," January 4, 2017, 12.
9. FEG Investment Advisors, 2017. Definition sourced via Wikipedia.com.

4

The Specifics of Market Efficiency

Markets populated by a large number of highly trained, profit-maximizing investors are likely to be efficient, meaning prices adjust rapidly to the arrival of new information, and the current price immediately reflects everything known at that time. The growth in the investment industry has almost certainly made markets more efficient, limiting the profit potential of stock selectors and effectively eliminating any competitive advantage that one investor has over another.

Efficient markets make it tough for active managers to gain a competitive advantage because prices change as soon as new information is released. The stock picker can outperform an efficient market only by predicting the future value and impact of factors affecting the companies they follow—an effort even most company CEOs know is exceptionally difficult to do for their own companies.

What the Research Says About Efficiency

As you might imagine, market efficiency has been extensively tested and hotly debated. Largely, this has occurred due to many questioning the philosophy upon which most mutual funds and professional investment programs have been based.

Some of the early work on market efficiency was completed by Burton G. Malkiel. In his book *A Random Walk Down Wall Street*, first published in 1973,[1] Malkiel surmised that stock prices behave like a person walking aimlessly down a street, shifting back and forth with no pattern to the movement.

© The Author(s) 2018
M. J. Oyster, *Success in a Low-Return World*,
https://doi.org/10.1007/978-3-319-99855-8_4

Just prior to Malkiel in 1970, Eugene Fama wrote an article in the *Journal of Finance* called "Efficient Capital Markets: A Review of Theory and Empirical Work."[2] In the article, Fama put the theory of efficient markets through a bit more rigorous analysis. Prior work on the subject had focused on price movements over time, but Fama attempted to define efficient markets as a fair game. The fair game equation specifically defined what is meant by prices fully reflecting all available information. This marked the beginning of the Efficient Market Hypothesis (EMH) that would be tested in a myriad of ways for years to come and is still being tested today.

In 2013, Fama shared the Nobel Prize in Economics for his work on market efficiency. The Nobel Museum said of his work:

> *For many of us, the rise and fall of stock prices symbolizes economic development. In the 1960s, Eugene Fama demonstrated that stock price movements are impossible to predict in the short-term and that new information affects prices almost immediately, which means that the market is efficient. The impact of Eugene Fama's results has extended beyond the field of research. For example, his results influenced the development of index funds.*[3]

Subsequent to his initial work, Fama refined the concept and further defined how the EMH is broken into three subsets or "forms" that could be tested independently of one another.[4]

- Weak form (EMH)
- Semi-strong form EMH
- Strong form EMH

The weak form (EMH) said that current stock prices reflected all available security market information. In other words, stocks are priced given what investors had observed in terms of prior price patterns, and no relationship between past performance and future results should exist. Gaining an advantage through observing past rates of return or any historical data (i.e., technical analysis) should not be possible if the weak form EMH is correct.

The semi-strong form EMH asserted that security prices adjust rapidly to the release of all public information. The semi-strong form takes the next step beyond the weak form by including nonmarket information. Nonmarket information covers fundamental factors such as dividend announcements, P/E ratios, stock splits, and economic news. If investors make decisions on any piece of information after it becomes public, the theory asserts they should not expect above-average profits.

The strong form EMH is built on the semi-strong form, due to it including all information, both public and private. It extended the assumption of efficient markets, in which prices quickly adjust to the release of information, to the point of a perfect market where all information is cost-free and available to everyone at the same time. The strong form EMH asserts that no group of investors has monopolistic access to all relevant information; no group should consistently be able to derive above-average profits. In other words, it assumes that the markets are devoid of inside information.

I'm sure that even the least skeptical reader is at this point saying to themselves that inside information makes its way into the financial markets, and even though it is illegal, some people are profiting from it. But don't forget what the strong form is actually saying. It asserts that no group has monopolistic access to all information. We can't realistically expect a person who has inside information on one stock to have inside information on enough stocks to consistently outperform the market. Moreover, as we'll examine in detail in Chap. 7, SEC regulators cracked down on inside information and preferential treatment through regulations such as Regulation FD (Fair Disclosure).

A whole host of tests have been conducted since the EMH was first developed to determine whether markets are truly efficient or not. If markets can be shown to be efficient, and no one group (save the exceptionally lucky) can be expected to outperform the others for any length of time, active management in its current form should cease to exist. After all, who in their right mind would invest their money with a high-fee active manager with less than a 50–50 chance of outperforming the market, when the same investor could get market-like returns for a lot less money?

Weak Form EMH

The weak form EMH has been difficult to disprove. Recall that the weak form suggests that past market-related information (stock prices, volume, etc.) should have no effect on future prices. Early tests focused on *autocorrelation*, which sought to find any connection between the rate of return on one day with the rate of return on some future day.

The results of short time horizons, including 1 day, 4 days, 9 days, and 16 days, were not statistically significant,[5] meaning that the information wasn't strong enough to suggest a connection between past and future returns. More recent studies have suggested that autocorrelation is stronger in small stocks, but the effect may be the result of small company stocks, many of which only trade sporadically, affected by the same significant news or event.

The effect may be less pronounced in large company stocks because they trade nearly all the time.

Other studies of the weak form EMH included the *run test*, in which positive stock returns were denoted with a + and negative stock returns were denoted with a −.[6] The actual amount of the stock return was disregarded. A run was considered two or more consecutive signs until the opposite sign occurred. The results of the runs were compared to expectations of randomly generated data. The results showed no significant difference between the observed stock price runs and the random runs, confirming the independence of stock returns over time.

Some have claimed that these tests were too rigid to identify the intricate price patterns examined by technical analysts. A second group of tests of the weak form EMH was developed in response.[7] As opposed to simple price patterns, certain commonly used trading rules were tested, but the results of these tests were similar. Most studies indicated that trading rules would not outperform a buy-and-hold strategy after deducting commission costs. Some caveats of these studies include the fact that many technical analysts use subjective overlays in their trading strategies, which cannot be tested. The subjective nature of human behavior might result in less consistency and ultimately below-market results after commissions, but that is impossible to test.

Certain technical analysis disciples point out that they don't use a "black box" approach, blindly implementing all signals generated by their system. Instead, they weave their own intuition and experience into their trading approach. Making this argument allows them to discount academic studies that suggest their philosophy is ineffective. Although several psychological research teams have attempted to develop novel techniques to quantitatively measure how much unconscious intuition can inform—and improve—our decision-making, no one has successfully created a single test to evaluate the ever-changing effects of human intuition and emotion. What the studies do suggest is that most technical analysis systems, based upon past price and volume data, are tremendously poor predictors of future performance after transaction costs are included. In Chap. 6 we will explore how human behavioral biases apply specifically to investment decision-making.

The Semi-Strong Form EMH

The semi-strong form EMH has also been widely tested. Recall that this semi-strong form moves beyond all market information to include all public information and asserts that prices immediately reflect this information.

Tests of the semi-strong form EMH have been done in roughly two distinct styles: tests of opportunities to predict future rates of return (either a time series or a cross section) and event studies.[8] Event studies have included stock splits, initial public offerings (IPO), exchange listings, and other announcements. Virtually all these studies seem to confirm the semi-strong form EMH and show that markets move quickly to adjust prices based upon new information. In recent years, information has become even more widely available and is disseminated instantaneously to anyone who wants it.

One event study that offered potential opportunity for outperformance was the event listing. The theory says that the listing of a stock on the NYSE provides prestige and liquidity, thus elevating the value of the stock thereafter. Although the fundamental value of the company would not change due to the listing, the stock can experience a moderate short-term advance in price immediately after the listing announcement. After the stock actually begins trading on the exchange, however, a decline can be expected.

This effect, when it has been observed, is usually small and short-lived, requiring great precision on the part of the trader attempting to take advantage of it. After all, a short-term boost may occur after the listing announcement, but how can you be sure you haven't already missed it, and how do you know how long it will last? The number of variables involved in this type of short-term trading would likely lead anyone familiar with the random behavior of stock prices to avoid the concept altogether.

Other tests of the semi-strong form, time-series analyses, have generally focused on factors such as price-earnings ratios, dividend yields, or other types of widely available economic information.[9] Of the numerous tests, several showed promise, seeming to suggest that markets were not efficient and investors utilizing certain factors could make an above-average profit.

Observing unexpected quarterly earnings was one such factor. A company that reported earnings in excess of expectations experienced "abnormal" returns, meaning that they rallied in addition to what would be expected, given changes in the overall market for the same period of time.

A wide variety of studies conducted throughout the 1970s and 1980s showed that stocks did not adjust immediately to new levels indicated by positive earnings surprises. Rather, the adjustment took time, time that a savvy investor could have used to take advantage of a positive move in the stock. Unfortunately, that study was conducted long ago, before professional investors dominated the market.

Many growth mutual funds employ this type of analysis. One possible explanation for this effect is that stocks don't immediately reflect the full impact of the earnings surprise. Another is that one positive surprise means more could follow. Profiting from the continuation of positive surprises requires a manager to accurately judge the true value of the company, a sketchy proposition at best. Still another reason for the effect could be the self-fulfilling prophecy of growth managers buying a stock en masse after a positive earnings surprise. Whether the delayed positive reaction to an earnings surprise illustrates a potential opportunity for investment managers or whether it is the effect of growth fund managers buying stocks believing that additional surprises are in the offing is difficult to determine.

Perhaps the most famous study of the semi-strong form EMH was conducted by Fama and Kenneth French. Their research led to "The Cross-Section of Expected Stock Returns," published in the *Journal of Finance* in June 1992.[10]

Fama and French found that both size and book-to-market were significant indicators of future returns when used either by themselves or together. Specifically, the research showed that investing in smaller stocks and stocks with higher than market book-to-price ratios (those at an attractive value) yielded above-average returns. The smaller names, as illustrated by the Fama and French work, can be expected to outperform the broad market over time but can be riskier. The unfortunate reality, however, is that the small cap premium does not appear to have survived discovery—another one of those good ideas that worked until everyone started using it and a concept we will consider in more detail later.

The Strong Form EMH

The strong form EMH takes the added step of saying that markets not only fully and immediately reflect all public information but all private information as well. In *Investment Analysis and Portfolio Management*, Frank Reilly and Keith Brown[11] show that tests of the strong form EMH have analyzed the performance of the following four major groups of investors:

1. Corporate insiders
2. Stock exchange specialists
3. Security analysts at Value Line and elsewhere
4. Professional money managers

The performance of these investors was tested to determine whether any group consistently received above-average risk-adjusted returns. To earn positive abnormal returns consistently, the group must have continuing access to important private information or an ability to act consistently on public information before other investors.

Although the test results were mixed, they leaned toward confirming the strong form EMH. The results of two groups (corporate insiders and stock exchange specialists) did not completely support the efficient market hypothesis because both groups have access to important information and use it to derive above-average returns. Unfortunately, most individual investors and mutual fund managers are neither corporate insiders nor stock exchange specialists.

With regard to corporate insider trading, the early studies, most notably those in the 1960s and 1970s, supported trading in line with insiders as a way to earn abnormal profits. By the mid-1980s, however, studies began to show that the effect had become diluted by excessive public attention. Once again, a good idea went by the wayside because too many people used it.

Yet another example is the Value Line rankings. Early studies on the subject indicated that following the Value Line rankings could generally lead to abnormal returns, but the effect has been diluted in recent years.

Perhaps the strongest indication that markets are efficient is the performance of mutual funds and professional money managers. Here's what Reilly and Brown said regarding the strong form EMH:

> *The vast majority of money manager performance studies, which have typically examined the performance of mutual fund managers, have indicated that the investments by these highly trained, full-time investors could not consistently outperform a simple buy-and-hold policy on a risk-adjusted basis.*

That's a strong statement and cuts to the very heart of the subject—the tools used by active money managers today may have worked at some point in the past but don't work anymore.

A Surprising Quote from Benjamin Graham

Ultimately, both sides of the efficiency argument can point at evidence to bolster their argument, but no clear advantage is enjoyed by either. Considering all the research in support of the EMH, however, an argument for is easier to make than an argument against. And it's getting easier all the time.

Despite long periods of being out of favor, the most notable exception is the Fama and French work that says small cap and value stocks should outperform the market over time. But if the best case for an investor who wants to outperform the stock market is to dump all their money into small cap value names, why do other kinds of mutual funds, like those investing in large cap growth names, still exist?

One reason is diversification. Although Fama and French showed that small cap value should be expected to outperform the market over time, it can't be expected to outperform all the time. For institutional investors, such as pensions and endowments, returns from stocks need to be more stable than what they might expect from small cap value alone. The theory is that when small cap value is out of favor, large cap growth may be in favor.

Of course, this is not always the case. In fact, small cap value and large cap growth are positively correlated, which means that more often than not, they move in the same direction because they both are groups of domestic stocks subject to interest rates, the economy, fiscal policy, inflation, and so on.

Anyone who witnessed the emotionally charged rise in technology names in the late 1990s, the stock rally preceding the Great Financial Crisis, and the astronomical returns posted in the decade thereafter realizes that markets aren't always perfectly efficient over the short term. As long as the markets are affected by human emotions and instincts, they will not behave rationally, instead constantly being tugged by the forces of greed and fear.

Over some period of time, prices tend toward fair value and given technology, competition and regulation, that time has become astonishingly short. It's easy to point out short-term detachments from fair value, but it is exceptionally difficult to develop a repeatable means of monetizing them. The problem hasn't been identifying periods when the market has been inefficient but seeing it in advance and investing to profit from it. Without the ability to predict the direction, magnitude, and duration of short-term market moves, which no one can do consistently over time, investors would be better off assuming the markets are efficient. Even those who believe the market can be timed admit it's a tremendously difficult proposition, so why bother?

Perhaps the most severe blow to those who don't believe markets are efficient came from a highly unlikely source. Benjamin Graham, the father of fundamental analysis himself, questioned the viability of stock picking just before he died in 1976. In a discussion with Charles Ellis for *Financial Analysts Journal*, Graham had an interesting answer to the following question:

Q: *In selecting the common stock portfolio, do you advise careful study of and selectivity among different issues?*
A: *In general, no. I am no longer an advocate of elaborate techniques of security analysis in order to find superior value opportunities. This was a rewarding activity, say, 40 years ago, when our textbook* Graham and Dodd *was first*

published, but the situation has changed a great deal since then. In the old days, any well-trained security analyst could do a good, professional job of selecting undervalued issues through detailed studies, but in the light of the enormous amount of research now being carried on, I doubt whether in most cases such extensive efforts will generate sufficiently superior selections to justify their cost. To that very limited extent, I'm on the side of the "efficient market" school of thought now generally accepted by the professors.[12]

When Graham made these remarks in 1976, the markets were far less efficient than they are today. If he was willing to disregard security selection as a means of outperforming the markets then, why should we consider it a worthwhile use of our time today or invest with funds that use that kind of analysis as the basis of their philosophy?

Let's recap what we have so far. Good investment strategies have been created and utilized by very bright managers, but those strategies became obsolete once everyone started to use them. In the absence of a clearly superior idea, we can't distinguish luck from skill. For the most part, studies show that the markets are efficient, which helps bolster the point that a competitive advantage is difficult to find and nearly impossible to exploit. The investment industry, steeped in highly trained and motivated professionals fighting among themselves, perpetuates market efficiency, making competitive advantages still harder to find. In such an environment, beating the market is a difficult proposition at best. To make matters worse, the stock market can no longer be expected to shroud all these problems behind double-digit returns, because future returns are poised to underperform the past. And we haven't even started talking about fees.

Notes

1. Burton G. Malkiel, *A Random Walk Down Wall Street: The Best Investment Advice for the New Century*, revised (New York: W. W. Norton and Company, Inc., 1999), 24–25.
2. Eugene F. Fama, "Efficient Capital Markets: A Review of Theory and Empirical Work," *Journal of Finance* 25 (May 1970): 383–417.
3. NobelPrize.org.
4. Eugene F. Fama, "Efficient Capital Markets: II," *Journal of Finance* 46 (December 1991): 1575–1617.

40   M. J. Oyster

5. Frank K. Reilly and Keith C. Brown, *Investment Analysis and Portfolio Management*, Fifth Edition (Fort Worth, Texas: The Dryden Press, Harcourt Brace College Publishers, 1997), 212.
6. Ibid., 213.
7. Ibid., 213–214.
8. Ibid., 215.
9. Ibid., 217–228.
10. Eugene F. Fama and Kenneth R. French, "The Cross-Section of Expected Stock Returns," *Journal of Finance* 47 (June 1992): 427–465.
11. Reilly and Brown, *Investment Analysis and Portfolio Management*, 235–241.
12. Charles Ellis and Benjamin Graham, "A Conversation with Benjamin Graham," *Financial Analysts Journal*, vol. 32, no. 5 (September/October 1976): 20–23 (Copyright 1976, CFA Institute. Reproduced and republished from *Financial Analysts Journal* with permission from CFA Institute. All Rights Reserved).

5

Fund Manager Fees

There may be fund managers who can squeeze a small bit of outperformance from the market, but how much is left for their shareholders after paying the fund managers' fees? Large active management fees might have been ignored when the stock market was posting upwards of 15 percent annual returns but will be hard to miss if the markets return only half that rate, or less. As Charles Ellis helps us cut to the chase, most managers' fees are more than 100 percent of the real value they add.[1]

The cost of portfolio management should be compared to the incremental, risk-adjusted return relative to a passive investment in a benchmark of that style. Index funds and exchange-traded funds make it easy to achieve market-like returns, so if you are paying higher fees for active management, you should expect outperformance. Most managers, however, have failed to beat the market over time net of fees.

So what exactly do those fees look like? Mutual fund fees come in a variety of shapes and sizes, and many can be buried deep in a prospectus. Let's first take a look at how mutual funds began. The Securities Act of 1933 was the initial major legislation to regulate the offer and sale of securities previously governed by individual states (blue sky laws). Then, the Securities Exchange Act in 1934 mandated that companies listed on stock exchanges must follow certain requirements such as registrations, proxy solicitations, audit, and margin requirements. The combination of both acts led to the structure of The Investment Company Act of 1940, passed by Congress to require registration and regulation of investment companies by the Securities and Exchange Commission (SEC). The Act sets the standards by which mutual funds and

© The Author(s) 2018
M. J. Oyster, *Success in a Low-Return World*,
https://doi.org/10.1007/978-3-319-99855-8_5

other investment vehicles offered by investment companies operate with regard to promotion, reporting, and pricing of shares for sale to the public.

An investment company can fall into three broad categories: (1) an *open-ended fund*, the mutual fund with which most investors are familiar; (2) a *closed-end fund*; and, (3) a *unit investment trust* or UIT. Exchange-traded funds can be open-ended funds or UITs that trade on an exchange. The principal difference between them is that the open-ended fund can vary the number of ownership shares it offers to the public, while a closed-end fund cannot.

The cost you are being charged as a mutual fund shareholder is the *expense ratio*. The expense ratio is the percentage of fund assets paid for operating expenses and management fees. According to Morningstar, the average expense ratio charged by actively managed large cap mutual funds in 2016 was 0.75 percent.[2] Part of the expense ratio that many mutual fund investors pay is called the *12b-1*. Mutual funds can charge a 12b-1 fee, which generally falls between 0.25 percent and 1 percent, for promotional and marketing expenses. Since you're reading this, chances are you don't need to have someone else marketing your mutual funds to you, so funds charging a 12b-1 should probably be avoided. And don't forget, the 12b-1 is charged every year, so you still pay for the fund to be marketed to you after you own it even if it is closed to new investors.

Another add-on charge that investors should probably avoid is the *sales load*. Load funds are sold in the over-the-counter market by broker-dealers who don't receive a commission but instead tack on a loading charge to the net asset value (NAV) the investor must either pay at the time of purchase or defer to a later date. In the old days of mutual fund investing (1980s), a common load was 8.5 percent, but more recently, loads are down in the 3 percent to 4 percent range. A lower load is still not necessarily a bargain, as we'll see shortly. Loads are broken into two categories—the front-end load and the deferred load. In general, a mutual fund's "A shares" come with a front-end load, while "B shares" usually carry a deferred load.

An investor choosing to buy into a fund must pay the front-end load at the time of purchase, while a deferred load is charged upon redemption if the investor sells out before some stated time period (five years, for example). The idea behind charging a front-end load is that the salesperson will explain the fund to the customer and advise them on its appropriateness. A deferred load is an alternative to a front-end load in that the fee is not paid until the shares are redeemed.

These fees are paid to a financial advisor, who then helps the investor determine the fund's appropriateness, but past performance suggests the best advice would be to avoid such costs altogether. The good news is that most investors do steer clear of those costs if at all possible. In terms of net assets, no-load classes represented 80 percent, or $9.6 trillion, of total long-term mutual fund assets in the United States at the end of 2016.[3]

Additionally, the size of load fees that investors pay have dropped in recent years. The maximum front-end load fee that shareholders might pay for investing in mutual funds has changed little since 1990 (still about 5 percent). However, the front-end load fees that investors actually paid declined from nearly 4 percent in 1990 to roughly 1 percent in 2016.[4] No-load mutual fund share classes received net inflows of $113 billion in 2016 while load mutual fund share classes experienced net outflows of $232 billion. This disparity, in large part, reflects a growing trend—investors paying intermediaries for advice and assistance directly out of their pockets rather than indirectly through funds.[5]

How Fees Combined with Behavioral Errors Can Impact Returns

For some investors, a load represents a justifiable expense for the advice that would come with it, but as we will see, the advice needs to be stellar to be justified. Let's say you buy into a fund with a 3 percent load. Only $97 of every $100 you started with is actually invested in the product. This way, you immediately lose 3 percent, which you hope will be made up by superior active management. As mentioned previously, this is more difficult than it sounds.

To earn back the cost of load, the fund that charged you 3 percent up front would need to outperform a no-load index fund by 1 percent every year for four years in a row, which is highly unrealistic. Even if it experienced an occasional lagging year, as all funds do, it would have to outperform by 1.1 percent one year and then lag by no more than 0.5 percent the following year, repeating the process for a total of ten years just to make up the 3 percent front-end load. Expecting an active manager to produce such strong returns is unrealistic.

An investment in a fund charging a deferred load of 3 percent would obviously have to outperform by a cumulative 3 percent before an investor would want to sell out. A 12b-1 of 0.75 percent automatically puts an investor behind the index by that much every year.

This model also assumes that the investor doesn't switch in and out of funds along the way. Studies have shown that most large cap actively managed funds lag the benchmark after fees, but the returns an investor actually experiences are even worse. The results of research done by Dalbar Inc. consistently show that the average investor earns below-average returns. For the 20 years ending December 2016, the S&P 500 Index averaged 7.7 percent annualized return per year. The average equity fund investor, however, earned only 4.8 percent.[6] And for that period at least, you can't explain it by failing to keep up with a runaway market because the 7.7 percent annualized stock market return falls below the long-term average of approximately 10 percent.

The Dalbar study also notes that the average retention rate for equity fund holders was just 3.8 years. It seems that investors simply can't bring themselves to hold a fund longer than four years on average but whipping into and out of funds can inhibit returns. Fund manager hiring and firing decisions are often based upon recent performance, but research indicates that common biases employed when drawing upon short-term relative returns can inhibit performance. As you can see in Fig. 5.1, managers underperformed their benchmark by 4.1 percentage points in the three years prior to being fired but then outperformed by nearly the exact same amount three years thereafter. Similarly, managers outperformed their benchmark by over ten percentage points in the three years prior to being hired but then only barely outperformed the three years thereafter.[7]

It's important to note that this study of pre- and post-investment manager hiring and firing analyzed the decisions made by plan sponsors, that is, "sophisticated" institutional investors. It seems that even those with greater

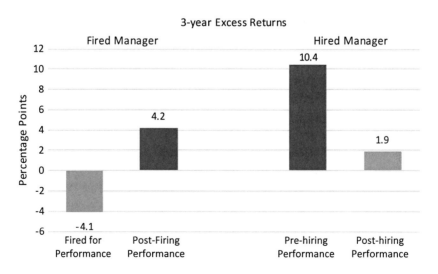

Fig. 5.1 Biases in manager hiring and firing

experience, resources, and access to information are just as human as individual investors. Part of the reason we engage in such self-destructive investment behavior is because of the way our brains are wired.

Investors are all too human and make the behavioral error of following the crowd. They hear about a hot fund that has booked stellar performance and jump on board with everyone else. Unfortunately, their timing is often dead wrong. In many cases, an investor will sell out of a fund after a period of poor performance believing the active manager is simply inept (which may be true) but not realizing that the manager's style may just be temporarily out of favor. Many good active managers underperform for three to five years or longer. For those unwilling to take a long-term approach with a manager, a better strategy might be to simply buy and hold the S&P 500 Index.

An instinct toward herding may have provided early humans safety and opportunity, but can inhibit investment performance. The fear of missing out can be powerful. Loss aversion represents another explanation for poor investment-related decision-making. We are willing to sacrifice a lot to avoid pain. Humans are wired to feel more pain from losses than joy from gains, and when faced with a loss, we are more willing to accept risk than when presented with a gain. Many of us simply can't take the pain of having to watch a losing investment any longer and we will sell it just to be rid of it, doing so at perhaps an inopportune time.

Hedge Fund Fees

The hedge fund industry's answer to fee issues is an incentive fee, also known as a *performance-based fee*. Many performance-based fees charged by hedge funds start with a management fee between 1 and 2 percent, then 20 percent of the profits the investor makes. Many of these also have a high water mark, meaning that they won't pay the manager a performance fee in a profitable quarter until the manager has made up a certain amount that was lost in prior quarters. This has great appeal to some of the more successful active managers who have departed their position as mutual fund managers in favor of hedge fund management positions. But, performance-based fees are not without their flaws.

Consider the hedge fund manager who is underwater and hasn't earned a performance-based fee in a while. This manager might be inclined to take on more risky positions than in the past to shock performance back into the black. Obviously, the risky positions could blow up in the hedge fund manager's face, making a bad situation even worse. Likewise, the investors wouldn't find out until too late because of the shroud of secrecy under which most hedge funds operate. In some cases, funds actually close once they are under-water, because getting back to even just seems too difficult. Some funds choose to start over rather than miss out on incentive-based fees until they can recover losses.

Hedge fund fees have declined in recent years but remain elevated relative to the average mutual fund. According to a report from Deutsche Bank, the average management fee paid for a hedge fund investment in 2017 was 1.56 percent while the average performance fee was 17.3 percent.[8] In part due to abysmal performance, hedge fund investors have pressured managers to lower or even eliminate certain fees. In an attempt to save client relationships, hedge fund managers have responded with creative solutions. Some funds offer zero percent management fee with 30 percent performance fee, which may sound like an appropriate alignment of interest between the fund manager and investor, but perhaps it also invites the excessive risk problem mentioned earlier.

It was introduced previously that Morningstar indicated that the average actively managed large cap mutual fund charges a 0.75 percent expense ratio every year, yet most of these funds have failed to outperform. By contrast, some index funds are far less expensive and fulfill their charge of keeping up with the benchmark. Index equity mutual fund expense ratios fell from 0.27 percent in 1996 to 0.09 percent in 2016.[9]

Translating these percentages into real dollars illustrates how fees can deci-mate returns. Let's compare two funds: an actively managed large cap fund and an index fund. The actively managed fund has a typical 0.75 percent expense ratio and the index fund charges an expense ratio of 0.09 percent. Although highly unlikely, let's say the active manager posts returns in line with the index for a 20-year period during which both return 7 percent per year before fees. The findings are that the index fund is clearly the better choice after fees are levied. If an initial investment of $1,000,000 was made in each fund, the index fund investment would be worth $471,837 more than the actively managed fund after 20 years. Even if you found one of the best actively managed funds that actually perform as well as the index, the higher fees will severely cut into profits.

At the end of 2017, in large part because of poor performance, a reassess-ment of fees was taking place across the entire investment landscape. Many actively managed mutual funds were seeing assets flow out as investment dol-lars departed for passively managed, lower-cost index funds. One can imagine that at some extreme point the indexing behemoth will have so decimated active stock picking that greater opportunities will be available for the few that remain, but active managers still outnumber their passive counterparts by a wide margin so it's hard to imagine that happening soon. Disruption can be difficult but can prove supportive of the greater good. Active managers, of both mutual and/or hedge funds, are offering concessions in the form of lower fees and/or zero management fees with an incentive tied to relative performance. Such fee arrangements can bring unwanted risks but their ability to more closely align the interests of managers and investors appears to be a positive development. So, as we move through the end of the twenty-first century's second decade, savvy investors should continue to seek ways to minimize performance drags due to fees. Unless the stock market substantially exceeds the returns expected in coming years, every penny will count.

Notes

1. Charles D. Ellis, "Symptoms and Signs," *The Journal of Portfolio Management* (Summer 2002): 16–21.
2. Press release from Newsroom.Morningstar.com. "Morningstar's Annual Fund Fee Study Finds Investors are Paying Less Than Ever for Their Fund Investments," Chicago, May 23, 2017.
3. Strategic Insight, "Monitoring Trends in Mutual Fund Cost of Ownership and Expense Ratios," 2017 Update, 5.
4. Sean Collins and James Duvall. 2017. "Trends in the Expenses and Fees of Funds, 2016," *ICI Research Perspective* 23, no. 3. (May). Available at www.ici. org/pdf/per23-03.pdf.
5. Ibid.
6. Lance Roberts, "Opinion: Americans are still terrible at investing, annual study once again shows," Marketwatch.com, October 21, 2017.
7. Source: FEG Investment Advisors. Data source: Goyal, Amit and Wahal Sunil, "The Selection and Termination of Investment Managers by Plan Sponsors," *Journal of Finance*, August 2008.
8. Chris Flood, *Financial Times*, "Hedge funds forced to cut fees to lure investors," February 18, 2018.
9. Sean Collins and James Duvall. 2017. "Trends in the Expenses and Fees of Funds, 2016," *ICI Research Perspective* 23, no. 3. (May). Available at www.ici. org/pdf/per23-03.pdf.

6

To Err Is to Be Human. To Make a Behavioral Error Is to Be a Human Investor

Among the other concepts discussed thus far, we have intermingled a few thoughts regarding how human behavior can shape investment decision making. As much or more than any other time in history, cognitive biases are being studied and utilized to help us make better investment decisions and perhaps limit some of our mistakes.

The human brain is an amazing thing. Our ability to influence and manipulate the world around us stems not from superior physical attributes like strength or size but rather by cognitive skills. Mammals weighing 130 pounds have an average brain size of 12 cubic inches. Modern humans exhibit brains averaging 73–85 cubic inches. A homo sapien brain accounts for about 2 percent to 3 percent of total body weight but it consumes 25 percent of the body's energy at rest. By comparison, the brains of other apes require only 8 percent of rest-time energy.[1]

Around 100,000 years ago, Earth was populated by at least six different species of humans but only homo sapiens exist today.[2] How did we win out and survive? Survival of the fittest certainly played a role. Just within the last 12,000 years our species made the transition to producing food by cooperatively changing the surroundings in order to do so. Unique abilities in how we communicate, process information, avoid danger, form groups, and collectively come together in support of a common cause all likely contributed. As investors, however, we are left with legacies from our ancestors that served them well as tribal hunters and gatherers but can inhibit our ability to make sound investment choices.

Markets are made up of human decision makers. Sometimes a trade can be triggered by a computer program, but that program was designed by a human.

© The Author(s) 2018
M. J. Oyster, *Success in a Low-Return World*,
https://doi.org/10.1007/978-3-319-99855-8_6

Investing is all about decisions made by people. The collective choices made by individuals deploying capital in the marketplace sum to a market's performance; likewise an individual's set of decisions to do one thing over another determine whether their goals will be achieved or not.

A cognitive bias is a systematic pattern of deviation from the norm of what is rational in judgment. By some accounts, there are nearly 200 documented cognitive biases[3] that affect human decision making. We aren't able to conduct a thorough treatment of all of them here, but we will focus on a few that apply directly to investing. We begin by seeking a means of summarizing and categorizing the large and continuously evolving group of documented cognitive, otherwise known as behavioral, biases.

In 2016, researcher Buster Benson compiled and classified[4] 175 different cognitive biases listed on Wikipedia into four different categories. With no established convention of classification at the time, he decided to group them according to the general mental problem that each was attempting to address. Most biases evolved for a good reason—generally to help our brains save time, energy, or both. According to Benson's research, it becomes easier to understand why cognitive biases exist, how they are useful, and the trade-offs (and resulting mental errors) that they introduce if you look at them by the problem they are trying to solve.

Benson's four broad categories of cognitive biases are as follows:

- Too much information
- Not enough meaning
- Need to act fast
- What should we remember?

Let's look at each of these in more detail.

Too Much Information (TMI)

Our senses are very effective at providing our brains with information. Too effective in fact. As powerful as the human brain is, it can't absorb and process all the information being fed to it. As a result, the brain is forced to work as efficiently as possible and make compromises. Some things we remember. Some things we forget. The process of determining what gets saved versus what gets pitched can lead to observable biases in human decision making.

One way the brain seeks efficiency is to focus more on things that are already established in our memories. An example of this is known as *frequency illusion.* If you buy a red coupe, for example, you may suddenly start noticing red coupes everywhere you go. The number of these cars hasn't actually increased, it just seems that way.

Another way that the brain manages TMI is that it prioritizes some bits of information over others; for example, the bizarre, weird, and funny thing that happens to stick out relative to that which is ordinary and expected. A related bias is the *picture superiority effect*, which refers to the phenomenon in which pictures and images are more likely to be remembered than words.

We are also drawn to details that confirm our existing beliefs and ignore details that contradict our established view. This is a big one in investing. Related biases include *anchoring*, which describes an overreliance on an initial data point and the *ostrich effect*, the avoidance of apparently risky financial situations by pretending that they simply do not exist.

Not Enough Meaning

Although we probably aren't aware of this process at any given point in time, humans develop from birth onward to learn how to deal with the bombardment of TMI. Basically, the brain is forced to narrow the stimuli down. After that occurs, we need to make sense of it all. In order to do this, the human brain will connect proverbial dots and fill in the blanks with things we think we already know. One way we do this is to find stories and patterns in data where they may or may not actually exist. Due to the fact that we are forced to narrow the flood of information down to the most important stuff, our brains need to reconstruct the world inside our heads so it feels complete. Unfortunately, this can result in inhibiting biases for investors that we might not even realize exist.

A bias that we will talk more about later is the *gambler's fallacy* and the related *hot hand fallacy*. Gambler's fallacy is the mistaken belief that, if something happens more frequently than normal during a given period, it will happen less frequently in the future. Said another way, human beings are influenced to act in certain ways based upon their observation of recent events. For example, if red has come up on a roulette wheel ten times in a row, we might be tempted to bet on black, but the next spin is no more likely to result in a red outcome than any other. The hot hand fallacy represents the idea that someone who finds success with a random event has a greater likelihood of success in future events. But that's not necessarily the case. This cognitive bias is so powerful, the SEC wrote Rule 156, which requires mutual funds to make the seemingly obvious statement that "past performance is not indicative of future results."

Need to Act Fast

Human beings evolved in difficult conditions. We didn't have the speed of a cheetah or the size of a wooly mammoth, but we survived on our smarts and in many cases, our ability to think, and to do so as quickly as possible. When new information came in, we had to swiftly interpret it, simulate a multitude of future outcomes and consequences, and then act. In order to achieve this in a way that maximized the probability of survival, the brain was forced to manage information in ways that were effective thousands of years ago but can inhibit decision making today.

For example, we tend to assign more value to things in the present than the future. If I offered you $1.00 today but $1.10 in a week would you wait? Many people wouldn't. What if I offered you $1.00 one year from now but $1.10 in a year and a week? Many people would be willing to wait the extra week in that case. The cognitive bias here is known as *hyperbolic discounting*. The strong preference for a reward that comes sooner rather than later can result in decisions that can inhibit long-term investment performance.

Another human behavior resulting from the need to act fast is the willingness to choose the least risky option or one that preserves the status quo within a group. With the exception of the few leaders that were commonly the cause than the consequence of communal living, the trait of not rocking the boat helped early communities continue to evolve. In investing, this can result in advisors and managers providing a palatable yet inferior allocation relative to a superior, out-of-the-box solution.

In a related way, we also have a tendency to focus our time and energy on things that are simple and avoid difficult problems. The *bike shed effect*, also known as *the law of triviality* helps explain this.

In his 1957 book *Parkinson's Law, or the Pursuit of Progress*, C. Northcote Parkinson describes a committee that met to discuss the construction of a new nuclear power plant. The agenda included three items: approving the plans for the plant, discussing a new bicycle shed for employees, and the refreshment expenses of the Welfare Committee. The committee spent two and a half minutes discussing the highly complex power plant, forty-five lively minutes debating the bicycle shed, and over an hour furiously debating the refreshments—the matter was eventually left unresolved and deferred to a further meeting. This bike shed effect is easily explained: true expertise on nuclear plants is rare, while everybody can have a say about bicycle sheds, and refreshments are clear and dear to all.[5] More practically, institutional investment committee meetings are often bogged down with contentious discussions of items of minimal significance to the success of the organization's mission while more influential, yet complicated matters are avoided.

What Should We Remember?

One way the brain seeks efficiency is to form generalities. We do this out of necessity, but the impact of implicit associations, stereotypes, and prejudice results in some of the most glaringly bad consequences from our full set of cognitive biases. The human brain is also forced to reduce events and lists to their key elements. We pick out just a few items to represent the whole.

We also store memories differently depending upon how they are experienced. Our brains will only encode information that it deems important at the time, but this decision can be affected by other circumstances that have little to do with the information's value such as what else is happening, how is the information presenting itself, can we easily find the information again if we need to, and so on.

As it pertains to investing, one of the most important cognitive biases falls under this category—*negativity bias* (and the closely related *prospect theory*, which we will discuss in more detail later). Negativity bias suggests that human beings feel more intensely from unpleasant thoughts and emotions than neutral or positive ones. Simply put, something very positive will generally have less of an impact on a person's behavior and cognitive awareness than something equally as emotional but negative in nature.

Behavioral Finance

The science of utilizing psychology to help explain shortcomings in investor decision making lies within the discipline of behavioral economics and more specifically, *behavioral finance*. The groundbreaking work on the subject was conducted by two Israeli psychologists, Daniel Kahneman and Amos Tversky, who demonstrated that people are anything but the rational human beings that the accepted economic models assumed them to be. Based upon this work, Kahneman won the Nobel Prize in Economics in 2002 (Tversky died in 1996).

In recent years, behavioral finance has gained greater acceptance as it has chipped away at the established models, and more accolades have followed. Professor Robert Shiller shared the Nobel Prize in Economics in 2013 for work that challenged assumptions of rationality. Professor Richard Thaler won the 2017 Nobel Prize in Economics for his research on behavioral finance and the benefits his work provided to the areas of investing and retirement planning, amongst others.

The behavioral finance scientists of today seek to understand and describe the human characteristics of market behavior and illustrate where traditional financial models have fallen short because they don't incorporate human biases and emotions.

One such traditional economic model, which serves as the driving force behind much of what's done in investing today, is the Markowitz Modern Portfolio Theory (MPT).[6] MPT does a great job of providing a general framework for describing portfolio construction that maximizes expected return for a given level of risk, but it is limited by three important assumptions that may or may not be true:

1. *Investors are risk averse.* Given a choice, they prefer less risk to more risk.
2. *Investors are rational.* Investment decisions are based upon all relevant information pertaining to a security's valuation.
3. *Investors consider asset integration when constructing portfolios.* A security is not only selected based upon its own characteristics but how its performance will affect the portfolio as a whole given the other securities in the portfolio.

The behavioral crowd looks at these a bit differently. Here's what they believe:[7]

1. *Investors are loss averse, meaning they prefer an uncertain loss to a certain loss.* Loss-averse investors are actually willing to take on more risk if it allows them to avoid a certain loss. Here is an example: You are given a choice between a guaranteed loss of $5000 or an equal chance of winning or losing $10,000. If you are like most people, you would take the chance, because we are so fearful of a guaranteed loss we are willing to risk having to pay twice as much. However, if given a guaranteed *gain* of $5000 or an equal chance of winning or losing $10,000, most people would take the gain and avoid the bet. In an investing sense, an all too human investment professional may take on more risk by holding a stock with deteriorating fundamentals while it drops, because selling it would mean accepting a guaranteed loss.
2. *Investors exhibit biased expectations and are overconfident in their abilities.* People sometimes have a biased opinion of something because of a personal attachment or an unrealistic sense of control. A professional stock picker

may overestimate the ability of a company's management after having visited them and met with them personally. Private oil and gas managers provide investors with trips to oil fields to tour the rigs and infrastructure in hopes that they make a personal attachment with the investments after seeing and touching them personally.

3. *Investors construct portfolios via asset segregation.* Fund managers and analysts dig deep inside the companies they follow in hopes of uncovering some bit of information the rest of the world doesn't yet know but spend far less time on how that stock fits in with the portfolio as a whole. Most fund managers claim they are stock pickers first and foremost, which may sound like a competitive advantage but can actually inhibit performance if all the holdings have similar characteristics.

Let's now dig into a few specific behavioral biases and talk about how they apply specifically to investment decision making.

Anchoring and Overconfidence

An important bias that shows up frequently in investing and is categorized under TMI is known as *anchoring*. Anchoring describes the tendency for people to rely too heavily on an initial piece of information when making decisions. In order to help improve the efficiency of information processing, our brains sometimes fill-in-the-blanks with *this is what this is*, and despite the advent of data to the contrary, we are slow to absorb new information.

Even though mutual fund managers are really smart, highly trained professionals, they are not immune to behavioral errors. Years ago in my investment manager research days, I was conducting ongoing due diligence of a bright, successful stock-picking fund manager. During our conversations over the course of a year or so, I frequently asked about a particular stock in his portfolio that kept falling quarter after quarter. In each of our discussions, I asked him whether he still liked the long-term prospects for the stock since the market clearly did not. Every quarter, the fund manager glowingly showered me with all the wonderful product details and financial merits it enjoyed. The company had a great business model, improving earnings, and was trading at an attractive value.

At one point, the stock was the fund's largest holding, but a 90 percent drop in value changed that. After the fund manager lost a substantial amount of his investors' money on this stock alone, he finally sold. When I asked him why he closed the position, he said the fundamentals had deteriorated.

Regardless of whether the fundamentals had deteriorated or not, he simply held on to the stock too long, believing the market would eventually come to its senses and prove him right. He was wrong and had become one of the many victims of the all too human trait of anchoring. It took an inordinate amount of evidence to the contrary to modify the thesis that the fund manager developed at the outset.

A separate bias, *overconfidence*, also played a role. Overconfidence is a particularly common problem in investing. One study showed that 70 percent of adult males think they are in the top 25 percent for leadership qualities.[8] The problems of overconfidence in investing may have more to do with overconfidence in males, who outnumber females in professional investing, but that's a different topic and is, thankfully, beyond the scope of this discussion. Overconfidence can prevent stocks from being sold after they have run up or after they have declined. It is hard to accept sometimes, but we tend to think we're smarter than we really are, and we're stubborn when we're wrong.

The mutual fund manager discussed previously followed the Benjamin Graham philosophy of buying a good company, whose inner-workings and industry he clearly understood, at an attractive value. He was simply wrong, and his refusal to accept his mistake cost him and his investors dearly. Perhaps a little bit of luck, or a bit more time would have allowed his thesis to play out as expected. Unfortunately, time is a luxury and unlimited time is a luxury that investment professionals do not possess. As Sir John Maynard Keynes once said, "*The market can remain irrational longer than you can remain solvent.*" Obviously, making money in the stock market is not as simple as buying good companies at an attractive value. A lot of smart people spend all day trying to do exactly that and still fail to beat the benchmarks.

Illusion of Control

A bias that falls within the *need-to-act-fast* category is the *illusion of control*. In addition to overconfidence, many investors feel an unrealistic sense of control over their investments after making an emotional connection or personal contact of some kind. Consider the study where one group of people was shown a card out of a blue deck, each being told that if their card was chosen later, they would receive $100.[9] Another group was given the same offer, but they were allowed to choose their card (from a red deck), hold it, look at it, and then put it back in the deck.

Each group was asked whether they wanted to sell their card, thus forfeiting their opportunity to win $100 if their card was chosen. Of those who were only shown a card (from the blue deck), 19 percent were unwilling to sell back their cards, and the average asking price of those choosing to sell was $2. However, of those who actually chose and held a card (from the red deck), 39 percent were unwilling to sell back their cards, and the average asking price was $9 per card.

The act of personal contact with a card clearly made it more valuable in the participants' minds. In comparable fashion, stock analysts who meet with the owners of the companies they follow, visit their plants, and talk to their employees, may fall prey to an unrealistic sense of control regarding their analysis of the company's stock. Doing so can lead to overestimating earnings prospects or underestimating the impact of negative events, both of which could have detrimental effects on the stock's performance. Compromised objectivity can be disastrous for investors, so it's important to understand how personal contact and the illusion of control can affect perception and the decisions that arise from that belief.

Gambler's Fallacy

One of my favorite investment researchers is Toby Moskowitz. Moskowitz collaborated on a paper with Daniel Chen and Kelly Shue titled (collectively CMK) "Decision-Making under the Gambler's Fallacy: Evidence from Asylum Judges, Loan Officers, and Baseball Umpires."[10] The "gambler's fallacy" as was described previously under Benson's "not enough meaning" category indicates how recent events influence the decision-making process. The work that Moskowitz and his collaborators conducted reviewed some impactful, potentially life-altering decisions, which would have you believe the decision makers would be less prone to bias. Yet it still showed up.

First, CMK reviewed the decisions made by judges regarding asylum cases. One would hope that the judges would decide whether to grant asylum or not based strictly on merit and the law. Yet they found, after normalizing the data for comparison, judges are up to 3.3 percentage points more likely to reject the current case if they approved the previous case. This translates to two percent of decisions being reversed purely due to the sequencing of past decisions, all else equal.

Second, CMK tested whether loan officers are more likely to deny a loan application after approving the previous application using data from a loan officer. They found that up to nine percent of decisions are reversed due to negative autocorrelation in decisions. In other words, if they granted multiple loans in a row, a subsequent application is more likely to be denied. Recent events carry an undue amount of influence on decisions.

Third, CMK tested whether baseball umpires are more likely to call the current pitch a ball after calling the previous pitch a strike and vice versa. They found that umpires are 1.5 percentage points less likely to call a pitch a strike if the previous pitch was called a strike. This effect more than doubles when the current pitch is close to the edge of the strike zone (so it is a less obvious call) and is also significantly larger following two previous calls in the same direction. Put differently, MLB umpires call the same pitches in the exact same location differently depending solely on the sequence of previous calls.

What does this mean for investing? The human behavioral bias that allows decisions to be influenced by recent events can cloud judgment and inhibit investment performance. We should as much as possible limit the amount of credence we give the recent past and focus on the fundamental factors that can be expected to influence the future. Just because emerging market equities, for example, was the best performing asset category for a three-year period doesn't mean it won't be so again this year. We should also not be fooled into thinking that just because the stock market exhibited strong performance for the decade following the Great Financial Crisis it will do so for the ten years thereafter.

In-Group Favoritism and FOMO

Another *not enough meaning bias* is the concept of *in-group favoritism* (or bias). In-group bias describes the idea that we tend to favor people in our group over outsiders. Early in human evolution, our ancestors banded together for safety, food, and procreation. When a nomadic Cro-Magnon stumbled upon a tribe of successful hunter/gatherers, the individual might feel a strong urge to join them and if accepted, would find favor with all things associated with the group relative to outsiders. We still feel an instinctive pull to join groups, especially with those having more success than we are. Investment history is replete with examples of massive herding behavior that is driven by a fear of missing out (FOMO). The instinct to join and not miss out is powerful and in some cases leads to investment bubbles as hordes of people all rush in at the same time.

Some investors, driven by the desire to join a successful group, might purchase a hot stock, commodity, or cryptocurrency by following the crowd and paying too much. If the investment starts to drop in value, as it often will after reaching an unsustainable price, bad cognitive behavior kicks in, prompting investors to hold it entirely too long. Booking a loss, however, means admitting you were wrong while simultaneously giving up any possibility that you might ultimately be proven right on that particular trade. After conducting hours of research on a potential investment and then committing capital to it, making such an admission takes strength that many investors simply don't have.

Agency Friction

One of the most significant behavioral errors made by individual and institutional investors alike is *agency friction*.[11] Agency friction is closely related to the bias *system justification theory*, which is included in the need-to-act-fast group. Agency friction is derived from an investor's desire to hold stocks of highly profitable and industry-leading companies, even though most studies indicate the laggards outperform the leaders over time. By the time a company has ascended to being a money-making industry leader, its stock price already reflects that ascent and may be predicting more growth and profitability than should reasonably be expected.

Many investors believe that owning highly profitable companies is a low-risk way to invest, but such is not the case. If expectations are high, which they usually are for the strongest companies, the company may not be able to grow enough to justify its high valuation, so the stock price has nowhere to go but down. The company may continue to make money and retain its industry leadership, but if future profitability fails to meet expectations, the stock will drop. Many people who tout the ownership of good companies fail to recognize this important risk.

Agency friction is a problem when the directors of an institutional plan like a pension board believe their investment managers should own stocks of industry-leading companies. The pension plan's investment managers may willingly comply with this perception. The fund manager or investment professional may recognize the risk in owning industry leaders and know that the stock prices of these companies may be overstating future earnings growth, but rather than rock the boat, they buy these names and avoid the "friction" of explaining why industry laggards are being held. Underperformance, which inevitably befalls all fund managers, is far easier to justify when the portfolio contains money-making companies than if the portfolio holds a bunch of losers. The losers, however, often offer far greater potential for future advancement than those stocks that have already made it.

Prospect Theory

As we delve into the final bias discussed here, we harken back to the behavioral retort to traditional economic models that says investors prefer less risk to more. That may sound like a reasonable assumption, but the traditional models describe risk in the form of performance variability, which can be either positive or negative. Behavioral scientists contend investors actually care less about variability and more about loss. For some reason, our brains are wired to feel more pain from a loss than an equal amount of joy from a gain.

The aforementioned early work in behavioral economics conducted by Kahneman and Tversky included a paper titled "Prospect Theory: An Analysis of Decision Under Risk".[12]

Figure 6.1 is an adaptation from one included in the Kahneman and Tversky paper, which serves to illustrate how people tend to experience more pain from loss than pleasure from an equally sized gain. Strong aversion to pain leads to greater risk-taking when faced with a loss than when faced with a gain. Investors "double-down" on losses and become protective of gains.

This bias and resulting investment decisions are easily observable in investment data. Prospect theory and loss aversion help explain why put options—contracts that provide the holder some measure of loss protection on an underlying security—tend to be more expensively valued relative call options, which provide the holder positive returns if the underlying security advances. People are afraid of experiencing losses, so much so, they are willing to overpay relative to fair value for protection against such losses. This idea will be discussed in more detail later as we describe how this overpricing can be monetized for investment returns.

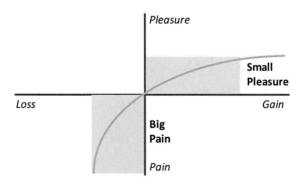

Fig. 6.1 Prospect theory illustrated. Source: FEG, illustrative interpretation of work by Kahneman and Tversky

Conclusion

Rather than just an exercise in describing our own human shortcomings, the knowledge of, then the real-time observation of, cognitive biases can help us avoid common mistakes that can inhibit investment performance. As AQR's Cliff Asness has said, investing is hard. As if market efficiency, competition, and fees weren't enough, those who seek to outperform the market through security selection must contend with their own behavioral shortcomings. No human being on the planet can avoid the negative effect emotions have on their behavior. Even the most seasoned professionals are subject to the forces of greed, fear, overconfidence, and pain avoidance, all of which serve to inhibit their ability to outperform. But by understanding then observing common behavioral biases in action, we hope to limit behavioral pitfalls in our investment decision making, as well as find opportunities to monetize mispricings that behavioral biases create.

Notes

1. Yuval Noah Harari, 2015. *Sapiens, A Brief History of Humankind*, Harper Collins Publishers, 195 Broadway, New York, NY 10007. 8–9.
2. Yuval Noah Harari, 2015. *Sapiens, A Brief History of Humankind*, Harper Collins Publishers, 195 Broadway, New York, NY 10007. 8.
3. Buster Benson, BetterHumans.coach.me, "Cognitive bias cheat sheet," September 1, 2016.
4. Ibid.
5. "Avoid Parkinson's Bicycle Shed Effect," Wikipedia.com. edited June 16, 2016.
6. Markowitz, H.M. (March 1952), "Portfolio Selection", *The Journal of Finance*, 7 (1): 77–91.
7. Amos Tversky, "The Psychology of Risk," *Quantifying the Market Risk Premium Phenomenon for Investment Decision Making* (Association for Investment Management and Research [AIMR] Conference Proceedings, 1990), 73–77.
8. Arnold S. Wood, "Behavioral Risk: Anecdotes and Disturbing Evidence," in *Investing Worldwide IV: February 21–23, 1993, Pasadena, California* (Association for Investment Management and Research [AIMR], 1993), 76.
9. Ibid.

10. Daniel Chen, Tobias J. Moskowitz, Kelly Shue, "Decision-Making under the Gambler's Fallacy: Evidence from Asylum Judges, Loan Officers, and Baseball Umpires," September 17, 2015.

11. Arnold S. Wood, "Behavioral Risk: Anecdotes and Disturbing Evidence," in *Investing Worldwide IV: February 21–23, 1993, Pasadena, California* (Association for Investment Management and Research [AIMR], 1993), 77–78.

12. Daniel Kahneman and Amos Tversky, "Prospect Theory: An Analysis of Decision Under Risk," *Econometrica*, Volume 47, Number 2, March, 1979. 263.

7

How Regulations Impact Investment Managers

The history of financial disasters is as old as time. They usually involved a boom period marked by financial institutions engaged in aggressive risk taking, a preponderance of excessive leverage and/or questionable lending practices that ultimately ended in a disastrous bust. Needless to say, trust in those institutions was eroded. Attempting to reestablish that trust, new regulations explicitly designed to prevent the painful tragedy from happening again were frequently enacted immediately following financial crises. In comparable fashion to the general who proves ineffective because he prepares only for the most recent war, regulations following financial crises are often overreaching and fail to prevent the next crisis because it might not look exactly like the last.

Stepping back in time about 100 years ago, the regulatory environment in which financial companies operated looked nothing like it does today. Banking and financial crises were generally more common and greater in magnitude than those seen in modern times. In 1933, in response to several thousand banks failing during the Great Depression, Congress passed, and President Franklin Roosevelt signed into law, the Banking Act of 1933, more commonly known as Glass-Steagall.

Many banks failed at the time in part because they held certain risky assets on their balance sheets including stocks. After the stock market crashed in 1929, bank depositors rushed to withdraw funds after learning of their bank's stress and possible impending doom, which exacerbated the problem. Glass-Steagall was formed in response with two important provisions: (1) the Federal Deposit Insurance Corporation (FDIC) was created to give depositors a sense

© The Author(s) 2018
M. J. Oyster, *Success in a Low-Return World*,
https://doi.org/10.1007/978-3-319-99855-8_7

of security and limit future runs on banks; and (2) banks were no longer permitted to use depositors' funds for risky investments as it formally separated commercial and investment banking activity.

The Volcker Rule

In 1999, the portion of Glass-Steagall that separated commercial and investment banking was repealed through the Gramm-Leach-Bliley Act, also known as the Financial Services Modernization Act of 1999. It would be a stretch to suggest Gramm-Leach-Bliley caused the Great Financial Crisis (GFC) although the deterioration of risky assets held on certain banks' balance sheets contributed to the stress. In 2010, in response to the ills of the GFC, one of the most sweeping set of regulations in the United States' financial industry (some would say too sweeping) was drafted into law—the Dodd-Frank Wall Street Reform and Consumer Protection Act, or Dodd-Frank for short. A worthy treatment of Dodd-Frank's nuances goes beyond the scope of this work and it impacts banking more than investing, but one area deems further attention—the Volcker Rule.

The Volcker Rule is a subset of Dodd-Frank named for the vocal proponent of the idea—Paul Volcker, former chairman of the Federal Reserve. The Volcker Rule prohibits banks from making certain kinds of speculative investments. Sounds a little like Glass-Steagall 2.0. Prior to the GFC, many banks operated proprietary (prop) trading operations in which a bank traded its own money in stocks, bonds, currencies, commodities, or anything else for that matter in hopes of boosting the bank's bottom line. Volcker's point was that since a functioning commercial banking system is important to the economy as a whole, banks engaging in high-risk speculation bring about an unacceptable level of systemic risk. In early 2018, there was a push to repeal the Volcker Rule, which would represent the latest in the cyclical history of deregulation, crisis, re-regulation, deregulation, and so on.

The Volcker Rule impacted the asset-management business in a number of ways. Many talented prop traders left banks to start or join hedge funds. More significantly, the regulation further skewed an important pricing anomaly that can lead to investment opportunities. In Chap. 6 we discussed how the powerful behavioral biases of loss aversion and prospect theory have led to demand for, then subsequent overpricing of, *put options*, which are securities that some investors buy to limit the risk of declines in investment value. Investors are so concerned with the pain of loss, they willingly overpay for put protection. Prior to the Volcker Rule, an activity in which many banks' prop traders engaged was generating income by selling overpriced puts.

Put prices have historically exceeded calls, a characteristic especially prevalent in index options. The disparity increased following the GFC in part because fears were heightened but also after the Volcker Rule removed downward pressure from banks selling puts. Additionally, banks frequently sought ways of limiting risk to comply with Dodd-Frank and buying puts served as an expedient means of doing so. More to the point, bank activity moved from put selling to put buying. The impact that shift from supply to demand had on price was substantial. Figure 7.1 helps explain this anomaly.

The Credit Suisse Fear Barometer (CSFB) measures the price comparison between S&P 500 index puts and calls where elevated levels of the index represent high relative prices of puts. CSFB levels at 10 indicate price neutrality between puts and calls. Following GFC, and then in earnest after Dodd-Frank became law in 2010, puts became highly expensive relative to calls. Despite exceptionally positive stock market performance at the time, put prices rose to approximately three-times greater than calls.

If the Volcker Rule were repealed, would this anomaly diminish? Perhaps to an extent, but it would take years before bank prop desks were running the size of assets they were pre-crisis, if ever. And even prior to Dodd-Frank back as far as the 1987 stock market crash, S&P 500 index put options have almost always been more expensively priced than calls. It stands to reason that regardless of regulations, human beings will continue to experience more pain from

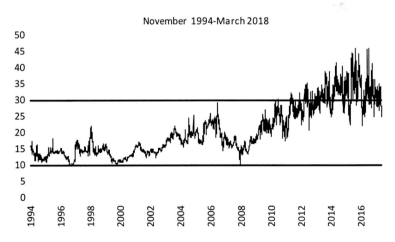

Fig. 7.1   The Credit Suisse Fear Barometer

loss than pleasure from gain, and the impact of those emotions will remain reflected in elevated put prices relative to calls.

A review of history can provide an interesting insight into how systemic financial disasters led to regulations and what unintended consequences followed. Other more localized crises have also resulted in regulations designed to repair public trust, and many of these have had a direct impact on the work done by professional stock-picking money managers.

Regulations and the Stock Picker

The most frequently discussed topic at meetings I've had with mutual fund managers is the group of companies whose stocks comprise the fund's portfolio. Managers love to talk about their fund companies and frequently speak of them with a doting affection that might otherwise be reserved for their children. In part, managers want fund researchers to know how much care and detail they put into their work (which is quite substantial in most cases), but they also want a researcher to be aware of how much they know about the inner workings of all the companies they follow.

As discussed in Chap. 6, *agency friction* can arise when a steward of an institutional pool of assets erroneously connects the current viability of a company to the future performance of its stock. The error in this thinking is that a company may be terrific but if the market already knows this, it will show up in a fair-valued or even overvalued stock price. In a Benjamin Graham sort of way, you should buy a stock and wait for the eventual ascent in price if you discover that the value of company is actually greater than the price reflected by the stock. Most professionals working for stock-picking mutual funds spend their time looking for undervalued stocks, digging through layers of a company, seeking that elusive mispricing. Unfortunately for the stock picker, this job became more difficult, thanks in part to some very shady businesspeople and a government seeking to eliminate their particular brand of fraud in the future.

The Impact of 2002

Every year sees its share of industrial shame, but 2002 may be remembered as *the* year of the corporate scandal. Even a casual observer of market-related news at the time might have become immune to otherwise shocking phrases such as *the largest corporate earnings restatement in US history* or *company XYZ's*

CEO has resigned amid allegations of fraud. Certainly Enron and WorldCom suffered through a tremendous amount of public exposure, but they weren't alone. Arthur Andersen, Tyco, Rite Aid, Adelphia, Dynergy, CMS Energy, Qwest, and many others had glaring corporate blemishes.

The scandals of 2002 weren't restricted to a single kind; the lawlessness wasn't just limited to "creative accounting." Companies reporting fictional profits from energy trades and analysts recommending stocks to curry favor for underwriting business also dirtied up the corporate world. At the peak of nastiness in the summer of 2002, amidst cascading stock prices and investor outrage, the US government was forced to act. In one piece of far-reaching legislation designed to show the voting public that corporate deception would not go unpunished, Congress passed the Sarbanes-Oxley Act, and President Bush signed it on July 30 of that year.

Sarbanes-Oxley became law and brought a new reality for corporate managers but has been met with criticism as market participants complied with it in the years that followed. Some believe it places too heavy a burden on smaller publicly traded companies and could ultimately inhibit their earnings, while others think it hasn't gone far enough in curbing corporate deception. A point that few people have considered, however, is the effect that 2002's scandalous activity continues to have on the work that stock analysts do. Digging a bit deeper into a few examples can help identify the ways that regulations following the early-2000s scandals changed the means by which stock pickers do their work.

Enron

The indignity of Enron was certainly the marquee scandal of 2002, but the company's problems began years before that. In 1985, Kenneth L. Lay orchestrated the sale of his company, Houston Natural Gas, to fellow pipeline firm Internorth of Nebraska and took control of the new company—Enron. Faced with huge debt brought on by the merger and operating in a highly competitive marketplace, the company knew it had to transform itself to grow. Enron moved beyond the selling and moving of gas to commodities trading. By 1995, Enron had become the biggest participant in the natural gas business, controlling one-fifth of the North American market.

In later years, Enron parlayed the techniques of making money in the gas business to other commodities such as electricity, wood pulp, steel, and so on. The company, awash in profits, set out to invest in a variety of different ventures, including building power plants all over the world as well as moving into the high-speed data line business.

These investments into hard assets totaled over $10 billion but were not producing profits. Receiving little from such an investment doesn't look very good on a company's books (and does nothing to help the stock price) so Enron's chief financial officer, Andrew S. Fastow, created a whole host of limited partnerships for the company that could, in theory, be treated as separate entities. Enron wasn't the only company to use these special purpose vehicles (SPVs), but it did use a lot of them. Company management was highly motivated to grow the stock price, and if that meant taking a few accounting liberties to make earnings look better, so be it. Any debts or assets that the company didn't want on its books could be dumped into the limited partnerships, making the company appear far more profitable than it really was. Even professional investors and analysts were oblivious to the accounting trick as they bought Enron stock with wild abandon.

But that was only the beginning. Enron frequently booked income from contracts that could take as many as ten years to complete. It manipulated accounts at the end of the quarter to make earnings look better, artificially drove energy prices higher contributing to the California energy crisis of 2000–2001, and frequently pushed accounting law to the limit.

So unique and complex was Enron's creative accounting that the company's auditor, Arthur Andersen, had a hard time keeping up. They either didn't realize what was going on, were misled by Enron, or were more interested in cultivating relationships than working to truly understand how the "profits" were earned.

Enron's stock had traded in excess of $80 in early 2001 but was down to roughly half that by midyear. As Enron stock started to slide lower in 2001, analysts and investors started digging deeper into the company balance sheets and asking tough questions about the SPVs. At that point, Andersen said Enron had to treat the partnerships as part of the company, which led to a $618 million loss in the third quarter of 2001 alone. The stock plummeted.

The Securities and Exchange Commission (SEC) opened an investigation, and investors jumped like rats from a burning ship. In October 2001, an Andersen partner directed the shredding and destruction of thousands of documents and emails related to Andersen's audit of Enron. On December 2, 2001, Enron filed for bankruptcy protection.

The details of what actually went on inside Enron and its relationship with Arthur Andersen are somewhat hazy, but it is crystal clear who was hurt. Long-time Enron employees lost not only their jobs but many lost most, if not all, of their retirement savings held in Enron stock. The real crime was perpetrated on the innocent employees who suffered as a result of the excessive greed and bravado of Enron's higher-ups. Thousands of Andersen employees also lost their jobs because many of the firm's other clients terminated Andersen after the Enron scandal.

As the law closed in on the notables at Enron, an outraged public closed in on lawmakers. The average investor was losing faith in corporate America. Congress moved in a very un-congressional fashion—quickly—to write up some laws that would tell the average citizen that this kind of activity would not be tolerated.

The Sarbanes-Oxley Act

On July 30, 2002, President George W. Bush signed the Sarbanes-Oxley Act of 2002. It flew through the Senate by a 99-0 vote and the House by 423-3. The details of Sarbanes-Oxley made it clear that lawmakers didn't want another Enron on their hands. Here are a few of the important points regarding Sarbanes-Oxley. First and foremost, a company's CEO and CFO must certify in every annual report that they have reviewed the report and that it does not contain any untrue statements or omissions of material facts. This cuts right to the heart of what Enron was doing, attempting to hide debt to make profits look higher than they were.

The penalties for not following the new rules? Any CEO or CFO who recklessly violates their certification of the company's financial statements faces up to a $1 million fine and/or up to ten years of imprisonment. If they willfully violate the certification, they can face up to a $5 million fine and/or up to 20 years of imprisonment. The best interests of a corporate executive lie in ensuring that the financial reports are correct and complete. This goes beyond a moral obligation—federal law now mandates massive fines and years of jail time for failure to comply.

There's more. If a company has to restate its financials, the CEO and CFO must forfeit any bonuses and other incentives received during the 12-month period following the first filing of the erroneous financials. Sarbanes-Oxley also discusses penalties for personal loans, insider trading, and document shredding, but it all comes back to the same thing. Clearly, there's a big incentive to come clean about how much money the company is making and to get it right the first time.

So what does all this mean for investing? Think of Sarbanes-Oxley for a minute, not as a company's CEO but as an analyst covering that company's stock. How does Sarbanes-Oxley affect you? Recall what most stock analysts do: they dig through a company's financial statements to piece together nuggets of information that ultimately form a mosaic upon which a stock recommendation is made.

A large part of any investment professional's education and ongoing professional study focuses on cultivating the ability to glean information from accounting statements. Why? … because they are complicated and highly subjective. Investment analysis, in the form of company valuation, relies heavily on determining the true value of an organization based upon what you can dig up in its financials. A good analyst should be able to tell you consistently that XYZ company is undervalued relative to the financials and it should be purchased, or company ABC is now overvalued based on the statements and should be sold. Some analysts are good and may make more correct recommendations than incorrect ones, but after Sarbanes-Oxley, there is less room for interpretation. When a group of financial statements is designed to paint a complete and accurate description of a company's financial condition, new information is immediately reflected in the stock price and new revelations coming from the same report thereafter will be virtually nonexistent. In other words, the elusive mispricings of companies became even more so after Sarbanes-Oxley.

WorldCom

But that's nowhere near the end of the story. Right about the time that Enron's creative accounting was eroding investor confidence in corporate America, fundamental trust in investment advisors also was being called into serious question. Investors began doubting not only the profits that companies reported but also the integrity of the analysts who were analyzing them. Certain financial advisors had more incentive to line their own pockets than serve the clients they were charged with advising.

The most significant example—and there were plenty—of misguided incentives involved former telecommunications giant WorldCom. WorldCom sprang up in the small town of Brookhaven, Mississippi, in the early 1980s after the breakup of AT&T. It was during this timeframe that AT&T was under court order to lease its phone lines cheaply to other long-distance service providers, and company founder Murray Waldron set out to take advantage of the situation.

Waldron started by setting up shop in Hattiesburg, Mississippi. Soon, he hooked up with Dave Singleton who had raised money for some local projects, including motels owned by a man named Bernie Ebbers. Ebbers and Singleton knew each other from the church they both attended and had worked together on some small business ventures. After Singleton suggested that Ebbers invest in Waldron's new company named Long Distance Discount

Service (LDDS), the partners began their business by taking out a $650,000 loan for a computer switch to route long-distance calls.

The low-cost long-distance industry mushroomed over the ensuing decade, and Ebbers ran his new company as he did his motel chain; he cut costs to the bone and bought out competitors. Growing through acquisitions allowed him to further minimize costs. Within ten years, Ebbers had combined 30 companies, and sales approached $1 billion.

Originally, the plan had been to sell out, but the opportunities for more and more growth were too juicy to pass up. Congress opened competition with the Telecom Act of 1996. Ebbers changed the name of the company to WorldCom and set off to make more acquisitions.

As the internet revolution began, the vast information superhighway was forming. This involved the construction of broadband lines to the tune of $300 to $500 billion. WorldCom was one of the companies that could profit from this expansion and the potential for growth was substantial.

But WorldCom couldn't do it alone. Management needed money, advice, and connections. Enter the Wall Street investment banker. The growth envisioned by WorldCom couldn't happen without money to finance corporate mergers. They needed to issue stock and bonds and sell them to investors. The broadband information superhighway was a potential goldmine for both WorldCom and investment banks, but they needed each other to make it happen.

Investment banking firms can make a substantial amount of money working with companies like WorldCom because such companies have an insatiable appetite for cash to build infrastructure and buy competitors. All this cash could be brought in through the creation of company stock. The investment bankers raised cash for WorldCom (less their take) and peddled the stock to investors. As long as the stock was strong, the cash could keep flowing in—both to WorldCom and the investment bank. Salomon Smith Barney saw the potential profits and wanted to make sure that it was WorldCom's exclusive provider of investment banking needs.

The arrangement was great for everyone. WorldCom made all its investment banking deals with Salomon, and Salomon kept a positive rating on the WorldCom stock. This only works if a very trusting relationship exists between the company and the banker. Salomon's telecom analyst Jack Grubman had a very tight relationship with Ebbers and was as well connected in the company as many insiders.

It was in Grubman's best interest to cultivate his relationship with Ebbers, because part of Grubman's compensation was based upon how much investment banking business he steered toward Salomon. In exchange for exclusive rights to their investment banking business, Grubman, one of the most widely respected telecom analysts in the business, hyped WorldCom stock to anyone who would listen.

The obvious problem with this arrangement is that analysts, who were being compensated on how much investment banking business they brought in, lost their objectivity. Grubman clearly lost objectivity on WorldCom. He continued to hype WorldCom throughout its decline and never did issue a sell rating. Grubman's case was one of the most glaring, but it was far from isolated. Here's what Arthur Levitt, SEC chairman from 1993 to 2001, had to say on the subject:

> *The analysts morphed from being the serious, almost nerd-like students of numbers and corporate strategies into being hypersalespeople, as an adjunct of the investment banking departments of the firms that employed them.*[1]

WorldCom provided Salomon Smith Barney with approximately $140 million in investment banking fees over four years. Grubman was said to have provided $1 billion in banking fees for Salomon across the telecom sector between 1998 and 2001.

The demise of WorldCom exposed the relationships between analysts and the investment banking divisions of the firms for which they work. It all started to fall apart in 2000 when WorldCom tried, unsuccessfully, to buy Sprint. Acquisitions had been the fuel for WorldCom's growth, but they had finally tapped out their potential. The accounting magic that WorldCom played made the company seem as though it was growing, enabling it to hide debt until another merger allowed the books to be cooked once again. The glut of telecom capacity was leading to lower long-distance prices, and the internet/telecom bubble was beginning to burst.

As WorldCom's stock price started to plummet, the company became strapped for cash. Citigroup, then parent company of Salomon Smith Barney, stepped in by leading the way on a $17 billion issuance of WorldCom bonds. WorldCom, in turn, gave some of this money to the banks to pay off some loans. In effect, the banks shifted their risk on WorldCom to the investing public. It got worse. In June 2002, accusations of massive corporate fraud from inside WorldCom rocked the company and the market. The company's earnings, it turned out, had been overstated by $9 billion.

Perhaps the most highly questionable aspect of the entire WorldCom scandal was whether Salomon's telecom analyst Jack Grubman knew earnings were grossly overstated, and if he did, why did he continue to hype the stock? WorldCom and its relationship with Salomon Smith Barney was one of many examples of misguided dealings between companies and investment banking firms that prompted analysts to make recommendations based at least in part on whether future investment banking business was in the offing.

Unfortunately, the investor was the biggest loser. Beyond the huge losses in stock and bond investments, the trust between the investor and the Wall Street analyst had been violated. Many investors no longer felt confident that buying a stock their advisor suggested was in the client's best interest or based upon some corporate-related incentive.

After a investigation ending in the spring of 2003, ten of the largest securities firms agreed to pay $1.4 billion to settle government charges involving abuse of investors during the 1990s. The agreement specifically indicated that Salomon Smith Barney (renamed Citigroup Global Markets at that point) and Credit Suisse First Boston improperly distributed shares in initial public offerings to corporate executives to gain investment banking business.

Jack Grubman received a lifetime ban from the securities business and was ordered to pay $15 million in fines. Henry Blodget of Merrill Lynch also received a lifetime ban and was ordered to pay $4 million. Both were charged with issuing fraudulent research reports, but both analysts and their respective firms consented to the charges without admitting or denying wrongdoing. One of the principal parts of the agreement was that no criminal charges would be filed.

The Fallout for Securities Analysts

Perhaps the most significant aspect of the agreement was how the life of the analyst was changed. Thereafter, analysts were no longer allowed to accompany investment bankers during sales pitches to clients. Reporting and supervisory structures for research operations were forced to remain separate from investment banking operations and compensation was required to be tied to the quality and accuracy of their research rather than how much investment banking business they brought in.

These changes were designed to keep analysts' recommendations on the up and up. Whether they actually accomplished that goal is anyone's guess. If they did, a competitive advantage that mutual fund managers had over the average individual was eliminated. Most fund managers do much of their research on their own. They love to talk about how deeply they research the companies they follow and understand their businesses. However, virtually all fund managers utilize some form of street research, meaning that they listen to what people like Jack Grubman say.

The average individual may find themselves on the receiving end of a sales pitch in which a broker tells them to continue buying a stock because the firm's analyst still rates it a buy. The fund manager has an advantage over the individual in the knowledge that most analyst recommendations are of the buy variety, and only rarely do analysts say to sell. Fund managers can interpret the true value of an analyst's report by reading between the lines and understanding if what was being conveyed in the report was objective analysis or motivated by some other incentive. Is the analyst working independently or are they compromised by the fact that their firm needs positive reports so the stock price stays elevated? Most individual investors lack the wherewithal to do this. After analysts were required to be more direct in their recommendations, and their compensation tied to the quality of their research, would they not then be more inclined to come clean about all aspects of a company's financial health?

In spite of the agreement with regulators, analysts may still feel some incentive to treat a company favorably to help secure investment banking business—albeit far less directly. But regulators pay very close attention to the recommendations analysts make and how they are compensated. If this attention improves the quality and clarity of research, the markets are bound to become even more efficient, adding further credence to the various forms of the efficient market hypothesis (EMH) mentioned earlier. If an influential analyst releases a report on a company, with material information capable of moving the stock, the price will change instantaneously. Ultimately, the opportunity to come closer to discovering the true worth of a company through insightful interpretation of an analyst's report will be gone.

So, Sarbanes-Oxley told corporate managers they had better be truthful about their earnings reports or they'll go to jail, and the brokerage settlement said analysts better be truthful and independent in their research. Both make it harder for professional investors to gain a competitive advantage through individual security research. As the quality of information got better, it became harder to find the diamond in the rough.

Regulation FD

Regulations have led to greater market efficiency and made it harder to uncover mispriced securities. The early 2000s represented a significant period of transformation in the world of professional stock picking, and the advent of Regulation FD (Fair Disclosure) levied perhaps the most impactful change. Regulation FD says that no company manager can have a conversation of material impact with any individual analyst or investment professional that could benefit materially as a result.

Regulation FD eliminates a significant aspect of the typical mutual fund investment philosophy because many funds acquire information directly from the companies they follow. Before Regulation FD, fund managers would boast of their tight relationships with the heads of the companies whose stock they own. Why? Because depending on the closeness of the relationship, a company manager might have given them a heads-up on an upcoming earnings report or the release of a new product. There was even a term for this—"whisper numbers"—which I always found dangerously close to inside information.

The practice of a company leading its better analysts on an upcoming earnings report skirted legality prior to Regulation FD, but since then is unequivocally illegal. The end result is an environment in which all parties have fair and equal access to all relevant information; in other words, a highly efficient market in which no one can gain a lasting competitive advantage.

Let's look at these three legal precedents together. Sarbanes-Oxley was designed to prevent another Enron. No longer can companies hide debt in outside organizations or otherwise misstate earnings. If you, as a corporate executive, say your company made a certain amount of money, you had better be right or face severe penalties. Sarbanes-Oxley made sure the true value of a company could be known by anyone. The hard work of sifting through mountains of paperwork suddenly became less impactful.

The brokerage settlement sought to prevent the shady dealings between companies and firms with both investment banking and financial advising businesses. The far too common practice of giving investment banking business to a firm in exchange for favorable coverage, hot IPOs, and huge personal loans became no more. Investment professionals who read between the lines in an earnings report and could gain a better understanding of the true worth of a company lost one of their key competitive advantages over less-informed professionals and individuals.

Finally, Regulation FD made it clear that no company could provide preferential information to any single analyst or investment professional. This took away the advantage gained by cultivating close relationships between the company manager and the investment professional.

Conclusion

Throughout history, regulations have changed markets in ways that would have been difficult to predict. Future regulations (or the elimination of them) may also unpredictably change markets. The trend for decades has been toward creating a marketplace where any interested party has fair and equal access to information, and the quality and accuracy of that information is worthy of trust. Years ago, a smart, hard-working stock picker could separate fact from fiction in accounting statements, understand, and then act on a stock analyst's true motivations regardless of what was said. Then, relationships could be cultivated to secure actionable advance information. With those advantages out the window, outperforming a benchmark by picking stocks became a much more difficult activity.

Note

1. Hedrick Smith and Rick Young, "The Wall Street Fix," *Frontline*, Public Broadcasting System, May 8, 2003.

8

Performance Doesn't Tell the Whole Story

Successful investing requires making at least a few good decisions and avoiding some bad ones. Many of us, either in our personal portfolios, as professionals on behalf of clients, or as a steward of institutional assets, have had to and will continue to decide between one investment manager or mutual fund and another. What criteria should be used? How much should past performance play into the decision?

An analogy about drawing upon historical performance when making an investment decision is as follows: Let's say I'm a heart surgeon and I regret to inform you that you require open-heart surgery. I then say "not to worry" because I have performed this exact surgery 300 times previously and every time the patient went on to live a healthy life thereafter. You might feel confident in your post-surgery outcome. Now let's say I start the conversation the same way but this time I tell you, "not to worry," I've performed the same surgery ten times in the past, all with successful outcomes. You might feel OK about your prospects but perhaps not as confident as you would in the first example. In a third scenario, what if I said, "not to worry," because I've performed the surgery once before with a successful outcome. In that case, you might not feel very confident at all. But that's exactly how we should think about past investment performance. Investment history is a data set of one. The outcome for a particular investment occurred the way it did only one time. Even if you looked at a large number of sub-periods seeking patterns, that analysis still sums to a singular event that will never play out precisely the same way again.

Beyond that, there is a flaw in the analogy because a level of commonality exists from one person's anatomy to every other that does not exist when comparing one period of investment history to another. The doctor who had

© The Author(s) 2018
M. J. Oyster, *Success in a Low-Return World*,
https://doi.org/10.1007/978-3-319-99855-8_8

performed just one surgery would find use in that experience to help guide future surgeries. Most people have hearts with similar anatomy, location of valves and arteries, and so on. In investing, there are some events and tendencies that have a certain probability of taking place, but the variability is vast and not necessarily persistent. A virtually infinite number of ever-changing variables constantly move and impact the potential for investment success or failure and there are very few things that are consistently repeated from one period to the next.

It is unfortunate that past performance does not provide adequate insight into future results because drawing upon it seems perfectly reasonable and natural. It's embedded in our instincts. Several behavioral biases discussed earlier help explain why we rely on past performance when evaluating potential investments. One is *illusory correlation*, which is the brain's way of seeing a relationship between variables when the variables aren't necessarily related. It is a shortcut that helps us process the flood of information streaming in through our senses.

Along those same lines, we try to make things as easy on ourselves as possible and nothing could be easier than simply comparing the past performance of a fund to other funds or to a benchmark. Another behavioral bias that helps explain why we base investment decisions on past performance is Parkinson's *law of triviality*, sometimes known as the bike-shedding effect (discussed in detail in Chap. 6). It suggests that a group of people will focus their attention on easy-to-understand issues or problems while spending less time on more complicated ones. It's hard work to dig into the subjective nuances of one potential investment versus another, but necessary because basing decisions exclusively on objective performance data can lead to poor performance.

Not only do we rely too much on past performance, we give special consideration to the performance that just happened. *Recency bias* describes the act of giving greater emphasis to events that have taken place more recently as opposed to those in the more distant past. Does very recent performance provide greater insight into a manager's ability? Maybe, but not necessarily.

So that's *why* past performance features so prominently in investment decision making. Now let's talk about *how* performance got to be what it was. Can we distinguish skill, which would suggest similarly strong performance could be expected in the future, from luck?

Skill or Luck?

Occasionally, you will see a mutual fund advertise its performance returns. "Over the past ten years, XYZ Fund has returned x percent, which is y percent over the S&P 500." Declarations like this are not uncommon because basic statistics tells us that some funds will have good performance, if only through sheer luck. The average investor may see this performance, think the outperforming fund's manager must be highly skilled, and make an investment in the fund. If asked about the purchase, they might say, "XYZ has had great performance, so they must be doing something right," but it is practically impossible to determine whether a fund's performance is the result of skill or luck.

The burden of proving skill should be on the fund manager, but the investor needs to know that favorable past performance does not necessarily indicate skill. A mound of evidence suggests that good performance does not necessarily persist. If a manager was truly skillful, performance should remain strong from one period to the next, but the examples of that are no more frequent than what can be expected merely by chance.

If you flip a coin 1000 times, you have about a 35 percent chance of seeing the same side come up 10 or more times in a row at least once. Does that mean that, during that streak, you were particularly skillful at coin flipping? Of course not, but a manager who outperforms their benchmark ten years in a row might be seen as skillful, when in reality, they may just be lucky. The point is that someone will outperform the benchmark ten or even more years in a row, but their performance may not be due to skill.

Short-term performance does not provide insight into skill or the lack thereof because nearly all managers exhibit both strong and weak periods at some point in their professional investing lives. In my first book, *Mission Possible, Achieving Out Performance in a Low Return World*, I investigated the ten-year returns of a broad large cap universe of 359 managers.[1] Of these managers, 98 percent posted at least one one-year period in the top quartile. (Eighty-six percent posted at least one three-year period in the top quartile.) This shows that being in the top 25 percent of your peer group is not necessarily indicative of investment skill, because nearly all managers are there at one point or another. Someone who was simply evaluating a manager based on their prior year's returns (or even three years), seeking only those who were in the top 25 percent of their peer group, would have invested in just about any fund, depending on when the research was taking place. Does it really make sense to evaluate funds based on a strategy that might choose one fund at one point and a different fund at a different point? A truly effective way to select managers would be to uncover their skillfulness, which would result in the same manager being selected, regardless of when the search was conducted. Such a process is notoriously difficult so most people simply look at historical returns.

Positive past performance does not necessarily indicate skill. Similarly, poor short-term performance does not necessarily indicate a lack of skill. Over the same ten-year period, 95 percent of all managers who posted top quartile returns over the long term—ten years in this case—experienced at least one three-year period below median, and two-thirds of them experienced at least one three-year period in the bottom quartile. This result shows the wide variability of fund performance and how even the strongest performing managers experience periods of underperformance. In other words, no managers post strong performance all the time, but that fact isn't widely understood.

Many investors buy into a fund following good performance and sell following poor. Recall Graph 5.1 in Chap. 5 showing that managers underperformed their benchmark by 4.1 percentage points in the three years prior to being fired but then outperformed by nearly the exact same amount three years thereafter. Similarly, managers outperformed their benchmark by over 10 percentage points in the three years prior to being hired but then only barely outperformed the three years thereafter. This performance-killing phenomenon can be explained by an overreliance on past performance when making investment decisions. Most funds that end up being long-term outperformers experience short-term periods of underperformance along the way. Investors who dump such funds after poor performance may miss out on the recovery.

Equity Styles

Another significant factor affecting mutual fund performance that isn't widely understood is the impact of equity styles. Prior to the 1990s, it was common to see US equity funds operate with a generalist style that could own any kind of stock—value, growth, large, or small. Over the years since then a trend of specialization took place. Now, most funds and ETFs are highly specialized—so specialized, in fact, that an investor can own a fund or ETF that focuses on nearly any sector, industry, style, or subcategory imaginable.

For broad generalization purposes, we can group funds into one of three style classes: growth, value, and core. Morningstar uses these styles in their boxes describing the normal area in which the fund invests. Growth stocks can be technology and consumer companies, while value stocks tend to include those with lower price multiples and often hefty dividends. Core includes a blend of both.

Generally, growth fund managers invest in companies that are increasing their earnings year over year. They buy into the momentum of a growing company in hopes that the stock price will continue to rise in response. A growth manager doesn't normally care a great deal about how expensive the stock is because they believe a good growth company can always push the stock price higher.

Value fund managers are all about buying on the cheap. Not to say they don't care about a company's fundamental picture, just that the valuation is a far more important consideration. In many cases, the value manager will seek out low-priced stocks that have been, they believe, excessively beaten down by the market. A catalyst like a new corporate structure or product line prompts the value manager to pull the trigger and buy the stock.

As specialization in the mutual fund industry has become ever more precise, most managers today focus on whatever style to which they attest is theirs and tend to not venture outside that box. If they do, they run the risk of being fired for violating their mandate as a manager filling a need in a broader portfolio. A large cap growth manager, for example, may have been hired to counterbalance a large cap value manager, so if the growth manager suddenly becomes a value manager, the portfolio will be overweighted to value and will be at risk of underperforming the market when value is out of favor.

Styles are highly cyclical, with growth and value alternating outperformance relative to each other. The effect of style cyclicality usually has a tremendous impact on a manager's portfolio, because even if they picked the greatest large cap growth stocks in the market, they may still underperform the S&P 500 when value is the dominant style. Does such a manager lack stock selection skill? Maybe, but that can't be determined by performance relative to the index because style, not stock picking, was at fault.

Many attempts have been made to isolate skill from luck by separating factor influences, such as exposure to the growth or value style, out of the manager's performance. What remains is theoretically due to security selection (i.e., skill). The evolution of this type of analysis will be discussed in greater detail in Chap. 11. Seeking evidence of skill by attempting to back out style represents a worthy attempt but is wrought with shortcomings because the effect of factors such as growth, value, size, or virtually anything else cannot be completely isolated. Notably, much of the security selection process used by even the most staunch bottom-up manager involves analysis of the more top-down factor exposures that would be removed in such an attempt to isolate skill. Many of the finest minds in investing, with access to the greatest academic research and technology, have spent years seeking to isolate skill from luck, yet an expedient and accurate means of doing so remains elusive. Such an exercise may offer a hunch about a manager's skill but never a definitive answer.

A manager's style of investing can allow them to post performance both well beyond and significantly below their skill level. Early in my investment manager research career, my due diligence efforts covered many large cap growth managers who overweighted technology and telecom names during the boom time in the late 1990s. The enjoyment of tremendous outperformance relative to the S&P 500 might have brought those managers praise from many who trumpeted their superior investment skill. But then after the tech bubble burst, many of the same managers experienced poor performance followed by a backlash of criticism by those who questioned their skill. In many cases, the managers remained true to their philosophy and style, but that style went out of favor due to the cyclical nature of growth and value. Were the managers skillful in the 1990s yet unskilled thereafter? That is difficult to say. Their performance may have been more a function of luck (both good and bad) rather than skill. This example further illustrates why investing with a manager following good performance, and selling after poor performance, can inhibit long-term returns.

Tracking Error

Tracking error can also hide skill (or a lack thereof). *Tracking error*, a measure of *active risk* (the risk of deviating from a benchmark), is the volatility of the return differential between an investment manager's performance and that of the benchmark against which the manager's performance is measured. Some examples can help illustrate how investment products managed with a great deal of tracking error may experience periods of outperformance simply due to luck.

Let's consider a poor performing fund that is expected to trail its benchmark by 2 percent over the long term. If its returns are normally distributed around that negative 2 percent relative to its benchmark (not an unrealistic assumption) the fund will have a 19 percent chance of outperforming the benchmark over any given five-year period, just by exhibiting a rather pedestrian tracking error of 5 percent per year. If the tracking error increased to 10 percent, the chance of outperformance becomes 33 percent—simply due to luck.

After a period of strong performance, some funds may lower their tracking error to reduce the risk of underperformance in hopes of preserving the growth in assets under management achieved during the good times. Such an action does a disservice to new clients who may have thought they were investing in an actively managed product, one that should experience tracking error relative to the benchmark but will now look very index-like. Such funds are commonly known as "closet indexers" and should generally be avoided like the plague. An investment that tracks an index is almost always available for a far lower fee than the typical active manager charges. An active manager, who charges active manager-like fees, should not behave like an index that could be had for far less money.

The Variables Behind Past Performance

In short, past performance is no guarantee of future results. Not even close, and not even over the long term. A lot of fund-management companies like to talk about their products' long-term track records, but such data provides little in the way of useful knowledge about a manager's skill. Without delving into the statistics involved, suffice it to say that ten years is nowhere near long enough to know with a high degree of certainty that an investment product's track record is significant, the result of skill, or simply due to luck. A ten-year statistical study would also assume that nothing had changed over the course of that period. That assumption is unrealistic because the world in which mutual funds live remains in a constant state of flux. Here are a few things to watch for that might make a fund's historical track record even less useful as a predictive tool for future performance.

Changes in the Manager's Philosophy

Even if the product has been steered by the same portfolio manager for many years, there is no guarantee that an investment manager has operated with the same outlook and temperament over their entire tenure. In early years, managers may seek to establish a name for themselves, but managers may temper their funds' volatility in the years approaching their retirement.

Cash Inflows

An investment product that posts strong returns will almost invariably experience an influx of new cash. If the size of assets being managed swells to an excessive amount, investment performance could suffer. For example, a manager who begins purchasing large amounts of a stock could push the price upward, lowering the expected return developed in the manager's original thesis. In addition, the sale of large blocks of a security can cause downward price pressure. Money-management firms can help mitigate this problem by closing the product to new investors before the asset size begins to affect performance.

Personnel Turnover

The returns posted at the beginning of a time series may have been due to the performance of a completely different team than the one in place at the end of the series.

Business Decisions Above Investment Decisions

Firms that spend exorbitant amounts on marketing may increase the size of assets their firm manages (and increase their aggregate fee), but investment performance will not necessarily improve. Marketing and client service responsibilities can affect a manager's investment focus. Many institutional investors like to see the portfolio manager at new business meetings, but a manager who is required to spend a great deal of time conducting marketing or client service work could lose focus on investment responsibilities, and the variability of those responsibilities may result in inconsistent application of their philosophy. In other words, performance periods when the manager has limited business development responsibilities should not be compared with periods of intense business development responsibilities.

Moreover, multiproduct firms will almost always have at least one product in favor. Fund families with dozens of different offerings will likely have several that are performing well over a given period, and these will be most widely promoted in advertisements. As we know from the study mentioned earlier, strong performance is not always followed by continued strong performance, so investors should evaluate highly promoted products with an especially skeptical eye.

New Products

Incubated products should also be scrutinized closely. A common practice, one especially prevalent in large management firms, is the incubation of new funds. Rather than rolling a new fund out to the public with no track record, a firm may provide some of its own money for the manager to invest at the beginning of a new product's life. This practice isn't fundamentally dangerous, as long as the investor realizes that the firm may have incubated several funds at the same time and the one they are now promoting is the one that posted the best track record over its incubation period. The best defense against such a strategy is to analyze why the fund outperformed. Was its style in favor? Did they avoid a single-stock disaster that befell similar products? Most importantly, the investor should ensure that the product's philosophy and construction process remain the same as during the incubation period.

Who Outperforms the Benchmark?

That having being said, how many managers actually outperform the benchmark over time? Thinking back to the S&P Global study cited in Chap. 2, over 92 percent of all actively managed large cap funds trailed their appropriate benchmark (S&P 500 Index) over the 15-year period ending December 2016. As bad as that is, survivorship bias makes the universe of funds look better than what an investor might actually experience because the poor performers that went out of business aren't included. The same S&P Global study indicated that only 34 percent of the funds that started that 15-year period remained in existence at the end, which suggests that 92 percent of the best funds that survived still underperformed the benchmark. Even without considering the survivorship bias, you could surmise that an investor has about a one in ten chance of finding a fund that will outperform over time and less than that if survivorship bias is considered—that assumes the investment environment for active managers will be no more difficult in the future than in the past, but substantial evidence suggests the contrary.

The perspective we can gain from this analysis is sobering. Evidence suggests that the stock market may only return 7 percent or so per year, although many investors are expecting more than 10 percent. To make up the shortfall through the use of actively managed mutual funds, an investor would need to find a fund that not only outperforms but does so by 3 percentage points on average year after year. Expecting this kind of outperformance from virtually any mutual fund is highly unrealistic.

If professional fund management is as critical to investment success as the industry would have you believe, they sure have a funny way of showing it. Jane and John Q. Investor are waking up to the fact that most fund managers don't beat the market, and their opportunities for doing so are getting worse, not better. It's easy to see why index funds, which simply buy and hold a broad market index like the S&P 500, have become so popular in recent years. Unfortunately, indexing will never outperform and therefore cannot make up the shortfall left if the stock market, as expected, advances at a slower clip than it has historically. Security selection is not the answer; indexing can help but may still leave investors with a bear market in expectations. The good news is that the solutions are out there, but they require a mind open to new ideas and a willingness to disregard old ways of thinking.

Note

1. Oyster, Michael J., *Mission Possible, Achieving Outperformance in a Low Return World*, Dearborn Trade Publishing, 2005, 72.

Part II

Solutions

So far we have spent the bulk of the discussion highlighting various challenges that investors will likely face in the future. The US stock market, of particular interest, stands to post returns well below historical averages. For a whole host of reasons, we shouldn't expect actively managed stock-picking funds to make up the difference. Alas, do not despair; numerous solutions exist … and more encouragingly, goals can be achieved in multiple ways. We will explore several of them in greater detail.

Successful investing requires effective decision-making. We spent time in previous chapters describing how common behavioral biases can lead to poor investment decisions. A different cognitive discussion can potentially help improve decision-making—relying on one's own intuition. When faced with a difficult problem, are you one to listen to what your gut is telling you and allow that to help inform your decision?

Earlier in my career, I would have found the idea of drawing upon intuition to make investment decisions nothing short of abhorrent. Decisions, I previously surmised, should be based upon verifiable facts. Education and experience have taught me that indicators, ratios, and other data points can serve as faithful guides but only if they have been tested and strong evidence supports their efficacy. But that's like leaving money on the table because our own intuition can serve as another tool in our investment toolbox. However, how we distinguish between the positive (or negative) influences of our own intuition and the dysfunctional nature of common behavioral biases can prove challenging.

At this point you may be contemplating one of two things: (1) Of course I use intuition in investing … how could I not? Or (2) If I claimed that I was making investment decisions for my clients based upon intuition, I would be fired in an instant! Although intuition is commonly utilized in a variety of industries, investing has not been categorically known as one of them. At the very least, having an inkling is not frequently cited as a decision-making tool. In a similar concept as the *agency friction* bias cited earlier, professional investors will not generally speak about intuition for fear of deviation from the norm. Finding it difficult to defend poor performance, investment managers choose to either not discuss the use of intuition or try to not use it at all.

The taboo nature of intuition in investing is unfortunate because utilized prudently, it can serve as a worthy check and balance to what the data is telling us. A dogmatic reliance on only objective data carries significant shortcomings. With greater awareness, and an opportunity to diversify our sources of investment expertise, intuition may grow in acceptance, which may improve the investment community as a whole. For the following chapter I leave you in the very capable hands of my wife, Catherine Lennon, who has spent the last 25 years of her marketing and writing career helping other business owners achieve their own success by teaching them how to listen to their intuition and the practicality of utilizing it in their business lives. She is far more versed than I regarding how intuition can support or impede the decision-making process.

9

Intuition

"The intuitive mind is a sacred gift and the rational mind is a faithful servant.
We have created a society that honors the servant and has forgotten the gift."
[Albert Einstein *1879–1955 Physicist and Nobel Laureate*]

If I had been given a dollar every time a family member or friend has told me to trust my gut in regard to my personal life, I probably would have enough saved to reach my IRA contribution limit for at least a year, if not more. I have often given that same (sometimes unsolicited) advice right back at them. Conversely, I can count on one hand how many times I have been asked, "So, what's your hunch on this?" in a business situation. Do you ever wonder why are we so quick to adhere to, say, a best friend's or a grandparent's direction for us in our personal lives but yet we may second-guess the validity of our own gut feelings, especially when it comes to business? Quite frankly, I never posed this question to myself until about ten years ago. Game changer.

In Chap. 6, several cognitive biases, such as *anchoring* and the *ostrich effect* are explored and how they can specifically impact our feelings, thoughts and thus, behavior. Part of knowing when to utilize your instincts or intuition in a business setting is being aware of what you already have a propensity for. Understanding who you are, what makes you tick, and that past experiences indeed shape behavior are imperative to know in our personal and professional lives; essentially, self-awareness, and self-trust go hand in hand.

© The Author(s) 2018
M. J. Oyster, *Success in a Low-Return World*,
https://doi.org/10.1007/978-3-319-99855-8_9

The Role of Trust

Trusting yourself is a pretty simple concept but it is one that many struggle with in practice, especially if you have lost the ability to do so with specific key individuals before or if trust has always been somewhat challenging for you with everyone. Why is this important? Because self-trust is the key to listening to what your gut is telling you, and without it you may potentially ignore every instinct or intuitive thought you have. Essentially, if you don't trust you, why would anyone else?

Sure, things can indeed go wrong when you trust yourself, but they can go really, really wrong if you trust yourself less. Erik Erikson (1902–1994), German-American developmental psychologist and psychoanalyst, is known for his eight stages of psychosocial development. According to Erikson, from birth to approximately 18 months is when that trust versus mistrust achievement occurs. He believed that everyone goes through eight crises in their developmental lifetime and all individuals must overcome or resolve them successfully in order to adjust well to the environment.[1] Trust is the first rung. Essentially, you can't move on to the others, such as rung two—autonomy versus shame/doubt—unless the first one is achieved. Erikson, who famed the term "identity crisis," went on to win a Pulitzer Prize and a US National Book Award for *Gandhi's Truth* in 1969. Today, he is still regarded as one of the most influential in the field despite not holding a college or university degree on the subject.

Going back to Erikson's first rung of trust: think of Calpurnia, wife of Julius Caesar for a moment. She had some trust in her ability of foresight and begged her husband not to go to senate in 44 BCE. She presented her ideas to him and asked him to feign illness. Caesar knew her to not be superstitious but replied that he wouldn't lie to his friends by pretending he was sick. He also is noted to have felt confident the next day and assumed that all the omens were simply "tricks of his mind." Caesar didn't trust her reasons for the conversation although Calpurnia did herself to a point or else she wouldn't have said anything to begin with. But, one wonders that if she had simply expressed that he not go on the grounds that she feared he would be killed and NOT ask him to lie, he might have listened otherwise. Also, if Caesar had not doubted the so-called tricks of his mind, things might have ended differently. Unfortunately, 23 stab wounds and some really famous words later, her intuition was confirmed.[2]

Then there's the example of Julia, Ulysses S. Grant's wife, in 1865. The Grants were invited to join the Lincolns at Ford's Theatre but Mrs. Grant urged her husband that they needed to decline and leave town immediately.

She later wrote, "I do not know what possessed me to take such a freak." She has often been credited with saving her husband's life.[3] Unlike Caesar, Grant actually took his wife's advice, preventing him from being an assassination target that fateful evening.

Despite the latest scientific research findings, which we will discuss shortly, there is still mystery surrounding the subject of intuition and many don't know how to define it or explain the scientific differences between instinct and intuition. It is through understanding this information that it should become clearer when it is feasible to use either in business. Note that it is not always practical. Sometimes these gut instincts help and sometimes they hinder our decision making.

Along with discussing the above, this chapter will also explore a brief timeline regarding how intuition has evolved from a historical perspective as well as offer ways to help you tune into it. So let's start with a definition and then explore the latter components.

Intuition Defined

The word intuition comes from the Latin verb *intueri* translated as "consider" or from the late middle English word intuit, "to contemplate." This root beginning sounds like the term is logical, rational, and purposeful and could very well be part of every informed decision already since it is formed by a collection of beliefs, experiences, and memories. But, read on.

The intuitive system is more "hardwired" into humans than commonly understood. It is automatic, really, mindless thought that doesn't require analysis or deep thinking. The official definition of intuition (according to Wikipedia) is the ability to acquire knowledge without proof, evidence, or conscious reasoning, or without understanding how the knowledge was acquired. Intuition cannot be described as a concept because it is not a general representation of what is common to a (possible) plurality of things. It is a singular representation of an individual—an individual that trusts him or herself.

Unfortunately, intuition can be silenced due to painful past experiences, such as being denied or forced certain feelings during prime stages of mental, physical, and emotional growth. This is where the inability to self-trust comes into play. For example, if a person has had an abusive childhood, excessive self-doubt and fear can mask gut intuition. Decisions are then not often seen with clarity due to a clouded thought process. The ability to have foresight (intuition) would thus be blocked due to the person's need to actively filter out stimuli that remind them painfully of their past. In all, you can't make a great present-day decision when you can't clearly see present-day solutions that may or may not be right in front of you. We are all human. It is highly unusual to come across an individual that doesn't have an exceedingly painful memory from some timeframe of life, so this "blocking" can happen to anyone in some way, shape, or form. It is this blocking that most of us are trying to overcome. The last thing you want to be is in a state of inaction; a type of gridlock where none of the paths look reasonable.

To many people, self-trust comes easily while others have seemed to master the usually disastrous art of second-guessing themselves. As Michael discussed in this chapter's introduction, it is unfortunate that this topic seems to be one of the most unsettling to so many business professionals in the area of finance. I have often wondered, is taking heed of what your head or heart is telling you too subjective for business decisions? Sometimes. Then again, sometimes not. I am hopeful that by shedding some light on the topic, utilizing your instincts and intuition will become more comfortable and less taboo to discuss in a professional setting. But first, how does intuition differ from instinct? One is a biological tendency and the other is not.

Intuition Versus Instinct

"Instinctus" or "impulse" is the body's biological tendency toward a particular behavior. It is innate. From a scientific standpoint, humans are considered animals with brains that are born with a "toolbox kit" of sorts. It is through these tools that we have survived as a species. We know the "fight or flight" response when danger approaches because the response is actually secreted into our blood systems by our adrenal glands. It is where the term "mother's instinct" comes from—offspring know automatically how to feed off their mothers and mothers know when there is something "awry" with them.

But first, you may be wondering why I am interested in the subject to begin with. My fascination has roots in how I was raised (strong lineage of openly intuitive foremothers) as well as having my intuition confirmed many more times than not, which would be a book in and of itself. My education and experience in business, economics, engineering, philosophy, psychology, and sociology over the last three decades also have played big roles. Speaking of ...

Red Flags and Green Lights

Although I am definitely educated and knowledgeable about the area of finance and investments, finance was not my collegiate area of study. Accounting was my major, at first. Accounting made sense at the time partly due to the influence of a parent being a CFO of a major NYSE corporation along with an overwhelming need of mine to organize money. Life experience as a summer intern at a CPA firm altered that vision. Apparently, I disliked numbers greatly and working in a spreadsheet program all day was not quite as exciting (or even remotely close) as I thought it would be. It's not that I needed excitement, but my gut was essentially screaming at me that something was indeed off. I changed majors without the blink of an eye; no second-guessing anything (other than how to wrap the paper cut due to the pile of paperwork that was involved to do so back in the late 1980s).

Somehow I actually graduated a semester ahead of schedule (can we say no social life) majoring in what was then known as industrial marketing (now B2B), with dual minors in human resources and operations management along with a certificate in international business. Then, I was hired full-time as a manufacturing engineer from the company I was a marketing co-op for and gained experience project managing clients such as Boeing, Ford, Reliance Electric, Reliance Medical, and so on. After a move into advertising to experience the agency side of B2B as well as Business-to-Consumer (B2C) companies, I am now freelancing assisting other business owners and managers with a focus on strategy, content creation, email marketing, and social media.

A commonality that Michael and I have is that I also like statistics (albeit to a slightly smaller scale than he does). I, too, have a scientific mind in terms of having the desire/need to back up ideas and experiences with possible facts. I prefer to watch something on The History Channel or the local public broadcasting station to over, well, pretty much anything. We have passed many a Sunday rainy afternoon doing so.

Through the years I have heard intuition described in a wide variety of ways from colleagues: (1) A quirky I-know-something-isn't-quite-right feeling but I'm not sure what; (2) A flush-in-your-cheeks sensation that is quite smoldering and leaves you speechless; (3) An empty abyss that seems inevitable no matter what you decide; as well as (4) A full throttle knowing that if you do take a certain path, you and many others will either revel in it or crash and burn. Talk about pressure!

For those of us that are the rarest personality, INFJs on the infamous Myers-Briggs scale, which will be discussed at length in this chapter, applying our intuition in our daily lives is just that, a daily occurrence. It doesn't matter if it is business or personal-related; it just is a natural way for us to feel and behave in a certain manner based on that feeling. Understanding that doing so may sometimes seem intimidating to others as they watch you being guided by some unknown force, your sixth sense essentially, will no doubt help you in all relationships.

There are basically two current schools of thought on intuition: (1) Humans have the ability to know their own instincts and be intuitive because the feelings are developed over time, shaped by past experiences; and (2) It's a gift (or curse) that you either have or you don't. Guess which one is more popular today?

When I sit down with a business owner or manager that is seeking advice on strategy and decision making, one of my first three questions to them is always, "Do you have any intuitive gut feelings?" on whatever topic we have on the table. Typically, after my question is posed to them, there is a lot of silence on their end that can last anywhere from mere seconds to enough time to get a refill of your caffeinated beverage of choice despite your doctor's advice. And then they start talking—mostly without organization—after which come some chuckles, a joke or two maybe, possibly a little bit more odd silence, until WHAM! Out it comes. Spoken words of instinct spew forth and they lay every gut feel they have ever had out on the table. You can't exactly put that type of information into a spreadsheet that will systematically solve a problem, but you can take notice of what is of importance to the individual and potentially why that is.

After having numerous conversations with professionals in management in a wide variety of industries—manufacturing, professional services (legal, financial), consumer products, as well as entertainment—the one commonality across all of these industries to me from a people standpoint has been this: no matter your nature of business, if it comes to constantly second-guessing your intuition, essentially ignoring your own red flags or green lights, success will not be yours for the taking. In the words of Ralph Waldo Emerson (1803–1882), "Self-trust is the first secret to success."

Suggestions to Consider Practicing

1. If something doesn't seem right, it probably isn't. Recheck your numbers if data is involved. Informally poll others on the subject at hand. Consider your life experiences. It's possible that one of your own cognitive biases is at play.

2. Everything you notice has meaning. Everything. The butterfly that flutters by you in the color pattern that just popped into your head a few seconds ago … that means something. You either saw it unconsciously prior to actually realizing you were seeing it or you had foresight that it would be there.

3. Realize that there is a difference between emotional wishful thinking and intuitive guidance. At its worst, passive wishful thinking can be as destructive as any sort of method of cognitive distraction. It involves day dreaming how things could be so without putting forth real effort to reach that goal. I, too, would love to have a fairy Godmother but we aren't in a Disney movie. The fairytale of being magically transformed by doing nothing isn't quite real.

4. Openly seek what is positive about a situation even if it doesn't look very hopeful. This is very hard to do at times for even the most positive personality.

5. Take action. When you feel stuck in making a decision, it is sometimes because the business analytics are saying to take one path but your instincts are whispering "nope." If you have a problem, do something about it. If you don't understand something or someone, seek to understand. Whatever you do, don't purposely stay in a state of inaction.

6. Learn to tell the difference between your intuition and your ego. The ego mind is there to protect and take care of you and you alone. From an investment manager standpoint, we all know that isn't ideal. Your ego mind is not in service to others and is extremely self-involved. Ego has been described as a guard dog that will never leave your side or change owners. On the other hand, your intuition may not be as loyal.

7. If you can, pay attention to your dreams. They may not make any sense at the time but if you can recall them, they can be very telling of your subconscious. When I was in college, I read a book on the topic of "Mind Control," which introduced the idea that we all have an ability to influence what we are dreaming at night. Essentially, if you are in a nightmare, you can change it. If you don't like fire-breathing dragons, try to change it into a fun unicorn. If you haven't already experienced this active type of sleep participation, try it. You may find that you have mystical superhero powers when you sleep AND when you're awake (not likely while awake but just saying that it's possible, just not probable). The entire concept of being asleep and learning to know when you are and then taking advantage of it can be helpful especially if you went to bed stewing over a decision that needs to be made. While I used to have this skill quite a bit as a youngster (probably had to do with more practice sleeping 13+ hours a

day to my now almost five), what I walked away with was the capacity to be somewhat cognizant while dreaming. And if that occurs, you can help solve a problem by using your practical intuition. (But, you probably don't want to tell anyone that a unicorn was part of your decision-making process.)

8. Really take notice of your five senses: sight, sound, smell, taste, and touch. It is through these senses that your, you guessed it, sixth sense of extrasensory perception, aka ESP, will be noticed. Some people have clear hearing, known as clairaudience. Others have clear seeing, known as the more familiar word, clairvoyance. And so on. Each sense is termed with a 'clair' prefix. One that I encounter frequently is clairgustance, which sounds disgusting but it is just the ability to taste something (such as a recipe you have never made), without ever making it or putting it in your mouth. Thankfully, I have always had an ability to cook well without much practice. Clairgustance is for those that don't go by recipes. They make their dishes by their intuition of taste and most don't know how to measure a liquid versus a mass and accurately write down their recipes for people despite being asked. Revel in this skill if you have it and practice it.

9. Start testing your gut feelings (of course with something that doesn't involve money—or anyone else's for that matter). Start small and work your way up. An example would be: you haven't heard from your mother and you REALLY feel that the next text that comes into your super busy phone will be her. And not only you are correct, but your intuition was confirmed within less than 30 seconds. Nine out of ten times I have guessed correctly in regard to my mom texting when she does, and there is no pattern to it as to time of day. I've tried to make sense of it, but I can't. It's just a thing. It's like a sense of vibration before it happens. Maybe she's sensing me thinking about it. Who knows. Anyway, my point is that you will be surprised how many times you are correct. Start small though.

10. If you are one of the unfortunate people that get headaches that lead you into a dark room or you get queasy in the stomach, intestinal cramping (and all that other unpleasantness) when something feels really off kilter, recognize that this could be plain stress calling you out or your intuition literally dialing you. I am a migraine person. I know that the majority of my migraines come AFTER a stressful event is over, rarely ever before or during times of immense stress. So, when these symptoms occur, I take notice of them. Even though you might feel really unwell to do anything at the time, try to ask yourself if/when this happens, "Why am I feeling this horrid?" It may serve you well by doing so.

What I call my 'Final Five' tips to help you strengthen your intuitive skills will be discussed before the conclusion of this chapter. But first, let's look at the historical background on the subject so those pointers will make more sense and be more memorable.

The Evolvement of Intuition

In prior centuries, intuition was largely known as a feminine domain partly due to men being trained to not rely on anything non-scientific, which intuition was inaccurately deemed to be. For centuries, intuition has been studied from a variety of philosophical and scientific angles. It has even been noted as rational and explained in a mathematical way. It is my hope that exploring how intuition has evolved will shed some light on the soundness (or not) of your hunches and make the subject more comfortable to discuss in the financial industry—without the risk of being inappropriately charged with "insider trading." This type of insider trading (as in inside your own head) should not land you in jail.

In Eastern Philosophy, intuition is mostly intertwined with religion and spirituality, and various meanings exist from different religious texts. In the West, intuition does not appear as a separate field of study, and early mentions and definitions can be traced back to Plato. In his book *Republic*, tuition is defined as a fundamental capacity of human reason to comprehend the true nature of reality. In his works, *Meno* and *Phaedo* he describes intuition as a pre-existing knowledge residing in the "soul of eternity," and a phenomenon by which one becomes conscious of pre-existing knowledge. He provides an example of mathematical truths and posits that they are not arrived at by reason. He argues that these truths are accessed using knowledge already present in a dormant form and accessible to our intuitive capacity.

Intuition has a very long history within the discipline of philosophy and a rather shorter one in psychology.[4] Since Plato, intuition has been considered a way of knowing which is fundamentally different from that with which we are most familiar. For Plato, Spinoza, Locke among others, intuition is a nonsensory way to the attainment of permanent, abiding, universal, ultimate truth or reality. Through intuition, one might be in direct contact with the final truths of the universe. In their view, the process of intuition is adamantly outside the normal conduct of daily life and reason as we know it, with reason, in fact, being antagonistic to the operation of intuition. It is quite a difficult philosophical concept to explain and I can't devise a graph or chart to do so, although I'm sure one exists somewhere in time. The point is that intuited truth during Plato's time was more important than truth through reason. Termed *philosophical intuitionism*, it places intuition entirely separate from reason, opposed to it actually, and leads to knowledge of realities from only what can be known through the senses. We could go into the whole body of work behind epistemology, the theory of knowledge, but that will be saved for another day.

Before I get into Keynesian economics, I would like to briefly discuss French philosopher Henri Bergson (1859–1941). This gentleman introduced two ways in which an object can be known: absolutely and relatively. Pertaining to each mode of knowledge is a method through which it can be gained. The latter is what Bergson called analysis, while the method of intuition belongs to the former. To Bergson, intuition is an experience of sorts, which allows us to, in a sense, enter into the things in themselves; the philosophy of true empiricism. Bergsen explains more of this thought in his 1903 essay *An Introduction to Metaphysics*. His view was one of the most provocative and influential of philosophical intuitionism.

Mathematical Viewpoint

There are currently two notions of intuition: the first is a point of view within mathematics which holds that ultimate proofs are self-evident and that no amount of algebraic manipulation can prove a geometrical axiom; it's proof must be self-evident. The second point of view is that intuition is a process whereby a mathematician can (and does) select from a host of alternatives, one of which will prove to be most fruitful. Do you agree with either of these?

Although considered a social science, the study of economics involves mathematics: analytic geometry, algebra, as well as basic arithmetic. One of the most famous English economists, John Maynard Keynes (1883–1946), was the most intuitive of economists. Many find it interesting that Keynesian economics has made a quick comeback since 2009. In *Keynes: The Return of the Master*, a book written by Robert Skidelsky, he is described as having "an extraordinary insight into the gestalt of particular situations. He possessed in marked degree the scientific imagination he ascribed to Freud, 'which can body forth an abundance of innovating ideas, shattering possibilities, working hypotheses, which have sufficient foundation in intuition and common experience, though unprovable.'" Keynes felt sure of his unprovable conjectures. He could be as excited as any economist at discovering correlations in data; yet, he was famously skeptical about economics—the use of statistical methods for forecasting the future. Keynes championed the cause for better statistics (which helped pave the path to big data) "not to provide material for the regression coefficient, but for the intuition of the economist to play on." He believed that statistical information in the hands of the philosophically untrained was a "dangerous and misleading toy."[5] Frankly, I do too.

Psychological Analysis

Among psychologists there are two points of view as well as two controversies. The first concerns the understanding of personality, by the direct intuitionistic approach as compared with an inferential-probabilistic approach. The former is a derivative of the mental testing movement, which began around the turn of the twentieth century in France and England and is represented currently in the study of psychometrics. Three psychologists of notable mention in the late 1800s and early twentieth century are Sigmund Freud, Alfred Adler and Carl Jung. Freud, who is known as the father of psychoanalysis, completely disregarded intuition by teaching that knowledge could only be attained through the intellectual manipulation of carefully made observations.

On the other hand, the founder of the inferiority complex, Alfred Adler, a former colleague of Freud, hypothesized that there is a single drive for perfection as the motivating force behind all of human behavior and experience. He suggested we not ignore empathy, intuition, and guesswork. I am more in tune with Adler's view and am guessing that he was a very secure intuitive soul.

Applying Adler's thought on whether or not a person would utilize their own intuition along with research, data, education, and so on in decision making depends on several factors: (1) Do they second-guess themselves or are they self-trusting; (2) Do they not feel the need to compare their actions to others; and (3) Do they allow themselves to feel strongly that they will be perceived as calm and self-reliant, essentially knowing that their pathway to success will be paved with an internal feeling of superiority. It is those that are confident in their thoughts, feelings, and actions that will succeed in Adler's view.

Personality Typing: Myers-Briggs Take on Jung

In the early 1900s, one of Freud's apprentices, Carl Gustav Jung, a Swiss psychiatrist and psychoanalyst, developed an interest in personality typing. Jung's work was based on the desire to help reconcile Adler's and Freud's theories and to define how his own perspective differed from theirs. Jung wrote, "In attempting to answer this question, I came across the problem of types; for it is one's psychological type which from the outset determines and limits a person's judgment" and that "Your visions will become clear only when you can look into your own heart. Who looks outside, dreams; who looks inside, awakes."

In Jung's theory of the ego, described in 1916 in *Psychological Types*, intuition is an "irrational function," opposed most directly by sensation, and opposed less strongly by the "rational functions" of thinking and feeling. He defined intuition as "perception via the unconscious" and using sense-perception only as a starting point, to bring forth ideas, images, possibilities, ways out of a blocked situation, by a process that is mostly unconscious. "Until you make the unconscious conscious, it will direct your life and you will call it fate." Fate or destiny is considered to be a supernatural power outside of anyone's control and predetermined. Relying on fate alone seems to be a very passive way to make decisions. Some personality types, though, are very comfortable with this idea. Speaking of personality types …

The subject of personality type theory and testing millions of people who now commonly refer to themselves by a variety of four letters of the alphabet, such as ENTP or, in my case, ISTJ, is a business in and of itself. Over 50 million people around the world are estimated to have taken the Myers-Briggs Type Indicator (MBTI), a personality-typing test that was first introduced in 1942 by the famous mother-daughter team. The aim of Isabel Briggs Myers and her mother, Katharine Briggs, was to make the insights of type theory accessible to individuals and groups. The MBTI is based on Jung's work in analytical psychology.

The four Jungian psychological types are Extraversion (E) or Introversion (I), Sensing (S) or Intuition (N), Thinking (T) or Feeling (F), and Judging (J) or Perceiving (P). The mother-daughter team addressed the two related goals in the developments and application of the MBTI instrument:

- The identification of basic preferences of each of the four dichotomies specified or implicit in Jung's theory; and
- The identification and description of the 16 distinctive personality types that result from the interactions among the preferences.

The test is an introspective self-report questionnaire with the purpose of indicating differing psychological preferences in how people perceive the world around them and make decisions. If you are interested in taking a shortened free version of the test, there are several websites that offer it (as of the writing of this chapter) such as humanmetrics.com and personalityperfect.com.

This is how it works. You are given a series of statements to agree or disagree with on a scale. Each statement presented to you has the same choices with the scale ranging from a firm YES to an adamant NO with a few less strong options in between. For example:

1. You are almost never late for your appointments

   a. YES
   b. yes
   c. uncertain
   d. no
   e. NO

2. It is difficult to get you excited

   a. YES
   b. yes
   c. uncertain
   d. no
   e. NO

And so on. There are 93 questions in the Standard English version but other languages may have more or fewer. After the test, you are given your type by letters with the percentage strength of each.

When I stated earlier that I just tested as an ISTJ, my scores broke down as this: Introvert (62 percent), Sensing (6 percent), Thinking (9 percent), and Judging (38 percent). My scores meant that I have distinct preference of Introversion over Extraversion but with only a slight preference of Sensing over Intuition as well as Thinking over Feeling and a moderate preference of Judging over Perceiving. But, is this personality test a valid measurement? I used to be an ENFP in my early 20s and am now the opposite. Let's see why this would happen.

The global popularity of the MBTI is astonishing. Here is a bit of history on the ladies behind the tool. Katharine Cook Briggs (1875–1968) began her research into personality in 1917. Upon meeting her future son-in-law, she observed marked differences between his personality and that of other family members. To maintain her relationship with her daughter, Briggs sought to better understand Myers and his differences.

Fast forward a couple decades. In 1944, Isabel Briggs Myers (1897–1980), a housewife who wrote award-winning mystery novels at the time, took a part-time job with the human resources director of a large Philadelphia bank in order to familiarize herself with the personality sorting instruments currently in use. She was able to learn modern practices and tested every person who applied for employment at the company.

Throughout the 1950s to 1970s, Myers presented her data and personality sorting methodology to a variety of educational institutions, publications, and psychologists. In 1962 she wrote *Introduction to Type*, a short but comprehensive educational book that is still in print. By the time of Isabel's death in 1980, their test was being widely used by organizations to improve employee interaction and career counseling, as well as by many others who wanted to improve their personal relationships.[6]

Her creation is everywhere and it is quite amazing that is the case. With no formal training in psychology or sociology, Myers concocted a test now administered in 20+ languages, and is routinely deployed by 89 of the Fortune 100 companies, the US government, hundreds of universities, and online dating sites like Project Evolove.[7] In the field of psychometric testing, a $500 million industry with over 2500 different tests in the United States alone, "there is not one expert that can explain why Myers-Briggs has so thoroughly surpassed its competition, emerging as a household name on par with the Atkins Diet or The Secret."[8] The MBTI is clearly the most frequently used personality inventory available. Taken together, the test and its administration is an industry unto itself. It is termed as "ideal for team and leadership development, conflict and stress management as well as career transitions and planning." But, is it good at defining you?

Many articles exist that challenge the test. It is a frequently Googled subject. The latest article in *Financial Times* questions "Is Myers-Briggs Up to the Job?" Huffington Post says, "Goodbye to MBTI, the Fad that Won't Die." *The Washington Post* questions "Myers-Briggs: Does it Pay to Know Your Type?" Go to a networking event and someone will undoubtedly ask, "So what are you? I'm an ESTJ." And, you will know exactly what they're talking about.

Philosopher Roman Krznaric notes that if "you retake the test after only a five-week gap, there's around a 50% chance that you will fall into a different personality category compared to the first time you took the test." This is bad news for the test's reputation, given that replicability is an essential part of scientific inquiry.[9]

"The content of the MBTI scales is problematic," according to the National Academy of Sciences. They concluded in 1991 that only the I-E scale has high correlations with comparable scales of other instruments and low correlations with instruments designed to assess different concepts, showing strong validity. In contrast, the S-N scale shows relatively weak validity. One of my first thoughts upon learning this was questioning what the difference is between

Sensing and Intuition to begin with? Empaths have the ability to feel emotions or physical symptoms of others even if they themselves are not going through the same events. A common trait of empaths is the *in*ability to discern between what is past, in the present, or what is to come in the future. Highly Sensitives have high sensory awareness and often feel extremely emotional or in-tune with their surroundings. Considering that only 2–3 percent of the population is considered to be empathic and 15–20 percent are considered to be Highly Sensitive People (HSP), the topic is worthy of discussion.

I would love to challenge a component of the MBTI: the S versus N that showed weak validity in the 1991 study. As Malcolm Gladwell, a Canadian journalist and writer wrote in the *New Yorker*: "Jung didn't believe that types were easily identifiable, and he didn't believe that people could be permanently slotted into one category or another. 'Every individual is an exception to the rule,' he wrote; to 'stick labels on people at first sight,' in his view, was 'nothing but a childish parlor game.'"

So, can a Myers-Briggs test help you understand the person you are, help employers place the best candidates in their companies, explain how you make your decisions, interact with others and how they interact with you? Sure. But even the best ideas need a little refinement from time to time. Challenging a component of this extremely popular personality test will take a book in and of itself. There are more relevant things to discuss on intuition.

Additional Research

In 1968, Vassar College conducted an in-depth study on intuition pursuant to a contract with the Office of Education, US Department of Health, Education & Welfare. The problem studied in the project was the theoretical concept of intuition and the behavioral phenomenon of intuitive problem solving. One of the most important conclusions in the study is that it is indeed possible to assert reliably that an individual has one or another propensity for intuitive problem solving, and it is possible to describe some of the concurrent and relatively long-term characteristics of behavior which are likely to be associated with that propensity. Thus, the empirical study of individual differences in intuitive thinking is empirically feasible and psychologically meaningful.

"The intuitionistic point of view obliges us to accept pure subjectivism and personal certainty as adequate criteria of truth along with empirical criteria of truth," a point of view that became under attack from neopositivistic philosophers. One of the most severe criticisms of the theory was from Mario Bunge (1962) who held that any point of view that proposes an absolutistic nonrational notion of truth is a "variety of quackery." What does all of this mean? Intuition has been scientifically considered since time was recorded to not be quackery and is becoming more acceptable for business professionals to openly utilize, even discuss, on a daily basis.

In a few pages of content, we have delved into the evolvement of intuition briefly from roughly 300 BCE to the late 1990s. Enter the 2000s.

In 2005, Malcolm Gladwell introduced the concept of rapid cognition or "thin-slicing," in his book *Blink: The Power of Thinking Without Thinking*. Thin-slicing is the process by which people make quick assessments of the world using a limited amount of evidence. In his work, Gladwell explained that an extremely large number of our decisions result from thin-slicing. There are advantages to this process but also some issues.

The conscious mind is great at looking at evidence and drawing conclusions. What is termed the *adaptive unconscious* doesn't work like that. While the conscious mind is good at studying a wide range of evidence and drawing conclusions from it, the adaptive unconscious assesses a very small amount of information (hence the term a "thin slice") and then makes an instinctive decision about how to respond. Basically, the adaptive unconscious acts instinctively as well as somewhat reflexively. What this means is that we don't necessarily know when we are using our adaptive unconscious, which can lead to prejudicial biases coming forth when we don't even realize it.

But in spite of that, rapid cognition also has some notable benefits. Perhaps most importantly, rapid cognition is rapid. There are many occasions when people don't have the time to weigh all available evidence. In such a moment, we need to use the adaptive unconscious to decide what to do. The adaptive unconscious is also more adept at interpreting subtle pieces of evidence such as facial cues, which the conscious mind often ignores. Human beings would have gone extinct long ago if rapid cognition hadn't helped them act in times of crisis. Later in this chapter I will discuss how executive leaders are more likely to utilize intuition for decision making when dealing with volatile crisis situations but not necessarily when a decision doesn't need to be made quickly.

When faced with an overwhelming quantity of variables, great decision makers aren't those who process the most information or spend the most time deliberating, but those who have perfected the art of thin-slicing, filtering the very few factors that matter. Think of the great business leaders of our time. Take Steve Jobs, for example. He was known for placing great emphasis on his gut feelings and incorporating most, if not all, into his decision making. He was a personality that did his best work by relying on his intuition and inner wisdom. What we can take away from this is that by approaching an issue from a variety of angles, your chance of making mistakes is minimalized. So, yes, your gut is important, but it needs validation.[10]

Over the last month or so, I have read the specific details of recent studies that are very telling, from a statistical standpoint, how the body is able to speak intuitively to the mind. There have been many experiments conducted, as the topic has been greatly explored in the last 20 years. There are specifically two that come to mind. Both have had an audience for their results in the subscribers of *Psychological Science*.

The first was a study performed by the Medical Research Council Cognition and Brain Sciences Unit, Cambridge, UK in 2011, which revealed how the body is able to speak intuitively to the mind. As mentioned in *Psychological Science*, the study involved a card game that was designed to have no obvious strategy in order to win. The objective was for participants to rely only on their hunches in order to learn how to win the game. Vital signs were measured while the game was taking place; a heart monitor as well as a finger sensor were utilized to measure sweat secretion. The researchers concluded that only those who listened to their heart rate eventually learned how to win the game. The rate would increase before they made a certain decision, but the players mistook the subtle body changes for intuition.[11] This, in part, might have been because of the phrases society has used to describe intuition. Have you noticed that the phrases "follow your heart" and "go with your gut" both describe physical body parts? Interestingly, in this study, the quality of the advice that people's bodies gave them varied. Some people's gut feelings totally hit the mark; they become proficient at the card game quickly. Other people's bodies told them exactly the wrong moves to make, so they learned slowly or never found a way to win. The idea is that we should be careful in following our instincts, because sometimes they can assist or hinder our decision making. But, does intuition even exist, can it be measured, and can it be improved over to time to help us in decision making?

Yes, according to multiple study results in 2016 by a team at University of New South Wales (if interested, the specific research methodology, results, etc. can be found in Lufityanto, Donkin, & Pearson's "Measuring Intuition: Nonconscious Emotional Information Boosts Decision Accuracy and Confidence," *Psychological Science*). So if we can use unconscious information in our body or brain to help us make better and quicker decisions, as well as have more confidence in the decisions we make, that leads me to think that practical intuition is not just possible, but that what has been trying to be proved for centuries (that humans can make successful decisions without deliberate analytical debate) is the start of *practical intuition*. What does this mean to us from a professional finance perspective today? Applying intuition in combination with rational analysis in our professional lives makes sense. I would term this practice as "practical intuition." Unfortunately, we haven't been formally educated on how to do this. It has long been my hope that colleges/universities will offer a course or more on the use of practical intuition in business. Why this isn't already a thing is beyond me. It's been discussed since Plato. Seriously, it's time.

Using Intuition in Decision Making

Being an effective decision maker requires a lot of things: collaboration, intelligence, leadership, life experience, and perseverance are naturally at the top of the list, but the most important skill, in my opinion, is being able to tell the difference between when intuition can accurately guide us or lead us awry. So, when do we listen to that inner voice or stomp it out? Following our intuition in our own personal life is one thing; being ultimately responsible to entities, investors, partners, vendors, and so on is quite another.

Enter the age of *Big Data*. When the amount of data available to business leaders over the past decade has so significantly increased, the possibility of overthinking a situation, of being in "data paralysis" is a much bigger concern than ever. Queens University, Smith School of Business Executive Survey findings support how valuable the combined use of intuition and experience, along with data analysis, are in *Intuition in the Age of Big Data*. Key findings of the survey include the following: 81 percent of the leaders at least somewhat agree that "Big Data" is changing how leaders make major business decisions and that important decisions are now based more on data and analytics and less on intuition and experience. Of those surveyed, 52 percent said they rely too much on data and analytics when making decisions and not enough on their intuition. On the flip side 41 percent indicated they rely on their intuition and experience more and not enough on data and analytics. The most interesting finding in this research is that 78 percent of business leaders must go with their gut and intuition when time is of the essence. They also tend to rely on intuition when making people-oriented decisions and when dealing with volatile situations—such as crises—where there is more focus on interpersonal and relational assessment than just data analysis. "What business leaders should recognize is that data analytics and intuition are not mutually exclusive. Even when we use data, intuition and experience are still critical in developing novel strategies to meet business challenges. Sometimes we can have too much or conflicting information, and it doesn't always provide a clear direction on what to do," explained Salman Mufti, associate dean and executive director of Queen's Executive Education.[12]

Final Five Take-aways

1. Understand that there are occasions when perfectionism is not an option, especially in times of crisis.
2. Expect intuition to randomly show up as well as appear when you ask it to. Your heart is 5000 times stronger magnetically than your brain.[13] Consider the reason why this is.
3. Don't overthink. If things are getting too complicated and you are in a data paralysis mode, take a walk to clear your head for a while and purposely think of either (a) absolutely nothing but what your five senses are telling you or (b) consciously focus on something simple, like the number one or a color and notice it wherever you are. I focus on the color blue because it evokes serenity, an invitation, and trustworthiness and typically makes me laugh thinking of Seinfeld's *Serenity Now* episode. After a while (30 minutes or so), go back to your question and answer it as quickly as possible. You will notice that if you don't let your brain get overinvolved, things will really come clearly to you.
4. Don't let fear or failure get you down. Walt Disney (1901–1966) believed he could build an empire on a dance star … that was a mouse! Just a hunch, but I'm thinking that this was not a linear decision. He took the plunge after he was fired from a Missouri newspaper for "not being creative enough." Even after his first venture went bankrupt, he still went with his gut and followed his instincts. For someone who still holds the record for the most Oscars won by an individual (32), that's pretty impressive.[14]
5. Realize that others' instincts and advice cannot compare to your own. In 1961, Ray Kroc became a business legend when he ignored his lawyer's advice and borrowed $2.7 million to buy out the modest fast-food franchise he helped build. Now more than 69 million people A DAY sit down or drive-thru at McDonalds.[15]

Conclusion

The fact that generations today may have not been taught to believe in, trust in, or expect intuition to show up is disheartening. Albert Einstein (1879–1955) once said, "The only real valuable thing is intuition." If that is the case, why intuition isn't automatically utilized in all situations and considered to be not just acceptable but applause-worthy in practice is puzzling. I mean, this is Albert Einstein talking! Mathematician, physicist, Nobel laureate—the first scientist's name that you are typically taught in grade school and actually know how to spell (even though explaining what $E = mc^2$ wasn't something you understood yet). What role, if any, should intuition have on your business? That depends, and it all really comes down to a matter of opinion and whether or not you would like to have it known that you utilize practical intuition. Some of the most inspiring business leaders of our world had no problem doing so. It could possibly work out for you as well, if you let it.

Notes

1. https://www.psychologynoteshq.com/erikerikson/.
2. http://www.dark-stories.com/eng/julius_caesar_beware_the_ides_of_march.htm.
3. https://Firstladies.org/biographies/firstladies.aspx?biography=19.
4. Office of Education, Vassar College, US Department of Health, Education & Welfare, June 1968.
5. Robert Skidelsky, *Keynes: The Return of the Master*, 2009.
6. http://www.personalityperfect.com/myers-briggs-personality-test/.
7. http://www.businessinsider.com/myers-briggs-personality-test-is-misleading-2014-6.
8. Merve Emre, "What's Your Type, Uncovering the Secret of Myers-Briggs," Digg.com. October 7, 2015.
9. http://www.businessinsider.com/myers-briggs-personality-test-is-misleading-2014-6.
10. Simon T. Bailey, Biz Journals, October 2014.
11. https://www.psychologicalscience.org/news/releases/trust-your-gut-but-only-sometimes.html.
12. https://smith.queensu.ca/insight/articles/intuition_in_the_age_of_big_data.
13. https://www.heartmath.org.
14. https://waltdisney.org/blog/walts-oscars-overview.
15. https://expandedramblings.com/index.php/mcdonalds-statistics/.

10

Focus on Asset Allocation

Perhaps the most frequent question I am asked after people find out I am in the investment business is whether I can help them with their 401(k). For those who don't normally walk through that particular jungle, the question of how much to allocate to each fund is a tricky one. Most companies who offer a 401(k) plan provide substantial information on the funds; a massive prospectus must be made available for each. But little if any guidance is provided regarding how much to allocate to different funds. Regardless of whether you are building a 401(k) plan, a personal investment portfolio or an investment mix for an institution, the *type* of fund, in most asset categories, contributes more to the overall portfolio's return than does the fund manager's experience, background, company, or any other individual characteristic. Deciding how much of a certain type of investment to include in a portfolio is known as the asset-allocation decision. If the US stock market of the future fails to post returns in line with long-term averages, effective asset allocation, at the portfolio level, can help make up the shortfall.

Asset allocation is simply the process of cutting up the investment pie into broad pieces such as stocks, bonds, and real estate. Depending on who you talk to, asset allocation can involve placing money with domestic or international stocks, private equity, various types of bonds, commodities, real estate, hedge funds, and a whole host of other categories.

Most investors spend an inordinate amount of time bike shedding through the minor details of their individual investments rather than evaluating how they fit together as a group. This harkens back to Chap. 6 where in response to traditional economic models that say *investors consider asset integration when constructing portfolios*, behavioral scientists indicated a belief that *behavioral investors construct portfolios based on asset segregation*. Although traditional

© The Author(s) 2018
M. J. Oyster, *Success in a Low-Return World*,
https://doi.org/10.1007/978-3-319-99855-8_10

finance would have us believe investors base decisions on the role an investment plays in the portfolio, behavioralists know that doesn't always happen. There may be some consideration of portfolio impact, but even many institutional investors spend far too much time on a fund's individual attributes. Over time, funds investing in a given asset space and style will generally exhibit similar returns because most of them are looking for the same things in the same group.

Gary Brinson et al. authored one of the most frequently cited studies attributed to asset allocation. According to Brinson's article that appeared in the *Financial Analysts Journal*,[1] over 90 percent of a pension fund's quarterly variability in performance is due to its investment policy (i.e., asset allocation). Pension funds generally define a strategic asset mix in their investment policy development process and then stick with it. They also regularly rebalance assets to maintain that mix and the investment managers they hire to implement their policy usually don't deviate much from their stated mandate, less risk termination; a point complemented by the discussion of *agency friction* in Chap. 6. The Brinson study showed that asset allocation contributes greatly to portfolio variability, but what about performance?

A later study by Roger Ibbotson and Paul Kaplan[2] showed that for balanced mutual funds (those investing in both stocks and bonds) and pension funds alike, very near, or slightly more than 100 percent of a fund's return was explained by the return of the policy (asset allocation) on average, meaning that the active decisions the funds make had either a nominal or slightly negative impact on total return. They point out that both groups *are not adding value above their policy benchmarks because of a combination of timing, security selection, management fees, and expenses.* Navigating the various studies that seek to explain the relevance of asset allocation can leave you with mixed feelings on the amount of impact it has, but virtually all studies on the subject indicate that an investment is greatly affected by the asset class in which that investment is made.

Much of the asset-allocation work done today is in the spirit of Harry Markowitz who showed that by combining two or more risky assets, the overall risk of the portfolio could go down as long as the two weren't perfectly correlated. His *Modern Portfolio Theory* won him the Nobel Prize and has been used at least in some capacity by virtually every allocator ever since.

Years ago, certain institutional investors were restricted to spending just the income generated from low-risk fixed income securities. Gradually, these institutions began drawing upon Markowitz's ideas and dipping their collective toes into the stock market pool when they had previously only invested in bonds. As the idea behind the Prudent Man Rule became more widely adopted, many institutions began investing in riskier investments including stocks. The Prudent Man Rule is derived from Massachusetts common law dating to 1830 when Massachusetts Justice Samuel Putman directed trustees *to observe how men of prudence, discretion and intelligence manage their own affairs, not in regard to speculation, but in regard to the permanent disposition of their funds, considering the probable income, as well as the probable safety of the capital to be invested.* Allocators took this to mean that any investment should be allowed in a portfolio as long as it was a prudent contributor to the greater good. The concept of diversification helped them enter the realm of stock investing by showing that a portfolio could be constructed with an appropriate level of risk despite including assets that by themselves exhibited risk beyond a tolerable amount.

Over time, both institutional and well-managed individual portfolios became more widely diversified, which helped smooth out returns when an asset class or two had the occasional hiccup in performance. And that's a good thing, because less volatility means greater returns, all else being equal. An example can show how that works:

Investor A and Investor B each buy a stock for $10 that they plan to hold for five years. Investor A's stock goes up by 10 percent in each of the five years, while Investor B's stock declines 12 percent in the first year, goes up 35 percent the second, up 5 percent the third, declines 8 percent in the fourth and jumps 30 percent in the fifth. The average yearly return for both stocks is exactly 10 percent, but Investor A's stock will be worth $161, while Investor B's stock will be worth just $149. How is this possible when they both returned an average of 10 percent per year? Look at it this way: a stock that falls from $10 to $9 per share loses 10 percent, but needs an 11 percent advance just to get back to even. Volatility is a quiet thief raiding investment portfolios.

It was mentioned previously that most mutual funds today invest in a given asset class and style, and don't deviate from that mandate. Markowitz's Modern Portfolio Theory is one reason we have so many highly specialized mutual funds today, because investors who sought the optimal asset allocation wanted to diversify as much as possible. At one point in investing history, there were generally only "stock funds" but for many years now, investors have had the opportunity to buy into an actively managed fund that focuses exclusively on small cap stocks with a value tilt, or a fund that buys only international growth stocks, or just about anything else for that matter. In most cases, these specialized funds rarely step out of their clearly defined asset boxes when selecting stocks, else they face the wrath of investment advisors who aim to keep a client's portfolio as well balanced as possible. If, for example, a small cap **growth** manager suddenly became keen on small cap **value** stocks, an investor's portfolio, of which the manager is only one part, may become overweighted to small cap value and at risk of poor performance if small cap value stocks don't perform well. This failure to diversify among several styles is one of the most common ways investors leave their doors open, inviting the volatility thief in for a visit.

Large fund companies have bought into the idea of specialization because it helps them smooth out the bumps in their income stream. A fund-management company that has enough different kinds of funds always has something to promote because at least one of their funds will always be in favor; so, too, do consultants who advise institutional investors like fund specialization because it allows them to place the fund in a predetermined box. Funds that don't fit neatly into a box are less expediently placed in a broader portfolio because they don't explicitly fill a specifically defined need.

Diversification is a great idea and it helps mitigate risk, but one shortcoming is that the correlation between different asset classes is not stable through time. Markowitz's work that says that combining two uncorrelated investments can reduce risk is correct, but most investment portfolios are constructed principally for returns. How? By taking on a lot of stock market risk. Even many of the most well-diversified investment portfolios carry a preponderance of equity risk because they need stock market performance to achieve long-term returns; but stocks can be volatile. Two investments that are largely uncorrelated over long periods of time may become more highly correlated when the stock market falls under price pressure. Consider a portfolio that includes large, small, growth, and value US equities, international stocks, emerging market equities, high yield fixed income, long/short hedge funds and private equity holdings. It sounds well diversified, but we should not expect any of those investment categories to provide much protection during a recession-fueled bear market in stocks. Each of those categories, although mutually exclusive, are exposed to stock market risk. In most historical examples of a substantial decline in stocks, all those asset categories declined at the same time.

The average annual return of the S&P 500 from 2009 through 2017 was in excess of 15 percent—a number sufficiently large enough to support the achievement of many an investment goal. But what if such strong returns do not repeat thereafter? What's an investor to do in an environment where stocks may return only 7 percent per year and there's limited benefit to diversifying across market caps and regions? Branch out into new territory. Look into areas that may have seemed too exotic or risky in the past but may offer solid returns with small or even negative correlation to equities. The point is this: An allocation to large cap US stocks will likely continue serving as a core position in retirement funds and other long-term investment programs, which is prudent, but investments with a high correlation to the stock market may not fare as well in the future and could come under stress during the inevitable periods when the stock market declines.

The following Monte Carlo simulation shows the benefit of combining low-correlation asset classes as opposed to combining highly correlated asset classes. Consider two stock-like assets, such as large cap domestic equity and developed international equity. They both average a return of 7 percent per year and experience 15 percent standard deviation. They are 80 percent correlated, which means 80 percent of the variability of one is explained by the other. A Monte Carlo simulation allows us to see the returns we might expect if assets were invested equally into each of these two stock asset classes. The simulation looked at 1000 separate examples that an investor might experience if they held an equal weighting in both assets over the course of a year. As you would imagine, the average return was 7 percent, but the standard deviation of these returns was 14.2 percent. This shows that if you combine two less-than-perfectly correlated asset classes, each with a 7 percent return and 15 percent standard deviation, your risk will be lower than if you had invested in only one of them.

That's helpful, but what if the two were virtually uncorrelated, meaning that the returns of one could not be explained by returns of the other. In this case, the study was repeated; two asset classes, each with a 7 percent return and 15 percent standard deviation, but this time, the correlation between the two was assumed to be 0 percent. The difference in what an investor would actually experience is significant. Once again, the average annual return was 7 percent, but the standard deviation of the total investment was just 10.4 percent.

Let's translate that into real dollars. Another Monte Carlo simulation allows us to see the growth of $1 million invested in the first example versus $1 million invested in the second. Both examples provide an expected return of 7 percent per year, but the second does so with far less volatility. Over the course of 1000 independent, 10-year period simulations, the $1 million invested in the first example grew to $1,963,808 on average, but the $1 million invested in the second example grew to $1,964,964. As was mentioned previously, volatility is a performance thief. Even though both portfolios had the same average annual return, the portfolio with the lower volatility added more dollars to the investment over time.

Reducing volatility helps, but over the long term, the increase in wealth creation strictly due to reduced volatility may not prove sufficient. In order to make up the bear market in expectations that the stock market may leave us with, we must increase returns. Investors seeking asset growth will need to look outside the normal stock-based asset classes.

Asset Allocation and Portfolio Construction Philosophies

How much return is needed and risk willing to be accepted differs from one investor to the next. We know that regardless of the methodology used, the inclusion of an uncorrelated asset into a portfolio can improve that portfolio's risk-adjusted return. That said, different investors approach the problem of how to allocate assets in different ways, each based upon their unique goals, constraints, competitive advantages, and risk tolerances. One philosophy is not inherently superior to another, but different investors with different needs should employ different allocation techniques that can work best for them. An understanding of different philosophies used by sophisticated institutional investors can help us understand and apply techniques that can improve the probability of success.

We will look at four different asset-allocation philosophies:

- The Endowment or Yale Model
- The Norway Model
- Factor or Canada Model
- Manager-Centric or MIT Model

The Endowment or Yale Model

David Swensen became the CIO of Yale University's investment office in 1985. Almost immediately, he began managing the institution's investment assets in unconventional ways. Swensen and Dean Takahashi developed an asset-allocation philosophy that has become broadly known as the endowment model because it has been so widely adopted by other institutional investors, most notably, university endowments.

Swensen was an early adopter of liquidity-constrained investments, recognizing that an illiquidity premium exists in certain areas of the investment universe. Although Yale's endowment represents the largest contributor to the university's ongoing operating budget, Swensen has been able to manage liquidity requirements and allocate to illiquid investments to tap into the performance premium (the illiquidity premium) they can provide relative to liquid investments.

Endowment models are well diversified and seek opportunities in less efficient markets through active management, while they utilize very little if any in fully liquid actively managed stock-picking funds.

The Yale model exhibits a strong belief in equities, whether public or private, but relies heavily on private mandates that can demonstrate a competitive competency accessing the illiquidity premium. As a general rule of thumb, endowment models allocate 50 percent or so to liquidity-constrained mandates. Although the fees of such "alternative" investments generally exceed those of their traditional counterparts, most exhibit fee schedules that include performance incentives for the manager, reflecting an alignment of interest between the manager and investor.

The endowment model is highly dependent upon accessing managers who through skill or access to information can be expected to outperform their area of investing in general. One advantage that Yale enjoys is the use of expertise and reputation to gain access to desirable managers. Many who seek to apply the endowment model do not have the same wherewithal and may experience less success than Yale. Uncovering, then gaining access to best-in-class managers, many of which have limited capacity/willingness to take on new investment capital, can be costly and require a large investment research staff to do so.

Additionally, liquidity constraints must be managed, recognizing the potential for near-term strain during periods of market stress. Yale notoriously entered the financial crisis of 2008 holding 70 percent of its assets in liquidity-constrained investments, which resulted in a near-term liquidity crunch for them and prompted some to declare the endowment model *broken*.[3] But Yale at least recovered practically unscathed with fiscal year 2009, a rare negative, seemingly inconsequential in the long term. Over the 20 years ending June 30, 2017, Yale's endowment returned 12.1 percent annualized, which exceeds domestic stocks (7.5 percent) and domestic bonds (5.2 percent) over that same time period.[4]

The Norway Model

Norway is one of the wealthiest countries per capita in the world, with vast natural resources, most notably oil and gas. In 1990, Norway's Government Pension Fund Global (GPFG) was formed as a savings vehicle designed to support the country's population over the course of multiple generations. In order to diversify the country's collective assets away from just resources, a portion of state-owned assets were sold with the funds channeled into the

GPFG, which then purchased investment securities. Investment returns are expected to provide the financial backing for Norway's government programs supporting the country's population over the long term. In 2017, the GPFG was the largest sovereign wealth fund on earth having grown beyond $1 trillion.

In many ways, the Norway model is the opposite of the endowment model. The GPFG focuses nearly exclusively on public equity and bond markets. They employ active management in only limited amounts with a strong focus on minimizing costs. The GPFG rebalances the fund back to targets in a highly disciplined fashion resulting in very little tracking error, and is highly transparent in terms of their allocations, which can be easily accessed through an interactive map on their website. It took me no more than 30 seconds or so to discover that as of the end of 2017, the GPFG owned over $8 billion of Apple stock. By contrast, the individual securities and private investments held in endowment model portfolios are almost always closely guarded secrets.

In short, the Norway model relies on market return (beta) for capital appreciation rather than outperformance (alpha). This represents an important differentiation relative to the endowment model. But that's not completely by choice, and they would be the first to admit it. The GPFG's sheer scale limits their opportunity set. In June 2017, Yale's endowment was a staggering $27 billion, but that's a mere drop in the bucket compared with Norway's $1 trillion. Yale, and others of similar size, must spend heavily on investment manager research resources to identify and access the most desirable managers with only limited capacity for new investment capital. While Norway theoretically could do the same thing, the costs would be astronomical and in their view, unjustifiable. While this misses an opportunity to draw upon an important resource in the form of their long-term focus, which would allow them to access the illiquidity premium, they instead choose to focus on inexpensive allocations broadly across deep and liquid markets around the world.

The Factor or Canada Model

In the mid-1990s, the Canadian government recognized that contribution rates to the country's pensions would be insufficient to support their aging population in years to come. Unless some significant changes were made, they surmised, their public pensions were on an unsustainable course. Solutions included modest increases in government contributions and a small reduction in benefits as well as the creation of the Canada Pension Plan

Investment Board (CPPIB), which was designed to oversee and invest the funds contributed to and held by the Canada Pension Plan (CPP). The CPPIB was designed to act largely like an independent company, enabling it to recruit top investment talent and retain them with competitive compensation packages. This provided the opportunity to devise and then implement certain investment-related innovations relative to the way pension assets were managed in Canada previously.

The Canada model shares some similarities with the endowment model but has some important distinctions. Most investors believe diversification at the portfolio level can improve long-term risk-adjusted returns, but rather than diversify by allocating among traditional asset class categories, the Canada model seeks diversification by allocating to different sources of risk. This concept is based on the idea that different assets are expected to earn different amounts of performance premia to compensate investors for bearing the underlying risk factors to which those assets have exposure.

An application of the Canada model seeks diversification among risks and return streams. It understands that even though equities and high yield bonds are different kinds of securities, they share a common risk (stock market declines).

Criticisms of the Canada model point to potential limitations of risk identification. Risk exposures are generally categorized as simple variations of fixed income or equity. This may prevent the allocators from recognizing all the disparate and potentially unintended risks that the portfolio may bear. Illiquidity, public policy, manager-specific and inflation are among many risks not easily identified through a mix of stock and bond market risk.

Manager-Centric or MIT Model

While all three models discussed so far rely at least in part on asset-allocation targets at the portfolio level, the manager-centric or MIT model turns that concept upside down. How an asset class performs levies a great deal of influence on the managers contained within but forecasting the future returns of an asset class is notoriously difficult.

One reason equity risk is held at a large percentage in so many investment portfolios is because the stock market generally appreciates over time, but it doesn't do so all the time. And the variability of performance is vast even over long lengths of time. Although rare, there have been periods in excess of a decade when the US stock market failed to produce positive performance. So how much should be invested in US stocks, and how much to invest in other categories? The cost of making a bad decision can prove catastrophic. In 2014, I was part of a team of asset allocators. In the spirit of overweighting that which was undervalued and seeking broad diversification, we held a large overweight in emerging market equities and a meaningful position in commodities. Soon thereafter, oil prices crashed amidst a glut of supply, the US dollar skyrocketed, and emerging market equities collapsed. Eventually those investments reversed ground but not before severe stress was placed on our client base. Investing is hard.

In 2011, the MIT Investment Management Company (MITIMCo) made the decision that they believe a higher and better use of their time and talents was identifying managers with a high probability of success as opposed to asset-class return forecasting.

The MIT model begins with the identification of what the allocators believe are exceptional managers irrespective of discipline. This involves a significant focus on manager underwriting in hopes of identifying specific traits. The mandate size per manager is then determined based upon their conviction to the individual manager and their conviction and attractiveness of space. Portfolio-level limits (guiderails) help ensure diversification, but that's almost an afterthought. To them, manager selection is paramount.

Advantages of the MIT model include a pragmatic recognition of their greater manager-selection ability versus asset-class forecasting ability, and they align their philosophy to that. With such a deep focus on managers and a willingness to draw upon their long-term focus to access the illiquidity risk premium, they have the opportunity to improve performance. One potential disadvantage is the unintended aggregation of risks to intolerable levels. Where Harvard seeks to understand, track, and then diversify sources of risk, MIT may discover certain unintended and/or uncompensated risks after the fact.

One difference between the MIT model and the Yale model is that MIT values liquidity where Yale draws upon their perpetual time horizon to access the liquidity return premium. In a February 2017 letter to alumni, MITIMCo wrote with regard to illiquid investments:

> A wise person once told us that if we were going to make a mistake, we should make the mistake that is easiest to reverse. We are comfortable sizing our liquid investments larger than our illiquid investments because we can change our mind more easily if we make a mistake.[5]

MIT does not avoid illiquid investments altogether, but they do subject illiquid commitments to a higher hurdle relative to fully liquid allocations.

Conclusion

The choice of how to allocate to different asset categories can serve as the primary driver of portfolio returns. Diversification can improve risk-adjusted returns over the long term, but the benefits can be shrouded by extreme asset category moves over shorter periods. If two different asset categories exhibit low long-term correlations between them, they may be expected to collectively provide stability for the portfolio as a whole, but may also experience similar behavior to one another having a concentration of the same risk during periods of stress.

Different investors solve the problem of how to allocate assets in ways that fit their asset size, return needs, risk tolerances, as well as other advantages and considerations. The four asset-allocation models described above exhibit significant differences but share some commonalities that we should consider in our own allocation decisions:

- Seek diversification to mitigate risk recognizing a need for equity risk in order to produce the desired long-term returns, while short-term displacements from fair value should be expected.
- Rebalance back to targets when allocations drift (Norway does this religiously, Harvard ensures they have the risk exposures they want, Yale does this less religiously than Norway and has limits on what they can do with illiquid commitments, and while MIT does not make broad category allocation targets, they maintain *guiderails* around broad category sizes).
- Utilize the illiquidity premium and active managers if you hold an advantage in terms of size, wherewithal, and an ability to discover then access exceptional managers; otherwise, rely more heavily on passive allocations within highly efficient asset categories in order to keep costs low.

Whatever model is chosen, or a blend of several, the asset-allocation decision should reflect a keen understanding of return needs, risk tolerances, and other considerations as well as a willingness to draw upon key competitive advantages to avoid competing on a level playing field with other financial market participants. Successful investing is difficult enough as it is. Any resource we have to gain an advantage over other investors should be responsibly exploited.

Notes

1. Gary P. Brinson, L Randolf Hood, Gilbert L. Beebower, "Determinants of Portfolio Performance," *Financial Analysts Journal*, July/August 1986, 39–44.
2. Roger G. Ibbotson and Paul D. Kaplan, "Does Asset Allocation Policy Explain 40, 90, or 100 Percent of Performance?" *Financial Analysts Journal*, January/February 2000, 26–33.
3. Joshua Humphreys, Ph.D. Senior Associate, Tellus Institute, and Lecturer, Harvard University, "Educational Endowments and the Financial Crisis: Social Costs and the Systemic Risks in the Shadow Banking System. A Study of Six New England Schools," Center for Social Philanthropy, Tellus Institute, iv.
4. "Investment return of 11.3% brings Yale endowment value to $27.2 billion," News.Yale.edu, October 10, 2017.
5. Alumni Letter, mitimco.org, February 2017, 2.

11

Indexing

Large cap US stock pickers have found it difficult to outperform the S&P 500 during most periods of their existence. Investors who own shares in such funds might not have questioned the underperformance when the rising tide of a bull market lifted all boats but may begin to decide that the fees are not justified if the days of stratospheric stock market performance come to an end. In fact, the flood of assets out of actively managed domestic equity funds has already begun and shows no signs of slowing. Where is the money going? Low-cost, passively managed index funds and ETFs, and for good reason. In short, indexing beats active management.

Indexing seeks to replicate the performance of a particular market or asset class by passively investing in a basket of stocks that represent that asset class. In most periods throughout investment history, the S&P 500 outperformed most actively managed large cap domestic equity portfolios. Here are some examples.

Recall from Chap. 2 the report from Standard and Poor's that said 92.15 percent of all actively managed large cap funds trailed their appropriate benchmark (S&P 500 Index) over the 15-year period ending December 2016. Active large cap stock pickers generally underperform the S&P 500 but manager peer studies versus benchmarks are influenced by the duration of the study and the specific period covered—they are *end-point sensitive*. Looking at the Lipper database of large cap managers for ten years ending March 2018, we see that 77 percent underperformed the S&P 500.

Managers will find more success relative to a benchmark in some environments, less in others. Regardless, as a group they generally underperform and studies such as this are often biased toward making the group of managers

© The Author(s) 2018
M. J. Oyster, *Success in a Low-Return World*,
https://doi.org/10.1007/978-3-319-99855-8_11

look better than they reasonably should. Rigorous analysis should consider the impact of survivorship bias. *Survivorship bias* is an overstatement of a group of funds' aggregate return because some of the poor performers went out of business and dropped off the list at some point during the analysis period. A research study conducted by Mark Carhart showed that survivorship bias overstated the 15-year performance of a universe of diversified equity funds by 0.9 percent per annum.[1] A similar study done by Burton G. Malkiel showed a 1.8 percent overstating of returns over a ten-year period.[2]

The fact that some of the worst performing funds went out of business made the group look about 1.5 percentage points better per year than someone actually investing in that asset class would have experienced. So, if we ratchet down the average performance of the large cap managers in the Lipper database by a conservative 1 percent per year, we see that only 6 percent of all funds outperformed the benchmark over that ten-year period ending March 2018. Expecting 6 percent of all large cap managers to outperform the benchmark going forward is probably optimistic, considering the environment for active management is getting harder, not easier. That makes indexing even more appealing.

Comparing a fund's performance to a core benchmark like the S&P 500 assumes that the performance of different styles like growth and value will even out over time, but styles can stay in or out of favor for extended periods. One way to more fairly evaluate a style-specific manager is to compare them to their appropriate style index. Over the ten years ending March 2018, 25 percent of large cap growth managers outperformed the Russell 1000 Growth Index but just 10 percent outperformed when a conservative 1 percent point adjustment for survivorship bias was made. That's about the same as looking at all large cap managers versus the S&P 500 and it does not inspire much confidence. Over the same period, however, value managers fared a bit better with 45 percent outperforming and even after adjusting for survivorship bias saw 11 percent outperform. Does this mean that value stock pickers are generally more skilled than growth stock pickers? I don't think so, here's why.

Historically and over long periods of time, equity styles generally don't balance each other out—the value equity style tends to outperform growth in terms of frequency (value outperforms more often) and magnitude (value tends to outperform growth by more than growth outperforms value). But, not always. The ten years ending March 2018 was a peculiar one in history in that despite being what most people would probably consider a long term, the Russell 1000 Growth Index outperformed its value counterpart by a staggering 450 basis points annualized. That exceptionally rare outperformance of growth could have been drawn upon by value managers to outperform the value benchmark. Even a modest amount of growth exposure in the value manager's portfolio could have served as a tailwind relative to the value benchmark. This at least partially explains why more value funds than growth funds outperformed, but let's be realistic. Fifty-five percent still underperformed and when adjusting for survivorship bias, we see that 89 percent lagged. Indexing would have been better.

Skill or Luck?

Active managers are faced with the challenge of justifying their fees relative to index funds. After all, if you're paying for skill, you should see skill represented in returns. But, what if the existence of some outperformers is not evidence of skill but rather chance? A Monte Carlo simulation can be devised to show what a group of randomly generated funds would look like, so if the Monte Carlo results look like the actual results, arguing that outperformance is derived from skill would be difficult.

Over the ten years ending March 2018, the average large cap mutual fund (according to Lipper data) returned 8.4 percent annualized. Approximately 95 percent of all returns fell between 5.6 percent and 11.4 percent, which implies a dispersion of returns about the mean of approximately 1.5 percentage points. Coincidentally, I conducted a similar study in 2003 that showed ten-year manager performance dispersion of 2.5 percentage points, suggesting that in the subsequent 15 years, active large cap mutual funds became less differentiated relative to one another. We will dig deeper into this concept in the next chapter that discusses active share.

The 1.5 percentage point dispersion among funds is a standard deviation that can be used to generate random returns in a Monte Carlo simulation. Over this same period, ten years ending March 2018, the S&P 500 posted an annualized return of 9.5 percent. If we assume that the S&P 500 provides a good representation of the group of stocks in which these large cap active managers invest, its return should serve as our jumping off point for the simulation. Our baseline Monte Carlo simulation, therefore, is a group of 10,000 simulated ten-year annualized returns that, as a group, return 9.5 percent on average (a return for stocks that has been typical in the past) and have dispersion (i.e., standard deviation) of 1.5 percentage points above/below the mean.

This simulation is a proxy for the average return of a randomly generated group of portfolios, derived from S&P 500 stocks, which are as different in terms of dispersion as what has been observed in reality. In this case, assuming normal distribution, 50 percent of the returns will be above 9.5 percent and

50 percent will be below 9.5 percent, with 95 percent (two standard deviations) of all returns falling between 8 percent and 11 percent.

But, it is important to note that this doesn't consider fees charged by active managers. In Chap. 5 we noted that the average fee charged by actively managed large cap mutual funds was 0.75 percent. If we make an assumption for fees of 0.75 percent, we can run a simulation to determine how many of the returns outperform the index if the group, on average, lags by their 0.75 percent fee. If the average group of ten-year returns is adjusted down by 0.75 to 8.75 percent, we find that 31 percent of the returns fall above the 9.5 percent mean we started with (aka outperform the index), simply by chance. Even though the random group's average return was less than the index, about 31 percent of them outperformed just because they were different.

We now need to include the effect of survivorship bias, conservatively estimated at 1 percent per annum. Taking survivorship bias into effect, we set the average of our random returns at 7.75 percent. The results indicate that 12 percent of the returns exceeded 9.5 percent, again simply by chance. What does this show? First let's recall that inclusive of fees and an adjustment for survivorship bias, we saw that 6 percent of the large cap managers in the Lipper universe outperformed over the ten years ending March 2018. However, a randomly generated group of ten-year return simulations that is designed to mimic the performance dispersion among large cap stock funds produced 12 percent that outperformed, simply by chance.

This exercise doesn't prove that active managers' returns are random, but if there was an advantage to active management, we might expect more of them to outperform the benchmark than would be expected by random behavior. Can we assume, therefore, that the security selection decisions managers make detract from performance and suggest indexing would be better? In a world where every percentage point will count, keeping costs low and avoiding things that drag on performance will be not just prudent but critical.

An Alternative to Active Management: Indexing

Most active managers fail to beat their benchmark (be it a core index or the appropriate style) and predicting who will is nearly impossible, so why bother? Indexing is a better idea.

Indexing works because it solves the main problem of active management: security selection. The efficiency of markets, competition, fees and costs, regulations, behavioral errors, and the wide availability and speedy dissemination of information all inhibit outperformance from security selection. Performing well in today's stock market is difficult enough, but investors further inhibit performance by making poorly timed buying and selling decisions. An investor may fail to experience even the average performance of a group of funds because they often bail out of a fund after poor performance and buy after good performance.

So to beat the S&P 500, an investor has to find the rare fund that will post outperforming returns then hold on to it despite the swings in performance that may make it look really awful, even for multi-year periods. Even the best funds have been known to spend three years or more well under the benchmark and in the bottom 25 percent of their peers. Why subject yourself to the uncertainty of knowing whether your fund is one of the many laggards or just in a slump while its style is out of favor? You would be tempted to stay with the fund because you know that switching in and out erodes returns, but holding an inferior fund for many years can levy a substantial cost in lost opportunity. Buying and holding index funds solves these problems, because core indexes like the S&P 500 have both growth and value styles and rebalance themselves as styles go in and out of favor.

The benefits of indexing don't stop there. If your sole interest in investing stems from an affiliation with a tax-exempt institution, taxes are not an issue, but most of us are subject to the almighty IRS. Index funds don't turn over their portfolios as much as active managers, resulting in a lower taxable impact. Active managers, who suffer from the behavioral bias of overconfidence, tend to do a lot of buying and selling of the stocks in their portfolio over the course of a year. They may think that doing so will justify their higher fees relative to index funds, but too much turnover can do quite a bit of damage to the returns their investors actually experience. Taxes can cost you up to 20 percent on long-term capital gains and, for some, nearly 50 percent on ordinary income, which would include short-term investment returns. US stock index funds exhibit about 9 percent asset-weighted average portfolio turnover and index ETFs about 15 percent. In contrast, non-index US equity mutual funds exhibit about 51 percent turnover.[3] Of course exceptions exist, but turnover will almost always leave the active fund investor with a higher tax bill than the index fund investor.

Index funds don't completely hide the investor from the tax collector, but they certainly help. Index funds will sell stocks when they fall out of the index, possibly resulting in a capital gain. However, index managers aren't selecting stocks that they think will outperform over time. Some may argue that the committee at Standard and Poor's that decides which stocks will be included in the S&P 500 Index are de facto active managers, buying the strongest companies in a given industry, but their approach is far more passive. They don't buy and sell names based on past performance or the expectation of future performance as active managers do. As a result, the index turns over its names far less frequently than most actively managed portfolios, benefiting the index investor.

Types of Indexed Securities

Making the case that indexing is superior to active management is easy, but the act of investing in index funds may not be. The number of index products has mushroomed in recent years, in part due to growing public awareness of active management's shortcomings. However, not all index funds are alike.

The largest percentage of assets held in index funds is benchmarked against the S&P 500. The S&P 500 has been around longer than most other benchmarks and is a well-diversified cross section of the US stock market. It does not include small company stocks, which may represent 15 percent or more of the total US stock market capitalization, but the S&P's coverage is fairly complete. As was discussed previously, index funds that seek to replicate the S&P 500 and don't charge loads or 12b-1 fees have been largely successful at their primary goal—tracking the returns of the benchmark as closely as possible.

The Vanguard 500 Index Fund, which through its collective share classes held over $400 billion in assets in early 2018, has exhibited about 9 basis points of tracking error over extended periods of time. Tracking error illustrates how differently a fund has performed relative to its benchmark, so a tracking error of 9 basis points means the performance of the fund was within 0.18 percent above or below the index 95 percent of the time. Although the fund usually fails to keep up with the index itself, it generally outperforms actively managed large cap domestic equity funds.

Index funds aren't the only way to index—not by a long shot. In recent years, Exchange-traded funds (ETFs) have grown in popularity. As their name implies, ETFs are funds that trade on an exchange. ETFs have sprung up all over the place, in large part because of their versatility, liquidity, tax-friendliness, and the wide variety of asset classes and styles in which they invest. For example, they can be bought and sold at any time throughout the day, the most recent price can be seen on your smartphone and they can be sold short or bought on margin, actions that cannot be taken with normal open-ended funds.

The first ETF, the SPDR S&P 500 ETF (SPY), was created in 1993 by State Street with the goal of offering a liquid means for their clients to gain access to a passive investment in the S&P 500. In early 2018, the SPY was the largest ETF in terms of assets under management with over $250 billion; a full 75 percent larger than the next largest ETF.

After State Street created the SPY, other organizations recognized the advantages that ETFs could provide relative to mutual funds and began launching their own. Although State Street was the innovator, Blackrock's iShares and Vanguard represent the two powerhouse issuers. By mid-2018, there were approximately 2200 unique ETFs holding $3.7 trillion, a staggering growth that was up from about $650 billion at the end of the financial crisis in 2009.[4] While ETFs represent a meaningful subset of the investment universe, they have yet to threaten the dominance of mutual funds and the $15 trillion of collective assets therein.

Although ETFs trade like stocks, they charge fees like many mutual funds, albeit much lower than those run by your average active manager. When selecting between an ETF or an index fund, differences in fees can help guide your decision, but for large cap domestic equity, it's largely a bike-shedding exercise. The iShares Core S&P 500 ETF (IVV) will cost you about 0.05 percent. The retail share class of the Vanguard 500 Index fund (VFINX), to which you can allocate as little as $3000, charges fees of just 0.14 percent. Those fees are miniscule but are even lower for institutional investors deploying millions of dollars, and the most sophisticated institutional investors (and those who advise them) negotiate directly with the fund managers to create customized funds or separate accounts. Even after considering transaction costs to buy an index fund or ETF, it's essentially free.

Another consideration when selecting between an ETF or an index fund is tracking error—how well has the investment tracked the index it is designed to replicate. Index funds tracking the large cap indices (S&P 500, NASDAQ 100) and the broad market (Wilshire 5000) indices exhibit very low tracking error. For example, the tracking error as measured by mean absolute return difference for VFINX relative to return on S&P 500 is only 5 basis points. For the same time period, ETF (IVV) exhibits on average a tracking error of 13 basis points.[5]

For investors with a long time horizon who don't care to short or lever up their index investment, the decision between an index fund or ETF to replicate a market capitalization-weighted index is largely irrelevant. By contrast, fees and strategy specifics should be considered when venturing beyond traditional cap-weighted index replication in the indexing or ETF world.

Exchange-traded funds (ETFs) offer the diversification of an index, can be traded like stocks, and charge relatively low fees. If it sounds like a great way to invest in the S&P 500, it is, but ETFs exist in far more asset classes than just large cap US stocks.

All traditional equity styles across growth and value, through small, mid, and large capitalization, have ETFs that track them. With ETFs, an investor can now isolate an investment in one of a myriad of different sectors or industries. Investment assets can be allocated to international developed equities without hedging currency, with currency risk hedged out completely or even international exposure with an actively-managed currency hedge such as the WisdomTree Dynamic Currency Hedged International Equity Fund (DDWM). You can get a broad exposure to emerging or frontier markets, target easily investible individual countries or some that are less so, government bonds, junk bonds, emerging market debt, gold and other commodities, MLPs, and on and on.

When has it gone too far? When are there too many ETFs? When demand no longer supports the marketplace. Although many ETFs fail to gain meaningful traction, many do, and the industry keeps evolving to meet changing demand. Exchange-traded funds (ETFs) began as a vehicle for tracking a cap-weighted index and the predominance of assets remain invested that way, but trends are moving into factor-based investing and even all the way to active.

As we will discuss in Chap. 14, market *factors* represent fundamental forces that underlie performance. Factors include broad generalizations about stocks that as a group tend to perform a certain way, and some groups of stocks that exhibit a type of characteristic (a factor) performed better than others. So, the question could then be asked of an active manager: "Did you outperform because you are a smart stock picker or because you simply tilted your portfolio toward a favorable factor like quality stocks?"

Market researchers have identified hundreds of factors but some of the more common ones include value, momentum, quality, and low volatility. Want to invest in a basket of stocks that exhibit lower volatility? There's an ETF for that, as there is for many others. The trend toward greater complexity in ETF offerings appears likely to continue as the marketplace progresses in its evolution away from traditional market-capitalization-weighted index replication into a whole host of unique strategies that apply countless different investment techniques.

The Future for ETFs

Whether in a brokerage account, IRA, or some other investment pool, ETFs offer tremendous opportunities for expedient diversification and access to specialized markets, strategies, styles, or factors, usually through a passive, low-cost vehicle. Institutional investors typically have a large asset base to invest, which can gain them access to the lowest cost index funds and many are nonprofit organizations with little to no tax liability and don't normally need daily liquidity, but that doesn't mean institutional investors should ignore ETFs. An institution may use ETFs as a place to park some money before allocating it to a different manager, such as a hedge fund that only accepts new money periodically. They might also utilize ETFs to target a specific subset of the investment universe or hedge risks to which they are exposed elsewhere in the portfolio. If you have an investment problem, there is probably an ETF that can help solve it.

And the future? It looks very bright for ETFs. According to Charles Schwab, over 60 percent of millennials have either begun replacing or begun considering replacing their individual securities with ETFs.[6] Millennials are generally cost conscious; a group that grew up with the internet and are accustomed to receiving items of value for free. They also like to view pricing throughout the day, for which ETFs have data available—stodgy old mutual funds are only priced once per day (#gasp). ETFs have grown well beyond the curiosity they were in the early 2000s. As the group retains its solid foundation replicating traditional indexes, continues to move into factors and then beyond into even more complicated strategies, still wider acceptance seems likely.

A Fundamental Truth of Investing

The final point to be made about indexing is perhaps the most important: indexing allows for inexpensive exposure to the stock market, which has shown to provide asset growth for those investing in it. You might call this a fundamental truth of investing. Stock prices go up over time. Stocks have advanced in just about any period you choose to measure, provided it's long enough to allow for short-term market noise to play itself out. The wheels of economic progress are almost always moving forward, pushed along by technological advances and efficiency improvements. Companies that issue stock can see their share prices jump if they come out with an innovative new product or find a way to cut costs. They're constantly trying to do both, pushed by the knowledge that failure to stay ahead of the competition will put them out of business. Only the strongest companies survive. This corporate need for success has driven the upward surge of the world economy, and it will continue.

Of all the pessimistic predictions of lower-than-average stock market returns for the future, few expect stock prices to go down. Not many people have suggested that stocks will fail to outpace inflation either. In the absence of complete and total economic disaster, stock prices going up over time is practically a foregone conclusion. Certainly the likelihood of revisiting the stratospheric market ascension that followed the Great Financial Crisis (GFC) or even long-term averages may be many years away, but the fundamental structure of the stock market gives it a natural tendency to ascend. We all know that the stock market doesn't go up every year, but it will go up over time. This trend is so ingrained in the capitalistic structure that it's worth hanging your investment hat on. A fundamental truth like this one may not work every time, but it will almost certainly work over time.

The idea of discussing the merits of stock picking versus indexing, the so-called *active versus passive* debate usually stops here. Passive proponents cite the shortcomings of active management and tout indexing as the logical solution. The arguments are compelling, and the data backs them up. There's no denying that active managers as a group have failed to outperform the index over time and the environment is becoming even more difficult for them. But these same arguments have been made for decades and were just as forceful then as they are now. So, why is only a fraction of all large cap equity assets invested in index funds? As human beings, we are driven by a need to do more and do better. It's in our nature.

Michael Douglas's character Gordon Gekko in the movie *Wall Street* made a now infamous speech in which he described *greed* as *good*. The soliloquy represented a scathing review of 1980s ills and excesses but offered a surprisingly rational assessment. "Greed, for lack of a better term," he said, "is good." Gekko surmised that greed would save the company in question as well as the country as a whole. "Greed," he said, "has marked the upward surge of mankind."

At first glance, it's easy to dismiss Gekko's moral ineptitude, but upon further review, some truth may be hidden in there somewhere. Instead of seeing *greed* and reading *misplaced priorities*, substitute *drive* or *ambition* or *desire* for greed. Greed, not just for money or power, but for life, love, knowledge, a garden patch, a redeemed social condition, or virtually anything in Maslov's pyramid is a natural instinct we can't just turn off. People not only want to beat benchmarks, they need to beat benchmarks—not only in their investments, but in life. Some benchmarks are high and some are low, but we're always trying to beat them. Simply giving in to the mediocrity of benchmark-like performance without trying to do better just doesn't seem natural.

The arguments made by the proponents of passively mimicking the stock market are compelling relative to traditional stock-selecting means, but we, as all too human investors, will never be completely satisfied unless we change the very nature of who we are. Thanks to the evolution of investment tools, we don't have to.

Notes

1. Mark M. Carhart, Jennifer N. Carpenter, Anthony W. Lynch, and David K. Musto, "Mutual Fund Survivorship," *New York University Research Paper*, November 28, 2001: Table 3.
2. Richard E. Evans and Burton G. Malkiel, *The Index Fund Solution: A Fireside Book* (New York: Simon and Schuster, 1999), 23.
3. James J. Rowley Jr. and Joel M. Dickson, "Mutual funds-like ETFs-have trading volume," Vanguard Research, November 2012.
4. Tom Lydon, ETF Trends, Capital Allocators Podcast with Ted Seides, June 2018, EP.56.
5. Rupendra Paliwal. "Tracking Errors of Exchange Traded Funds and Index Funds," WCOB Working Papers, Jack Welch College of Business, Sacred Heart University, April 2014, 17.
6. Max Chen, "Why Millennials Like ETFs", ETFTrends.com, June 25, 2018.

12

Active Share and Private Equity

To this point, we have spoken in broad generalities about the difficulties active stock pickers face when trying to outperform a benchmark and how low-cost, passive ETFs or index funds can serve as a solution. But that's not the end of the story. Human beings not only hold a natural instinct to seek outperformance, we may need it to reach our investment goals if future stock market performance results in a bear market in expectations.

An important clarification worth making here is that the challenges associated with picking stocks we have highlighted have been exclusively focused on those who do so in the large cap domestic equity market as represented by the S&P 500. In Chap. 4, we talked about the specifics of efficiency, and one could argue that the large cap US stock market is the most efficient in the world. Information is disseminated instantaneously and completely such that every interested market participant enjoys equally unfettered access to it. Regulations have deliberately levelled the playing field where the professional investor previously enjoyed an advantage and because the professionals are so smart, hard-working and do such a terrific job utilizing Benjamin Graham's fundamental analysis, they limit the opportunities for everyone.

That's not to say that every market in the world is as efficient as the large cap domestic equity market. Even in the US, mid-cap and small cap stocks are not as picked over. The same could be said of international markets (although developed international is highly efficient) and emerging and frontier markets. Just because it is really hard to outperform the S&P 500 by selecting stocks doesn't mean it can't be done. And, just because one market limits advantages by being highly efficient doesn't mean that advantages can't be found elsewhere in less efficient markets.

© The Author(s) 2018
M. J. Oyster, *Success in a Low-Return World*,
https://doi.org/10.1007/978-3-319-99855-8_12

Active Share

We have painted active stock pickers with broad brush so far, but substantial differences exist among them. Some professed active managers look very much like the index that represents their marketplace; others look nothing like it. It is worth describing the differences because the magnitude of activeness can hint at a manager's probability of outperforming.

In order for a stock-picking manager to outperform a benchmark, their portfolio must differ from the benchmark. Sources of benchmark deviation come in one of two forms:

- Stock selection
- Factor timing

Stock selection, as the name implies, represents bets on individual stocks where factor timing describes factor allocations that differ from the benchmark, such as a tilt toward value or away from highly volatile names. With these two descriptors, we can quantify how active an investment manager is relative to the benchmark.

In a 2009 research paper,[1] Martijn Cremers and Antti Petajisto introduced the concept of *active share*, which describes the magnitude of difference in terms of its holdings between a stock fund and its benchmark. Many stock-picking mutual funds hold stocks that are in the benchmark but at a different weight. They might also hold some stocks that aren't in the benchmark. Active share is shown in percentage where an index fund would exhibit active share at or close to zero and a fund with holdings and weights that deviated greatly from the benchmark would show a higher number. Active share for stock portfolios will range from 0 to 100 percent as long as there is no shorting or leverage.

We have talked before about tracking error, which is the standard deviation of relative performance. We can expand on tracking error here because tracking error describes the volatility of a fund's performance that isn't explained by the benchmark. It shows the impact of factor bets. Some examples can help clarify.

Let's say you have a stock portfolio that owns every stock in the benchmark but in just one industry. In that case, you might have low active share but high tracking error. You aren't attempting to outperform by picking stocks as much as you are betting that your single industry allocation will outperform the index and you will probably deviate a lot from the benchmark along the way.

Now let's say that your benchmark has 15 industries. You have an allocation to each in the exact weight as they are in the benchmark but with only one stock per industry. In this case, your active share will be high because your stock selection deviates significantly from the benchmark but you probably won't have much tracking error because many stocks in the same industry will experience similar performance as others in the same industry.

With this framework, we can describe different types of active managers and do so with a visual that I recreated deriving from the Cremers and Petajisto paper.

The most active portfolio is one that deviates from the benchmark in terms of stock selection resulting in high active share and does so in a concentrated way isolating in just a few factors or industries. These are the concentrated stock pickers shown in the upper right-hand side of Fig. 12.1. The upper left portfolio, diversified stock picks, has high active share but is diversified across factors in similar fashion to the benchmark. The lower right portfolio may deviate from the benchmark because of its active factor bets but not because of security selection. The closet indexing portfolio is not highly active in terms of either security selection or factor bet.

So which one is best? In 2013, Antti Petjisto updated the original Cremers and Petajisto work from 2009 with newer data and found a repeat of the conclusion to which they had arrived previously—stock selection as indicated by high active share is rewarded in the stock market, and the most aggressive stock pickers are able to add value for their investors even net of all expenses.

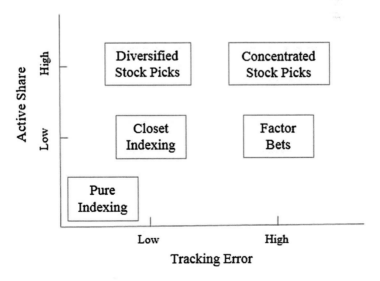

Fig. 12.1 Types of active managers

In contrast, factor bets, as indicated by high tracking error, are not rewarded in the market; on average, those funds have destroyed value for their investors.[2]

So not all active management is bad and stock selection isn't necessarily a pathway toward investment destruction. Identifying a manager that will outperform a benchmark in advance of that outperformance is an exceptionally tall order, but you are more likely to when you focus on managers with high active share. Subsequent to the initial studies on active share, Martijn Cremers wrote a paper[3] in 2017 that, among other things, found that the level of expenses seems unrelated to performance for high active share funds. In other words, keeping investment fees low is important but for many high active share funds, you get what you pay for. Cremers also found that only active stock pickers with long-term conviction have been successful while short-term stock pickers generally underperform. This can help narrow down a manager search in that you should look not simply for high active share managers, though that is a fine idea independently; you should seek those with limited turnover. Success then requires a long holding period and a willingness to ride out the inevitable periods of short-term underperformance that prompt many a behavioral error in investors who sell out of a good fund at the wrong time.

Tracking error, by contrast, is less telling. Tracking error has often been used to describe how active a manager is relative to their benchmark. Though the research suggests there is a positive correlation between magnitude of activeness and outperformance, simply seeking the high tracking error managers is insufficient. The *factor bets* group that Petjisto described had high tracking error but low active share and their performance was abysmal. In other words, they isolated their bets to overweighting and underweighting factors, which suggests factor timing is probably a bad idea. This is a subject we will delve into more deeply in Chap. 14.

In his 2013 paper, Petjisto also took issue with closet indexers, which he defined as those having active share less than 60 percent. He made the point that about half of the components in an index will outperform and about half will underperform. If a manager's portfolio is, therefore, more than 50 percent comprised of the index (i.e. has an active share of less than 50 percent) some positions are being held not for outperformance but to reduce the risk of deviating relative to the benchmark. Petjisto mentioned that he set the closet indexer cutoff at an active share of 60 percent, which implies that an active manager should be able to select investments from what they consider the top 40 percent of all stocks on the basis of their future alphas.

The problem with closet indexers is not necessarily that they hug the benchmark, it's that they charge their investors active management fees to do so. Closet indexers are the least active of the actively managed universe and they charge lower fees than average but still more than 1 percent according to Petjisto's study. That's just a poor value proposition.

The trend in manager type is also important to watch. In 1980, there were virtually no closet indexers and about 60 percent of all funds exhibited active share in excess of 80 percent. This harkens back to Chap. 3 when we discussed the massive growth in the mutual fund business in terms of number of funds and assets they manage. There were 743 equity mutual funds in 1987 and nearly none of them were closet indexers. By 2006, the number of funds had grown to 3748 and the number of closet indexers was then up to nearly 50 percent. More recently, investors are dumping closet indexers in droves, not necessarily in favor of high active share names—allocations to managers above 80 percent active share as a percentage of active equity funds has remained largely unchanged in nearly two decades—but rather in the more general trend away from active management toward indexing.

Why did the universe of equity funds move from exclusively high active share to a substantial percentage of closet indexers? It might be due to the growth in assets. The S&P 500 is a capitalization-weighted index meaning that the names with the highest percentage weight are the largest market cap stocks. Those are generally the most liquid, so if you have a ton of money to push around, you probably will put more with the largest most liquid names, less with the smaller. That makes you look like the benchmark and reduces active share. If you have a lot of assets under management, you can still be different than the benchmark but you risk inhibiting your returns by adversely moving the prices of low-liquidity names when you buy and sell.

Another possible reason that the domestic equity mutual fund industry moved away from high active share toward closet indexing is behavioral—agency friction. If I, as a fund manager, have a primary goal to avoid getting fired and/or preserve the amount of assets under management I have amassed, I carry an incentive to keep my deviations relative to the benchmark to a minimum. You, as my fund investor, may be happy when I outperform by five percentage points over a three-year period, but you will fire me if I underperform by that amount. If I only underperform by one percentage point, you might not be happy but you may be more willing to give me the benefit of the doubt. Small relative underperformance might not be so bad that you would be willing to go through the effort of finding a replacement fund.

The final point about active share has to do with the Fidelity Magellan fund. When Magellan was managing over $100 billion in assets in 2000, it

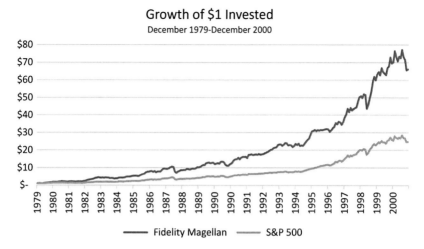

Fig. 12.2 Fidelity Magellan versus S&P 500: 1979–2000. Data source: Bloomberg

was like one of those 800-pound gorillas that couldn't sit wherever it wanted because it moved the markets through trading activity. The fund got that large because performance leading up to that point, particularly during the 1980s when it was managed by Peter Lynch, was really good (Fig. 12.2).

Magellan's active share was above 90 percent in 1980 and remained above 60 percent almost uninterrupted for the next 15 years.[4] Then something changed. Starting in 1996, the fund's active share was reduced in earnest and fell below 40 percent where it stayed until 2005. Over this period, performance for the fund looked nothing like it did previously. In fact, it looked a lot like a closet indexer, which it was—hugging the benchmark and trailing by about as much as it charged in fees (Fig. 12.3).

I don't know if the powers that be at Fidelity made the conscious decision to turn the fund into a closet indexer out of need given the enormity of the assets it had amassed or if such a decision was intended to reduce the risk of large underperformance in hopes of preserving assets; but, if that was the case, it didn't work. Performance from 2006 through 2017 looked almost identical to 1996–2006 and despite periods where the fund increased its active share in response to closet-indexing criticisms, investors voted with their feet. In early 2018, the fund's assets under management were down to just over $17 billion. A respectable sum to be sure but a far cry from those heady days in the early 2000s.

All of this is intended to help guide the decision-making process when selecting managers and funds in which to invest. Considerable qualitative analysis is necessary to uncover a manager with a decent probability of future

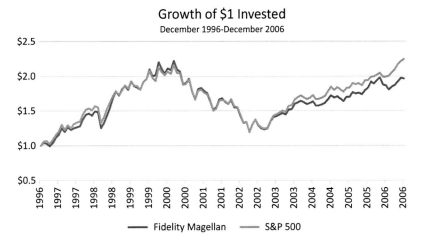

Fig. 12.3   Fidelity Magellan versus S&P 500: 1996–2006. Data source: Bloomberg

success, but some quantitative data can help as well—not past performance, rather a view of active share seeking those with the highest percentage combined with minimal turnover.

The means exist for increasing the chances of finding a manager who can outperform in an efficient market, but you can also enjoy success by fishing in less efficient pools. One such method involves private equity.

Private Equity

Let's say I offered you the opportunity to invest in something to deploy your hard-earned capital in the marketplace. Here's the deal: I need you to commit a large sum of money and you have to agree that you can't get it back for 10 or even 15 years, if not longer. When I say, "Send me money," you have to send it and I may not tell you exactly what I'm going to do with it. You may lose some or even all of what you commit and the chances of being in the red at least in the first five years are high. Every year, you will pay me 2 percent of whatever amount you commit and if the investments actually post a positive return, you may not see it until a decade from now and when it does, I get 20 percent of your profits. Given all of that, would you do it? Many investors do. Those are the rules of the game for private equity (PE).

We use the term *stocks* synonymously with *equities*. They both denote ownership stakes in companies. Stocks represent fractional portions of a company's value that are publicly traded meaning that anyone with the necessary amount of money can purchase one and the exchange that facilitates that purchase is highly regulated to ensure fairness. No special access or knowledge is necessary. *Private equity*, like public equities, represents ownership in a company but the ownership stake is not available for purchase by the general public. PE is inclusive of venture capital, which is generally where investment capital is allocated to start-up or early-stage companies, and buyout, which involves the purchase of part or all of a more mature company or a financial restructuring of some kind.

Private equity funds cobble together different ownership stakes in companies like mutual funds do but not just anyone can buy in. They are structured as partnerships with a general partner (GP, the investment manager) and limited partners (LP, the investors). The fund structure allows the GP to invest in just about anything but the number of investors is limited and they generally need to be accredited or qualified, meaning they must have at least $1 million of net worth excluding primary residence among other criteria. Accreditation and qualification rules differ for individuals and business but are generally designed by regulators to say something to the effect of, "We aren't looking out for you on this investment as much as we would on a mutual fund, so if you want to invest in it, that's on you."

With the high fees and long-term commitment, why would anyone invest in private equity? Because private equity affords limited partners the opportunity to earn a higher rate of return than that which could be had in the public markets. Part of the value proposition with PE is that rather than simply buy a portion of a private company on behalf of the LPs and sit on it, the GP will in many cases enact changes to the company that will unlock value, thus improving the return to the investors when it comes time to sell.

Private companies avoid certain regulations to which publicly traded organizations are subject. Remember Sarbanes-Oxley from Chap. 7? Privately held companies don't have to comply with that because they don't distribute publicly disseminated earnings reports. We discussed how Sarbanes-Oxley and other regulations had flattened the playing field for everyone where the professional money manager had previously held an advantage. That made the marketplace more efficient, but the world of private equity is more opaque and as such, less efficient. Someone with detailed knowledge of the inner workings of a private company can enjoy a competitive advantage. Information isn't available to everyone and distributed fairly and instantaneously. Those who have it can profit from it.

Private companies are also able to take a longer view of things making choices that can benefit them over the long-term as opposed to being forced into the quarter-to-quarter short-termist scrutiny that public companies face.

Given the privacy to pursue value creation opportunities, the results are observable, with private equity-backed companies exhibiting average *earnings before interest, taxes, depreciation, and amortization* (EBITDA) margins from 250 basis points to over 600 basis points better than their public market comparables.[5]

The marketplace for private companies is vast as the number of stocks has been going down in recent years. Over the past 20 years, the number of publicly listed US companies has been nearly cut in half, from a peak of 8090 in 1996 to 4331 at the end of 2016, with delistings outpacing new listings in all but one year over this period. About 60 percent of delisting activity was driven by mergers and acquisitions (M&A). Private equity's fingerprints are all over that statistic, as the universe of private equity–backed companies able to act as strategic acquirers was on the rise.[6]

So let's cut to the chase: has private equity outperformed public equity? Probably, but the question is more complicated than it might sound. First let's think about how private equity investing actually works. An LP commits, say, $10 million to a fund giving the GP the right to call that capital and invest it when and into whatever he or she sees fit. In the first year, perhaps $1 million of the LP's commitment is called. The LP sends it in and the GP invests it into a start-up pharmaceutical company developing a new drug. What was the LP's return on investment that year? Did they lose 10 percent? Nothing? How do you account for the value of the investment into which the money was deployed?

For the next five years, the remainder of the $10 million commitment was drawn from the LP and the GP invested it in various private enterprises. Suddenly in year six, the pharmaceutical company was bought by a larger organization and the initial investment of $1 million turned into $3 million. Is the return on investment 30 percent in year six? What about the value of the other investments? The point is that private investments, unlike their public counterparts, aren't valued on an ongoing basis. You really don't know for sure what something is worth until it's sold and when it is, a big cash flow comes into the account, which distorts the performance return if a traditional time-weighted method is being used. One solution to that problem is what's known as *internal rate of return* (IRR).

Determining the percentage return on investment in a stock is fairly straightforward. The value is easily known as its listed price at the beginning of the time period in question and also at the end. Adjusting for any cash flows, the return is the ratio between the stock's value at the end and the beginning. The value of private equity investments is not well known and often large sums of money are either called or distributed, which would make the return look different than it reasonably should if calculated using the same methodology one might use for a stock. IRR takes the lumpiness of cash flows into consideration. In a very strict sense, IRR is the discount rate at which the net present value of all the cash flows (both positive and negative) from the investment equal zero. IRR is not just influenced by the size of a cash flow but by when it took place. Once calculated, the IRR of a private investment can be compared to the rate of return of a liquid investment like stocks.

Academic research is filled with papers highlighting the flaws with using IRR as a measure of returns for private equity. As at least a partial solution to that problem, PE returns are also commonly compared to a public market equivalent (PME). For example, if a buyout-focused private equity firm conducted most of their activity on small-to-mid-sized US companies, their performance might be appropriately compared to the Russell 2000 Index, a benchmark comprised of publicly traded small cap US stocks.

Figure 12.4 was adapted from a 2016 study from leading alternative investment database provider Preqin:[7]

The year in which a new fund was created is known as its *vintage year*, and the bars in the Fig. 12.4 represent vintage year performance, which illustrate how well each group had done since that year through December 2015. The Preqin Median Net IRR shows the returns of all private equity (excluding direct lending) with the other bar showing the performance of the S&P 500. Funds launched after 2012 did not have a meaningfully long period of time for their returns to be relevant by December 2015. This graph shows that PE

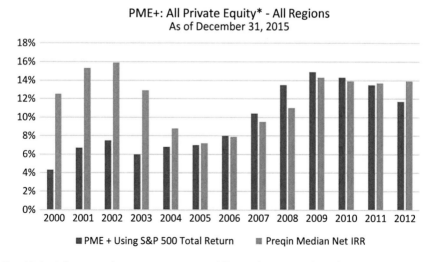

Fig. 12.4 Private equity returns versus public market equivalent (PME). Data source: Preqin. *All private equity is defined as private capital excluding direct lending

funds launched in the early-2000s outperformed the PME by substantial margins but save a limited number of years, have largely matched the public markets since then.

But this doesn't tell the whole story. Different academic research studies provide different answers to the question of whether private equity outperforms public equity but broad generalizations provide little in the way of actionable knowledge. Just as there are different kinds of active stock pickers that then experience different levels of relative performance, private equity returns are highly fragmented and not normally distributed. After a thorough review of a wide variety of research publications on private equity performance, the Center for Economic and Policy Research (CEPR) concluded the following in their February 2017 report:

> *The most positive academic findings for private equity compare its performance to the S&P 500: They report that the median fund outperforms the S&P 500 by about 1 percent per year, and the average fund by 2-to-2.5 percent. The higher average performance is driven almost entirely by the top quartile of funds—and particularly the top decile. With the exception of the top performing funds, returns do not cover the roughly 3 percent additional return above the stock market that is required to compensate investors for the illiquidity of PE investments. When PE funds are compared to indices of smaller publicly traded companies whose size is comparable to most PE-owned portfolio companies (the S&P 500 is comprised of much larger corporations), then the average PE fund barely performs better, and the median fund just matches stock market returns.*[8]

The takeaway here is that the *top-performing* private equity funds can be expected to outperform the public markets while the liquidity lock required to invest in an *average* PE fund is probably not justified by a commensurate level of outperformance. So how do you find the top-performing funds in advance? Conventional wisdom says, and in stark contrast to mutual funds, past performance *does* provide decent insight into future performance.

In the mutual fund world, you generally have one fund per strategy. Maybe a few different share classes with different fees for different mandate sizes but generally just one fund. In private equity, a manager will establish a fund that invests in some things for a few years and then after 75 percent of it has been committed to whatever investments are to be made, the manager can start fundraising for a new fund, which will usually exhibit a Roman numeral in its name one higher than the predecessor fund. For example, in 2015 "Private Equity Manager, L.P. IV" was enacted. Then after a few years you might see "Private Equity Manager, L.P. V." Each is a different partnership with potentially different limited partners and almost certainly different investments held within. By some measures, good performance from one vintage year fund can suggest good performance from subsequent funds from the same manager in the same strategy.

Pitchbook is a leading private capital database company that tracks every aspect of the public and private equity markets, including venture capital (VC), private equity, and mergers and acquisitions. In their "Global PE & VC Fund Performance Report" that included data through the third quarter of 2017, they indicated that 39 percent of managers with initial top quartile funds went on to have top quartile returns in successor funds. That number should only be 25 percent if return distribution among funds was random. Pitchbook also found that 34 percent of bottom quartile funds were followed by another bottom quartile fund (Fig. 12.5).

This represents strong evidence of persistence in private equity manager performance. Why would that be? In private equity world, success or failure is not limited to simply price at purchase and price at sale. Many private equity managers provide direct influence over the privately held companies and will make changes that can increase the value of the company. A manager who can do that well has the potential to unlock value and repeat the process multiple times with multiple companies. Also, the market for privately held ownership in companies isn't really a market at all. There is no exchange where you can go to buy a share in a private company. Those opportunities must be found, and the better private equity managers are more adept at finding them. Successful private equity managers will often be made aware of opportunities to buy private companies in advance of other potential owners, which can

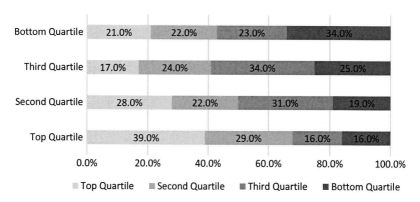

Fig. 12.5 Successor fund performance quartile sorted by initial fund quartile. Data source: Pitchbook

lead to better investment performance, which then provides opportunities for an early view of subsequent opportunities, and so on.

But it's not all roses for private equity. For some of the same reasons the stock market may disappoint in years to come, so too may private equity. Private equity benefited from the declining interest rate environment since the early 1980s that was punctuated by the quantitative-easing-fueled squashing of rates post Great Recession. Many PE funds use borrowed assets (leverage) to support performance. As the cost of that borrowed money goes up, returns will be inhibited.

In 2018, after a long economic recovery and stock market ascension, stock multiples (price/earnings ratio for example) had become elevated, which should temper expectations for returns thereafter. Prices paid to acquire assets had also become elevated in private equity. The median valuation-to-EBITDA multiple for PE acquisitions was 10.9x in 2016—highest since the 2008 financial crisis.[9] Also, an inverse relationship exists between the magnitude of private equity commitments and subsequent performance, which makes sense. In an environment where only a small amount of investment capital needs to be deployed, GPs can invest highly selectively, allocating only to the most attractive opportunities. Average investment quality goes down when lesser deals are done because capital needs to be put to work. In 2017, global *dry powder*, the money that private capital funds have raised but not yet put to work, was nearly $1 trillion, the highest ever. Dry powder may represent prudent discipline but does not enhance returns. Investors expect market-beating performance from their private equity managers, but they won't get it if their committed capital is not being put to work. Dry powder increases when managers refuse to deploy capital in unattractive ways, which is appropriate but also indicative of the state of private equity in general. In such an environment, private equity return expectations should be modified lower relative to historical averages.

In a world where stock markets are efficient and artificial intelligence, big data, and high frequency trading continue to change the landscape relegating fundamental analysis even further into obsolescence, private equity stands as an investment strategy in which differentiated access to information and opportunity can provide outsized returns. That said, private equity tends to correlate with public equity. Prices for private companies are similarly elevated to stocks, and the absence of exceptionally low interest rates could press returns below historical averages. The average private equity fund may post disappointing returns alongside the stock market, but doubtless there will be managers with demonstrated histories of finding attractive opportunities and enhancing returns through operational influence, which will earn outperformance for their limited partners.

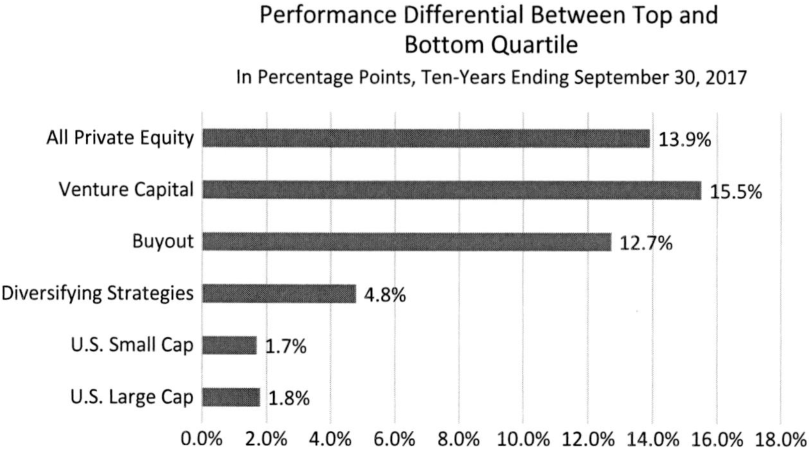

Performance Differential Between Top and Bottom Quartile
In Percentage Points, Ten-Years Ending September 30, 2017

Fig. 12.6 Performance differential between top and bottom quartile managers. Source: FEG Investment Advisors. Data sources: Lipper, HFRI, Thomson One; Private Equity Data for vintage years 2005 through 2014, performance available through September 30, 2017, returns in USD, net of fees

Finding such managers, however, can prove challenging and failure to do so can leave investors with a gaping hole in their investment portfolio. The difference between top quartile and bottom quartile private equity managers is vastly greater than for other asset categories. Correctly selecting the top quartile private equity manager would have provided an investor with nearly 14 percentage points higher returns than if they had selected the bottom quartile one. In large cap domestic equity, that difference was just 1.8 percentage points (Fig. 12.6).[10]

Conclusion

Outperforming the S&P 500 poses a difficult challenge, but not an insurmountable one. Stock picking is generally a poor way to seek outperformance but some managers who demonstrate a high degree of conviction in their holdings by deviating meaningfully from the benchmark, with a willingness to hold the positions for a long period of time, have been able to beat the benchmark. Additionally, private equity can offer investors the opportunity to outperform but manager selection is key.

If the stock market of the future produces lower returns than historical and more recent averages, outperformance will be critical. Every basis point will count. But outperformance alone isn't enough and it's quite difficult to find an outperforming manager in advance. So, we have to do more. We have to find ways of enhancing the return of our investment portfolios that go beyond just outperformance. Let's switch gears now and talk about a few ways to do that.

Notes

1. Martijn Cremers, and Antti Petajisto. 2009. "How Active Is Your Fund Manager? A New Measure That Predicts Performance," *Review of Financial Studies*, vol. 22, no. 9 (September): 3329–3365.
2. Antti Petajisto. 2013. "Active Share and Mutual Fund Performance," *Financial Analysts Journal*, vol no. 69, no. 4 (July/August): 73–93.
3. Martijn Cremers, "Active Share and the Three Pillars of Active Management: Skill, Conviction and Opportunity," *Financial Analysts Journal*, vol no. 73, no. 2 (Second Quarter 2017): 61–79.
4. Antti Petajisto. 2013. "Active Share and Mutual Fund Performance," *Financial Analysts Journal*, vol no. 69, no. 4, (July/August): 73–93.
5. Andrea Auerbach, "CA Answers: Is Private Equity Replacing Public Equity?" Cambridge Associates Research, November 7, 2017.
6. Ibid.
7. The 2016 Preqin Alternative Assets Performance Monitor, Sample Pages. 2016 Preqin Ltd. www.preqin.com.
8. Eileen Appelbaum and Rosemary Batt. "Update: are Lower Private Equity Returns the New Normal?" Center for Economic and Policy Research. February 2017. 10–11.
9. Ibid.
10. Michael J. Aluise, "Private Investing and the J-Curve, Short-Term Pain for Long-Term Gain." FEG Insight, FEG Investment Advisors, June 2018. 7.

13

Momentum

When viewed in an inertial reference frame, an object either remains at rest or con-
tinues to move at a constant velocity, unless acted upon by an external force.
—Sir Isaac Newton, *Philosophiæ Naturalis Principia Mathematica*, July 5, 1687.

In the seventeenth century, Sir Isaac Newton described three laws of motion that explain how bodies with mass behave in the physical world. The revolutionary publication laid the groundwork for classical mechanics and served as the accepted description of mass, gravity, and motion until Einstein published his theory of relativity over 200 years later.

Newton's first law describes the concept of inertia, that is, momentum—a body in motion stays in motion until acted upon by an outside force. Momentum appears in countless ways throughout our daily lives, and momentum can also explain changes in investment pricing. The opportunity to recognize and then apply that concept to enhance investment returns and/ or reduce risk is our focus here.

Much of this chapter was originally published as: Oyster, Michael J., "The Persistence of Performance, Momentum as a Tool for Sub-Category Asset Allocation," FEG Investment Advisors, September 2015.

Background, the Evolution of Momentum

Throughout the history of finance, academic research has improved practical investing by identifying sources of return that might have previously been confused with skill. Said another way, an investor can outperform a market through expert security selection or by taking a long-term bias toward risk factors that can provide the outperformance. Let's recount some of these, keeping the conversation in the long-only equity world for the time being.

One of the most straightforward ways an investor can outperform a stock market over time is to use leverage (borrowing) to take more market-related risk than the market itself. This concept has been described with the Capital Asset Pricing Model (CAPM), which was developed through the work of multiple academics including William Sharpe[1] building upon early research by Harry Markowitz's[2] description of Modern Portfolio Theory.

In part, CAPM quantifies an asset's sensitivity to the market through a quantitative measure known as beta. Investments with a beta greater than 1.0 exhibit a higher-than-market risk for which an investor should expect compensation in the form of outperformance. Researcher Michael Jensen set out to derive a risk-adjusted measure of portfolio performance that estimates how much a manager's forecasting ability contributes to the fund's returns. Market outperformance at the expense of greater-than-market risk is not necessarily indicative of skill. After adjusting for market risk, a better description of potential manager skill can be seen.

After taking into consideration an investment portfolio's market risk (beta) relative to the market's return less the risk-free rate, what remains is the portfolio's risk-adjusted return as described by Michael Jensen[3] and has come to be known as Jensen's alpha.

Building upon Jensen's work, Eugene Fama and Ken French[4] suggested that beyond just market-related risk, additional identifiable factors exist that that can further explain sources of outsized returns. Specifically, Fama and French found that certain cross sections of the equity markets exhibited outperformance beyond what should be expected from beta alone.

The identification of two additional performance-describing factors, (1) size and (2) book value to market value, thereafter changed the way investing was done and how performance was analyzed. Today, virtually anyone who would like to deconstruct the investment performance of an equity portfolio can run it through a "Fama-French three factor model" to determine what portion of total return was the result of exposure to those factors.

The three factors in the Fama-French model are:

- Beta (exposure to market risk)
- Size (exposure to market capitalization risk)
- Book to market (exposure to valuation risk)

Looking at the idea a slightly different way, when excess portfolio returns are adjusted, likely downward, due to the performance-improving impact of exposures to the three factors, any remaining outperformance may be due to skillful security selection. At the very least, it can be instructive to see what portion of an investment manager's relative performance was due to simple exposures to certain factors.

But this isn't the end of the story. Building upon the Fama-French three factor model, Mark Carhart (yes, the same really smart guy from Chap. 11 who was part of a group that documented how much the performance of a group of mutual funds was overstated due to survivorship bias) published a paper[5] that described a four-factor model that included a one-year return momentum factor that explained performance beyond the three Fama-French factors. The momentum factor itself isolated stocks that had been performing well for the past year from stocks that had been performing poorly. Since then, a new model, commonly referred to as the Fama-French-Carhart four-factor model, can be used to attribute investment portfolio returns to beta, size, valuation, and momentum.

Although it only hints at the depth of the research involved, the first line of Carhart's seminal paper on the subject provides a strongly worded summary:

"Persistence in mutual fund performance does not reflect superior stock-picking skill."
—Mark M. Carhart, "On Persistence in Mutual Fund Performance," *The Journal of Finance*, March, 1997.

In other words, a researcher could determine if a fund was outperforming a benchmark by tilting toward the stocks that had good performance and away from poor performers. But more than that, Carhart's work gives us a potential opportunity to improve performance—by tilting toward stocks with favorable momentum. That's good, but can that work in other asset categories as well?

Evidence of Momentum

Momentum is not just an equity thing. A massive amount of academic research has been conducted on the subject of momentum across a variety of asset classes and regions, and the evidence of its efficacy is strong. Momentum has been found to be pervasive in US stocks as described in important early work by Cliff Asness[6] among others,[7] foreign equities,[8] emerging market equities,[9] global government bonds,[10] corporate bonds,[11] commodities,[12] currencies,[13] and residential real estate.[14]

The research does not indicate a single, most effective means of using momentum (although many focus on a common lookback period—more on this later), but rather suggests a multitude of methodologies, many of which illustrate how momentum can explain returns. This suggests something fundamental and foundational about the concept of momentum that goes beyond a statistical anomaly that may appear useful in one period or in one region but not repeatable later or elsewhere.

There is far more evidence to support the *if* momentum is a strong enough factor to explain investment returns than the *why* it does so. Momentum does not easily lend itself to the traditional notion that outsized returns are the result of taking greater risk. The three factors in the Fama-French model each carry with them an elevated amount of risk that rationalizes their respective contributions to outperformance—beta higher than 1.0 means greater-than-market risk, and both smaller companies and cheaply priced companies exhibit a greater risk than their larger, more highly priced counterparts.

Attaching a risk to momentum that would justify its higher return is difficult, but buy low/sell high philosophy implies recent winners may be riskier than recent losers. One specific possibility is that high momentum stocks are more reliant on earnings growth, which makes them more susceptible to shocks.[15] In addition, strong correlations among momentum stocks suggest there may be a common source of risk.[16] That might explain some of it but there may also be some behavioral effects at play.

While risk may partially explain the momentum effect, investor psychology and human behavior likely contribute as well. A significant amount of research has been conducted with the goal of describing why behavior drives momentum, as well as work that draws upon psychological research on behavior and biases that can help explain decision making.

A Basis in Behavior

Human beings may be slow to react to new information, a concept Amos Tversky and Daniel Kahneman described as *anchoring*—the bias that keeps individuals tied to their initial estimate.[17] The psychological resistance to change one's opinion (despite new evidence suggestive of doing so) potentially leads to a slow reaction to new information. Markets are exceptionally efficient, particularly the large cap domestic equity market. But if markets were truly and completely efficient, prices would rationally and immediately reflect the impact of new information. Anchoring suggests that new information diffuses into prices gradually, which might partly explain why recent price performance can persist.

Somewhat counter to the concept of underreaction, certain researchers point to overreaction to explain the momentum effect. Kent Daniel, David Hirshleifer, and Avanidhar Subrahmanyam put forth a more direct explanation of momentum that addressed both underreaction and overreaction through a theory based on investor overconfidence, and variations in confidence arising from biased self-attribution.[18] If an investor overestimates his ability to generate information, or to identify the significance of existing data that others neglect, he will underestimate his forecast errors. The authors also show that positive return autocorrelations (momentum) can be a result of continuing overreaction.

The ability of recent performance to explain future returns is a phenomenon that can be observed in a variety of markets across the globe. Much of the underpinning for momentum is likely rooted in behavioral biases, many of which are deeply seated in the human psyche, suggesting that the effect may persist through time and momentum is unlikely to be arbitraged away by overuse.

Momentum has the ability to improve investment decision making, but it isn't perfect. In spite of the evidence describing the efficacy of momentum, Kent Daniel and Toby Moskowitz point out inevitable periods when the opposite is true.[19] These periods of time when a momentum strategy fails, the so-called *momentum crashes* tend to occur in what the authors refer to as *panic* states following market declines and when market volatility is high. Daniel and Moskowitz found that momentum returns are negatively skewed, meaning that there are more really awful examples than equally positive ones, and the crashes can be pronounced and persistent.

Importantly, the researchers indicated that when stocks are cascading lower, experiencing downward momentum, that momentum may quickly change course *crashing* a momentum-driven strategy with a sharp market rebound that detracts from momentum's effectiveness. They did not, however, find significant instances of positive price momentum *crashing* downward. Specifically, every one of the worst 15 applications of a momentum strategy occurred when the lagged two-year market return was negative. The worst examples occur in months where the market rose, often in a dramatic fashion after having previously established downward momentum. Downward momentum, it seems, may fail to persist after reaching an extreme.

Although easier said than done successfully, one way to potentially protect against the downward momentum reversals described by Daniel and Moskowitz is to identify extremes in panic and take a contrary position.

One may be able to identify examples of US stock market panic by pointing to exceptionally high levels of the Cboe Volatility Index (VIX). As investors rush to buy protection in the midst of a stock market decline, the VIX, which represents the implied volatilities of S&P 500 Index options, tends to surge. After reaching historically high levels (many around the 45 level, with the notable exception of a price spike to over 80 in 2008), the stock market tends to recover smartly, at least for a brief period. In many of these cases, a telling sign that downward momentum might soon be reversing was seen in the form of demonstrated investor panic, so a contrarian stance was warranted.

Applying Momentum

Investors worldwide have used momentum in an effort to make better decisions with most of the work being applied to individual security selection. Far less pervasive is research on applying momentum to subcategory asset-allocation decision making, which is our focus here. Before delving into how we might apply momentum to help guide category weights, let's first more specifically define some methodologies for momentum calculations. There are two broad categories of momentum:

- Cross-sectional momentum (relative strength) is the effect that suggests that an asset's past *relative* performance informs its future relative performance; and,
- Time-series momentum (absolute) is the effect in which an asset's *own* past performance informs its future performance.

Research from Gary Antonacci is also important as we think about applying momentum because he showed that both approaches to applying momentum can improve portfolio construction, but a combination of the two is better. With cross-sectional momentum, a security or asset-class performance is compared to other securities and classes in a relative way. Those that have exhibited better relative performance are expected to continue to outperform. Time-series momentum suggests that if a security or asset class is performing well as compared to its own history, that strong performance should persist. Time-series momentum includes trend-based metrics such as moving averages. In the case of both cross-sectional and time-series momentum, the persistence of recent price behavior is expected whether positive or negative.

Antonacci's paper titled "Risk Premia Harvesting Through Dual Momentum"[20] showed that both absolute and relative momentum can enhance returns, and that combining absolute and relative momentum gives the best returns. Additionally, Antonacci found that applying absolute momentum helps avoid volatility and drawdowns. That suggests an important application for investors who are sensitive to capital preservation or who are looking for stability in performance to support regular spending needs.

Independent Research

A wealth of academic research supports the case that recent price performance may persist and that the effect is at least partly rooted in investor behavior. Although there is less of it, there is also research that suggests that both cross-sectional and time-series momentum can be shown to add value when making portfolio construction decisions and applying both types of momentum simultaneously improves performance further. With these ideas in mind, I conducted some independent research on applying momentum when making portfolio construction decisions.

I began with monthly data on 28 asset categories across domestic and international equities including large, mid, and small, core, growth, and value US equities; developed, emerging and frontier equities; hedged equity; core domestic fixed income; high yield bonds; bank loans; international developed and emerging market sovereign debt; REITs; MLPs; commodities; and absolute-return hedge funds.

From these asset categories, I formed a hypothetical, equal-weighted *baseline* portfolio that was rebalanced monthly (disregarding transaction costs and recognizing that while the two hedge fund indices post monthly returns, it is largely impractical to rebalance liquidity-constrained hedge funds on a monthly basis). I observed performance back to the beginning of 1980 with the knowledge that data was not available for all categories over the entire period, but each category was included as early as possible.

I then applied a number of momentum overlays in order to observe whether the momentum effect would be seen among asset categories within a broader portfolio. The first step was to determine the appropriate *formation period*. The formation period is the range of time in the past that is observed to determine the magnitude and direction of price momentum. Much of the academic literature focuses on a 12-month formation period across a variety of assets. More specifically, Antonacci showed that Sharpe ratios, observed on eight discrete global asset categories based upon the use of a momentum strategy, were highest at a 12-month formation period among the nine different lookback periods he tested.[21] For these reasons, the formation period I used in my study was 12 months.

Next, I applied a cross-sectional momentum overlay to the baseline portfolio. Specifically, I ranked the asset categories according to their prior 12-month risk-adjusted returns, that is, the total return divided by the standard deviation of returns. Dividing by standard deviation serves as a normalization that helps ensure that differences in volatility do not influence the momentum effect. A quick aside: prior to starting this study, I was fortunate to have a conversation with Mark Carhart. I told him I was trying to utilize momentum to help make better subcategory asset-allocation decisions and thought who better to ask on how I should do that than him. He suggested the ranking methodology I described above. A few months later, I asked AQR's Cliff Asness the same question. Asness did his doctorate thesis (under the tutelage of Gene Fama no less) on combining value and momentum. To hear Cliff tell the story, the idea of proposing a thesis that combined momentum with value to the larger-than-life (and a little prickly) pillar of the Efficient Market Hypothesis was more than a little unnerving. Fama told him that "if it's in the data, write the paper." I had frequently been utilizing value criteria for subcategory decision making but I needed to combine it with momentum, so Asness was a great person to ask as well. He suggested the ranking criteria above just exactly as Carhart did, so I figured I was on to something.

Based upon the cross-sectional momentum value for each, the top 25 percent ranked categories were tapped and equally weighted among themselves to form a new portfolio that I called *CS Top*. A hypothetical portfolio formed by equally weighting the asset categories in the lower 75 percent was named *CS Bottom*.

From this point, I built upon the cross-sectional ranking by incorporating a time-series momentum factor. The ranking system utilized to form the CS top and bottom portfolios was augmented by including a measure of how each asset category was performing relative to the category's own historical average. Specifically, I formed a new portfolio from the top 25 percent ranked categories relative to one another as well as being based upon their respective returns compared to their own historical averages. The normalization by dividing by standard deviation used in the formation of the CS portfolios was applied in this case as well. These were also equally weighted among themselves to form a portfolio called *CSTS Top*. I named the hypothetical portfolio formed in similar fashion from the asset categories in the lower 75 percent of this test *CSTS Bottom*.

Transaction costs were not considered for the purposes of this study and all portfolios were rebalanced monthly. Table 13.1 and Fig. 13.1 below summarize statistical comparisons between them.

This research provides support for the idea that applying momentum to portfolio construction decisions by favoring those with more positive price momentum and avoiding those with less favorable momentum can add value over time, while reducing volatility and vastly limiting maximum drawdown.

Inspired by a point that Antonacci made in one of his papers, I sought to further refine the momentum factor (CSTS Top) by excluding any signal that

Table 13.1 Performance of portfolios formed through momentum-sorting techniques

All data in %	Baseline	CS bottom	CS top	CSTS bottom	CSTS top
Annualized return	11.00	9.78	14.12	9.55	14.87
Standard deviation	12.17	13.48	11.30	13.04	12.30
Sharpe ratio[22]	0.52	0.38	0.84	0.37	0.83
% Positive months	66.67	64.80	69.93	64.34	69.4
Maximum drawdown	−44.58	−49.40	−25.84	−47.81	−31.99

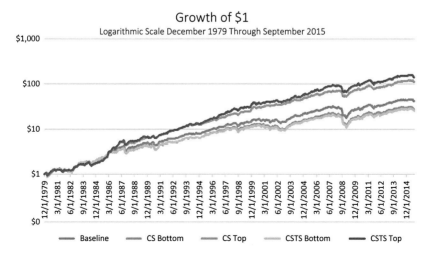

Growth of $1
Logarithmic Scale December 1979 Through September 2015

Fig. 13.1 Cumulative asset growth

Table 13.2 Performance of portfolios formed through momentum-sorting techniques screened for positive readings only

All data in %	CSTS top	CSTS top positive
Annualized return	14.87	15.10
Standard deviation	12.30	11.90
Sharpe ratio[23]	0.83	0.88
Maximum drawdown	−31.99	−20.22

may be in the top 25 percent based upon cross-sectional momentum, but experiencing negative absolute time-series momentum. This new portfolio we referred to as *CSTS Top Positive*.

Screening out all examples of negative time-series momentum reduced the number of signals that had previously formed CSTS Top by approximately 15 percent. Therefore, relative to CSTS Top, the utilization of this signal to make portfolio construction decisions could lead to a greater concentration of higher-conviction ideas, which an allocator could manage through conscious distribution of one's tracking error budget. Notice in Table 13.2 how it improved upon the CSTS Top portfolio.

Returns and standard deviations are modestly improved but maximum drawdown has been sharply reduced. If we consider how this tool might be applied to portfolio construction decisions and designate a benchmark weight as the base case with drawdowns in this study equating to underperformance, one can postulate that the use of CSTS Top Positive could limit the magnitude by which a portfolio might trail its benchmark contrasted with how a portfolio might otherwise perform without the factor's use.

Conclusion

Inspired by the groundbreaking research of Cliff Asness, Mark Carhart, and many others, I looked at how momentum could be used as a tool for improving total portfolio performance by tilting toward asset categories that are performing well and away from those that aren't. The results of the research suggest that when applied in both cross-sectional and time-series ways, momentum can improve returns, reduce risk, and lower maximum drawdowns.

Momentum is pervasive across and within asset categories around the globe. A wealth of academic research exists that explains the existence of momentum, but less on why it does so. Behavioral biases such as slow reaction to new information as well as overreactions to existing trends most likely play an important role. Finally, momentum can enhance returns and reduce risk, but momentum represents only one factor among many that needs to be considered to improve the probability of investment success. Portfolios should be constructed in a way that maximizes the expected return per unit of risk, with risks understood and tied to investment goals, and assets allocated through an approach that diversifies both sources of risk and return. Next let's look at how expanding beyond momentum into other factors can help improve investment performance.

Notes

1. William F. Sharpe (1964). Capital asset prices: A theory of market equilibrium under conditions of risk, *Journal of Finance*, 19 (3), 425–442.
2. Harry Markowitz (March 1952). "Portfolio Selection," *The Journal of Finance* 7 (1): 77–91.
3. Michael C. Jensen, "The Performance of Mutual Funds in the Period 1945–1964," Journal of Finance 23, No.2. 1967, pp. 389–416.
4. Eugene F. Fama and Kenneth R. French (1992). "The Cross-Section of Expected Stock Returns," *Journal of Finance*, June 1992, 427–466.
5. Mark M. Carhart (1997). "On Persistence in Mutual Fund Performance," *Journal of Finance* 52: 57–82.
6. Clifford S. Asness, 1994, "Variables that Explain Stock Returns," Ph.D. Dissertation, University of Chicago.
7. Narasimhan Jegadeesh and Sheridan Titman, 1993, "Returns to Buying Winners and Selling Losers: Implications for Stock Market Efficiency," *Journal of Finance* 48, 65–91.
8. K. Geert Rouwenhorst, 1998, "International Momentum Strategies," *Journal of Finance* 53, 267–284.
9. K. Geert Rouwenhorst, 1999, "Local Return Factors and Turnover in Emerging Stock Markets," *Journal of Finance* 54, 1439–1464.
10. Clifford S. Asness, Tobias J. Moskowitz, and Lasse Heje Pedersen, 2012, "Value and Momentum Everywhere," *Chicago Booth-The Initiative on Global Markets*, Working Paper No. 80, Chicago Booth Paper No. 12–53.
11. Gergana Jostova, Stanislava Nikolova, Alexander Philipov, and Christof W Stahel, 2010, "Momentum in Corporate Bond Returns," FDIC Center for Financial Research, Working Paper No. 2010-04.
12. Craig Pirrong, 2005, "Momentum in Futures Markets," University of Houston working paper.
13. Lukas Menkoff, Lucio Sarno, Maik Schmeling and Andreas Schrimpf, "Currency Momentum Strategies," Bank of International Settlements, Monetary and Economic Department, BIS Working Papers No. 366, December 2011.

14. Eli Beracha and Hilla Skiba, 2011, "Momentum in Residential Real Estate," *Journal of Real Estate Finance and Economics* 43, 299–320.
15. Timothy Johnson, 2002, "Rational Momentum Effects," *Journal of Finance* 57, 585–608.
16. Antti Ilmanen, Ph.D., Ronen Israel, Tobias J. Moskowitz, Ph.D., "Investing with Style: The Case for Style Investing," AQR Capital Management, LLC publication, December, 2012.
17. Amos Tversky and Daniel Kahneman, 1974, "Judgment under Uncertainty: Heuristics and Biases," *Science* 185, 1124–1131.
18. Kent Daniel, David Hirshleifer, and Avanidhar Subrahmanyam, 1998, "Investor Psychology and Security Market Under- and Over-Reactions." *Journal of Finance* 53, 1839–1886.
19. Kent Daniel and Tobias J. Moskowitz, "Momentum Crashes," Columbia Business School and NBER, and Booth School of Business, University of Chicago and NBER, respectively. Preliminary Draft: February 10, 2011, Latest Draft: June 16, 2015.
20. Gary Antonacci, "Risk Premia Harvesting Through Dual Momentum" (October 1, 2016). *Journal of Management & Entrepreneurship*, vol.2, no.1 (Mar 2017), 27–55. Available at SSRN: https://ssrn.com/abstract=2042750 or https://doi.org/10.2139/ssrn.2042750.
21. Gary Antonacci, "Absolute Momentum: a Simple Rule-Based Strategy and Universal Trend-Following Overlay," Portfolio Management Associates, LLC. First version: April 18, 2012. This version: January 28, 2013.
22. The risk-free rate for Sharpe ratio calculations was approximated by US 91-Day Treasury Bills.
23. The risk-free rate for Sharpe ratio calculations was approximated by US 91-Day Treasury Bills.

14

Smart Beta

In Chap. 11 we talked about indexing, and how the low-cost means of earning market-like returns will usually outperform the average stock picker. In Chap. 12, we showed how managers who build portfolios with high active share can outperform as can private equity funds, but manager selection is critical and fees are high. Thankfully, these don't represent the only means by which market outperformance can be had. A systematic tilting toward factors that have demonstrated an ability to provide unique, outsized returns represents another way to beat the market. Such strategies are commonly classified as *smart beta*.

Recall from early in Chap. 13 the discussion regarding how the identification of certain characteristics of stocks held in a portfolio could represent the explanation for that portfolio's outperformance rather than skillful security selection? Many years ago, researchers identified market risk as source of outperformance. A manager may have outperformed the market, but if they did so by simply taking market risk, they should not necessarily claim that stock selection skill was the cause. Fama and French said in addition to market risk, you should also back out market capitalization (size) and valuation when seeking to identify skill because tilts to those factors can explain outperformance as well. Mark Carhart showed that in addition to market risk, size, and expensiveness, momentum can explain returns.

It almost feels like a negative accusation to say to a stock-picking manager, "Well, when you back out those factor exposures, you really didn't outperform. You just tilted toward factors, so you don't really have stock selecting skill." But we can look at these phenomena through a more positive lens. What if we deliberately and unapologetically tilted toward factors that we believe can provide outperformance? That's what smart beta does.

© The Author(s) 2018
M. J. Oyster, *Success in a Low-Return World*,
https://doi.org/10.1007/978-3-319-99855-8_14

Smart beta strategies were around long before people started calling them that. Some people resisted the term but then finally relented (more on that later). The subcategory types that fall under smart beta in general are not agreed upon but there is some acceptance that the following four should be included:

- Equally Weighted
- Fundamental-Weighted
- Factor-Based
- Low Volatility

We won't cover all of these in great depth, but we will dig deeper into two of them—fundamental-weighted and factor-based—because they are among the more widely accepted forms of smart beta and more importantly, offer the possibility of outperforming the stock market without any individual stock picking required.

Fundamental Indexing

Let's start with the problem smart beta was designed to solve. In the early 2000s, prolific researcher and investor Rob Arnott founded his asset-management firm Research Affiliates. Arnott was highlighting the shortcomings inherent with traditional, capitalization-weighting techniques that formed the basis for most indexes at that time. Before we talk about those shortcomings, let's recount the problems that cap-weighting solved relative to its predecessor.

The Dow Jones Industrial Average (DJIA) dates to 1896 and was designed to gauge the performance of the industrial sector of the US economy, and in practicality, a measure of the domestic economy in general. But it's price weighted, meaning that of the 30 stocks included therein, those with the higher price earn a higher weighting in the index calculation. It's easy to calculate without computers but rationale for its weightings is practically arbitrary because the price of one share of stock says very little about the company.

In 1923, Standard and Poor's introduced the *Composite Index*, which after expanding the number of holdings to 500 large US companies in 1957, formed the S&P 500 Index. Like the DJIA, it provides a general sense of the US economy but is calculated based upon corporations' market values as opposed to just stock price. The S&P 500 Index is capitalization or *cap-weighted*. The market capitalization, which is stock price times shares outstanding, represents what the market believes the value of the company to be. The larger market cap names garner a higher weighting in the index, the smaller names a lesser allocation.

Now back to Arnott. If a stock in a cap-weighted index performs exceptionally well, its market cap will become greater earning it a larger allocation in the index. In a self-reinforcing sort of way, the index's calculation methodology will add more weight to stocks as they go higher thus becoming more expensive. The opposite is also true in that stocks that are declining will see their allocation in the index reduced. This can lead to an index composition that overweights overvalued stocks and underweights undervalued ones. Smart, long-term investing that seeks to buy low and sell high might take issue with that methodology. Arnott certainly did and in 2005, along with Jason Hsu and Philip Moore, published a paper titled "Fundamental Indexation,"[1] which described an index designed not from cap-weighting names but rather allocating to stocks based upon company fundamentals.

Through Arnott and Hsu's company Research Affiliates they launched the RAFI™ Fundamental Index™, which considers sales, cash flow, book value, and dividends as weighting criteria rather than just market capitalization. The original paper that focused on the large cap domestic equity market showed that if the Fundamental Index™ had been in existence from 1962 through 2004, it would have outperformed the S&P 500 by about two percentage points annualized. Let's put that in perspective. A manager who outperformed by two percentage points over the S&P 500 for the ten years ending March 2018 would have been one of the best 3 out of every 100 active large cap stock pickers over that timeframe (not adjusting for survivorship bias). That could certainly help mitigate a bear market in expectations if stock market returns in the future will fail to best long-term averages.

I remember when Arnott and members of his team visited our Cincinnati offices as he had just started to promote fundamental indexing. After hearing his presentation, we were waiting by the elevators and I told him I thought his ideas were going to revolutionize equity investing. I remember, though, thinking as I said it, do I actually believe that or am I just being nice? Although I was certainly taken by the elegance of the idea and the evidence that it could work, I wondered if anyone would actually buy it. After all, equal-weighted indexing, the idea of holding every stock at exactly the same weight, had been around for a long time but had gained very little traction because it was so hard to implement. Cap-weighted indexing seemed fine as it was and if you wanted outperformance, there were plenty of active managers to sift through. Turns out, his work and that done by others did create somewhat of a revolution. In early 2018, there were approximately $159 billion invested in RAFI™ strategies and smart beta strategies in general crossed over the $1 trillion in assets threshold in late 2017.

Around that same time in 2005, professor Jeremy Siegel of the University of Pennsylvania's Wharton School came out with a book titled, *The Future for Investors: Why the Tried and True Triumphs Over the Bold and the New*. One idea in the book to which he gave significant attention was to seek market outperformance by emphasizing dividend-paying stocks. Siegel joined asset-management firm WisdomTree soon thereafter as a senior investment strategy advisor. Then in 2006, WisdomTree launched a group of ETFs that they called *fundamentally weighted*, in that they tilted toward higher dividend-paying stocks. Where Arnott's Fundamental Index utilized multiple types of fundamental criteria, WisdomTree built their index based on dividends alone. RAFI and WisdomTree were the pioneers in fundamental indexing, but there were more to come as the types of smart beta strategies began to expand.

The Beginning of the Arnott/Asness Rivalry

I have a great deal of respect and admiration for asset-management firm AQR's founder Cliff Asness. You would be hard pressed to find anyone in investing as clever and entertaining in their writing and speaking, but even as dynamic as his personality is, it pales in comparison to his intellect. Asness and the many other highly capable researchers at AQR have built their firm based upon sound academic research that is effectively applied. AQR stands for applied quantitative research, which is really the heart of what they do.

One of the things that makes Asness so great is that he is never shy about offering an opinion. He takes a strong stance on a point of view and always has evidence to back it up. In 2006, Asness took the opportunity to weigh in on the debate that had already started to simmer between cap-weighted indexing and fundamental indexing. In an article in *Institutional Investor* magazine,[2] he described himself in the middle between Vanguard Group founder Jack Bogle and Princeton University economics professor Burton Malkiel as the chief defenders of traditional indexing, and Arnott and Siegel on the side of fundamental indexing. Asness cited the merits of the "active bets" made by fundamental indexes but took issue with calling it an index because it wasn't truly passive—it was built with conscious tilts toward some areas of the market and away from others.

Then he dropped a hammer that would set the stage for an academic rivalry that would continue for years thereafter. In that *Institutional Investor* article from 2006, Asness made it clear that he believed Fundamental Indexing was not some new creation, rather it was simply a repackaging of a long-standing means of outperforming—tilting toward value. Asness cited an Arnott publication titled "Just Another Value Index? Not," then retorted with: "Well, Fundamental Indexing is 100 percent exactly, precisely, without question, just a tilt away from market cap based purely on valuation. That makes it hard to even begin addressing these claims beyond the schoolyard riposte, 'Yes, it is value investing, do the math.'"

So if you're Rob Arnott and/or Jeremy Siegel, you might be a little bit miffed at this. Cliff Asness just dismissed your groundbreaking new concept as the same car just with a new paint job. As time went on, Arnott continued to tout the merits of fundamental indexing while Asness talked about quantitatively-based factor tilts, which he had been implementing for years in AQR's hedge fund strategies.

Although the term smart beta had been around for several years, it did not rise to prominence until about 2013 when professional services provider company Towers Watson distributed a publication[3] delineating smart beta from bulk beta (passive cap-weighting) and alpha (outperformance from active management). Their paper also expanded the smart beta concept beyond just the stock market to alternatives when it was becoming clear that much of the performance enjoyed by high-cost hedge funds could be explained by exposure to styles or factors that could be replicated at a much lower cost.

In a progression that began from describing outperformance as coming from stock market risk, small cap, value, and momentum, we can further describe sources of return from quality, carry, low volatility, and a whole host of other factors. This provided an umbrella (smart beta) under which both Arnott and Asness could find a home. Smart beta could include both Fundamental Indexing as well as the quantitative tilts toward various factors that Asness employed; though he still didn't like the name. It took a few years but he finally relented recognizing that the industry was coalescing around the term smart beta, so he had to just go with it. But despite the broadening category that smart beta was becoming, Asness still insisted that it wasn't anything new.

In 2014, Cliff Asness partnered with John Liew to pen an article titled, "Smart Beta, Not New, Not Beta, Still Awesome."[4] While Asness may not have immediately jumped in with both feet on the term, he absolutely recognized the merits in the methodology. The opening statement of that 2014 article describes his point of view well:

Let's be blunt. Smart Beta is mostly re-packaged, re-branded quantitative management. That's not to say we don't like it or think it's not good for investors. We love quantitative management, having spent our careers pursuing these types of strategies. However, we work in a business where good ideas are constantly repackaged as something new. Smart Beta is the latest example. It takes well-established, quantitative investing styles, or factors, and implements them in a simple, transparent manner often, though not always, at lower fees than what we've seen in the past. That certainly sounds like a worthwhile repackaging, and it's not surprising that Smart Beta has received great attention.[5]

Rob Arnott seemingly had little reservation about adopting the smart beta moniker tucking his Fundamental Index™ neatly under its tent. In fact, Arnott is sometimes referred to as the "godfather" of smart beta. Now that Cliff Asness' quantitative factors or styles could be housed under the same broad heading, you would think he and Arnott would have much to agree upon. Alas, that would not always be the case as we will discuss in more detail shortly. First, let's dig deeper into what it means to be a factor-based smart beta strategy.

Factor-Based

An effective way to classify an investment is to describe what sets it apart from other investments. At the broadest level, there are equities, bonds, and real assets such as commodities and real estate. Within broad categories, investments can be further subdivided based upon the characteristics they exhibit relative to other investments therein. In some instances, investments that can be characterized in a certain way tend to outperform investments that are characterized a different way. These characterizations are sometimes referred to as *factors*.

In Chap. 14 we discussed how Eugene Fama and Ken French built on just market risk to define two outperforming subsets of equity returns—size and valuation. They described this sub-grouping as the *cross section* of equity returns, and the concept has also been referred to as *dimensions* of return. An important aspect of Fama and French's work was that the dimensions of return they identified were independent of market risk and independent of each other. That's a critical aspect of a factor—it should be unique.

There are practically countless ways of classifying investments. Not all of them should be considered factors and not all factors are worth following. Different groups draw upon different qualifications when determining what factors are worth investing in and each has its own merits. I particularly like the way AQR goes about answering the question. In order for AQR to accept that a potential factor is viable, it must demonstrate positive characteristics when tested according to these three things:

- Economic Intuition
- Evidence
- Implementation

Intuition here is related to but not exactly how Catherine described it in Chap. 9. With regard to factors, economic intuition asks, does it make reasonable sense that a factor would behave the way it has? Let's look at value for example. Should a group of stocks that exhibit attractive valuations outperform the broader market and their more expensive counterparts over time? Probably. Value stocks can be overly beaten up while expectations for growth stocks are excessively high based upon recent performance. Expecting a reversion to fair value over time, value should outperform growth, so the value factor seems reasonable and tests well according to economic intuition. Intuition tests of other factors include similar considerations but specific to their particular subset of the investment universe.

A big part of economic intuition is the idea that there is no free lunch. Outperformance is compensation for risk. Risk is a part of investing and the higher return you seek, the greater amount of risk you must accept. One challenge when seeking viable factors, and across all of investing for that matter, is determining whether the risk is justified by a commensurate amount of expected return. It's difficult to say that a factor is viable if you can't assign a risk to it that explains its outperformance as compensation for that risk.

Economic intuition isn't enough. Just because something *should* perform a certain way doesn't mean that it *has*, or it *will*. There has to be evidence in the historical data. That said, a potential factor that shows strong historical performance but has no economic intuition supporting it is not useful. Remember the Vanguard study from Chap. 1 showing that a portion of stock market returns could be explained by rainfall? Just because an anomaly exists in the historical data does not mean it will in the future. Unfortunately, some researchers who go looking for the next big factor will screen a return series by a large number of factors looking for evidence that a certain characteristic coincided with outperformance. This is known as data mining and it is wickedly dangerous. A researcher may show historical data providing evidence that a certain style or factor outperformed over time to an unwitting investor only to find out that it wasn't a viable factor after all. More on this later.

The third test of factor viability has to do with implementation. It may have performed well in the past and make logical sense that it would, but can it be actually implemented in an investment portfolio? Are there a sufficient number of securities upon which to draw in order to build an investment strategy that employs the factor? Is there enough liquidity? Are there derivatives that can be utilized to fine-tune the desired exposure? Cost considerations are also vitally important.

Researchers who are prudent and objective in their search for factors usually end up with a small number that they believe will be viable sources of outperformance in the years to come. No one has a monopoly on which factors are expected to prove most effective but those who offer investment products that draw upon factors for investment returns usually include some form of the following three (also referred to as *alternative risk premia*):

- *Value*—The tendency for inexpensive investments to outperform more expensive ones;
- *Momentum*—The tendency for an investment's recent price performance to persist.
- *Defensive/Low Volatility*—The tendency for lower risk investments to generate higher risk-adjusted returns.

But that hardly makes for an exhaustive list. Some organizations offer exposure to a factor known as *carry*, which is the tendency for higher yielding assets to outperform lower yielding ones. Another is a focus on higher *dividend-paying* names—remember WisdomTree? There are factors that identify an opportunity for outperformance arising from companies who are aggressively *buying back* their own stock and ones that seek to tilt toward *lower-liquidity* stocks. And there are many more factors, including the premium of option prices relative to fair value. This *Volatility Risk Premium* (VRP) is not as widely known and utilized as some of the others. It will be a focus in subsequent chapters.

One that is conspicuously absent from many lists of viable factors is *size*— the thought that small cap stocks should outperform large cap stocks. But small has not outperformed large for a very long time and evidence of its effect barely exists over even a long period of time. From December 1989 through June 2018, small cap US stocks outperformed large stocks by just 0.15 percent annualized. An expected premium from small cap equities is simply not as prominent as it once was and there are a few important reasons why.

There was much excitement in the early 1980s when the early work on the size effect was being done. At that time, it seemed clear that a premium from small cap stocks existed that could not be explained simply by stock market risk. Investment assets soon flowed into small cap stocks, which like many times in investment history then diluted the effect due to excessive popularity. In 2018, Ron Alquist, Ronen Israel, and Tobias Moskowitz (collectively AIM) wrote a paper titled "Fact, Fiction and the Size Effect"[6] that said among other things that the size effect diminished shortly after its discovery and publication.

This quote from the paper is interesting—*the size effect continues to receive a disproportionate amount of attention relative to other factors with similar or stronger evidence behind them.* That's a textbook identification of the behavioral bias of anchoring. People continue to believe that a premium from small cap exists despite a mountain of evidence to the contrary.

AIM went on to say that having looked at over 90 years of US data, there is no evidence of a pure size effect, and moreover, it may not have existed in the first place. They cited data errors and insufficient adjustments for risk and liquidity. But they also allow that size can be made much stronger when viewed in conjunction with other factors such as defensive/quality. This hearkens back to a similar point made by Cliff Asness in 2015[7] when he was looking at the size factor. The idea is this—*quality* is a known factor that can take a variety of forms but commonly describes the phenomenon where the stocks of higher quality companies (strong gross profitability and return on equity, low debt to equity, etc.) have historically outperformed their *junkier* counterparts. Small cap stocks, it turns out, are junkier than large cap stocks, so when you account for that, the size premium re-emerges.

The marketplace for smart beta has evolved so significantly that a large number of asset-management firms offer a myriad of products that are built with multiple styles or factors as well as products that focus on just a single factor. In this way, an enterprising do-it-yourself investor could build an investment program out of pure factor exposures, but the interrelation between them is important. The goal would be to use those to provide a diversification benefit relative to one another. Value and momentum, for example, are negatively correlated, which makes the combination of the two a nice addition to a portfolio of factors. The question would then be how much to have of which and should an investor attempt to time factors in hopes of allocating more capital to factors that are expected to perform well and away from those expected to perform poorly. That brings us to the next chapter of the Arnott/Asness rivalry.

Factor Timing

The greatest prize fights are always when the two most powerful fighters square off. Rob Arnott and Cliff Asness are giants in the field of smart beta so when they disagree on something, people pay attention. One area of high-profile disagreement involves factor timing—should you seek out opportunities to overweight/ underweight factors or simply hold them at strategic targets. The only reason an investor might attempt factor timing is if they believed they could improve performance as a result of doing so. But that comes with risk, and the risk in this case is concentration—you sacrifice diversification when you overweight a factor giving it a higher degree of concentration in the portfolio as a whole. If you are wrong, there is a diminished amount of offsetting other stuff to cushion your fall.

One of the initial salvos in the factor timing debate came in 2016 when Rob Arnott wrote a paper (the third in a series) with Noah Beck and Vitali Kalesnik titled, "Timing 'Smart Beta' Strategies? Of Course! Buy Low, Sell High."[8] As the name implies, the authors suggest a methodology of seeking out undervalued factors just as one might seek out undervalued investments in general. They also warn against the risks of performance chasing and factors developed through data mining techniques.

In 2017, Cliff Asness responded with a criticism of Arnott's reliance on book-to-price as a measure of valuation and that factor timing might be even harder than market timing because the composition of the factors turns over so much. It also may take a very long time for valuations to mean revert, which is also the case in equities in general.

Some strong words were exchanged but Arnott and Asness were not terribly far apart on this debate for one important reason—both recognized the risk associated with the loss of diversification when concentration in a single factor grew too high. Even Arnott suggested that timing bets should be only modest. So who is right? Should you attempt to time factors? I will leave that for you to decide, but regardless of whether you do or don't, it is important to recognize the risk and ensure that the return enhancement you expect is justified considering the risk you have to take to achieve it.

But the sparring between Arnott and Asness didn't end there—not by a long shot. In April 2017, Arnott was quoted in a Bloomberg article saying that he believes Asness has done some outstanding work over the years but that he's "insufficiently skeptical about the pervasiveness of data-mining and its impact even in the factors he uses."[9] Let's pause for a moment and let that sink in. In quantitative research, data mining is sacrilege, so to suggest another researcher is "insufficiently skeptical" about it is a stinging accusation.

Asness was upset and responded with the following on his blog at AQR. com:

That is, he says I'm a data-miner. That may seem like an innocuous little comment actually prefaced with a kind of compliment. It's not. It's a damning accusation that's provably false, backwards in fact.

I have met and chatted with both men on several occasions. They are both brilliant and forces of nature in the world of investing, and I would place them alongside the pillars of the craft in all of investment history. Their ideas have changed investing for the better, but we are forced to ask—are their ideas, like many great ideas before them, so good that they ultimately lose effectiveness due to overuse? Smart beta represents a tremendous way of seeking outperformance over the stock market. Has it, and/or will it, survive discovery?

Has/Will Smart Beta Survive Discovery?

Cliff Asness, in the aforementioned *Institutional Investor* article from 2006 in which he dismissed fundamental indexing as nothing new, offered some wisdom dripping with perspective.

> *If Fundamental Indexing grows too successful, it will suffer after the spreads between cheap and expensive stocks narrow. In the extreme its success could sow the seeds of its own destruction.*

Today one could substitute *smart beta* for *fundamental indexing* and not change the truth of that statement. As smart beta strategies grew their collective assets under management beyond the $1 trillion dollar mark in 2018, performance of many had been suffering and warning bells were being sounded. Some warnings, in fact, had begun years prior with one coming from an unexpected source.

In 2016, Rob Arnott, Noah Beck, Vitali Kalesnik, and John West wrote a paper titled "How Can 'Smart Beta' Go Horribly Wrong?"[10] In it, the authors point to changes in valuations as a source for factor returns that may not repeat in the future. The value-addition that a factor is expected to provide could be *structural* and thus repeatable, or *situational* in that valuations simply rose over the period in question. If rising valuations explained the strong performance, a factor's viability should be called into question. Arnott and his collaborators also went as far as saying they see a reasonable probability of a smart beta crash as a consequence of the soaring popularity of factor-tilt strategies. In investing, there are few words as inflammatory as *crash*, so they really wanted to get their point across.

An associated concern with smart beta is that as a group, the average effectiveness gets diminished after Johnny-come-lately funds rush to market trying to distinguish themselves among the substantial number of existing smart beta strategies. Such new strategies might look good on a back-test but fail to deliver after going live with real money. This risk was highlighted (among other places) in 2017 when a study by Antti Suhonen, a finance professor at Aalto University in Finland, published a report warning that many smart beta strategies did not perform as well as they were predicted to do. According to the study, there was a median 73 percent deterioration in Sharpe ratios, a measure for calculating risk-adjusted return, between back-tested and live performance.[11] It is buyer beware in smart beta today because you never know that your shiny new smart beta strategy is actually just a data-mined piece of garbage until it's too late.

Conclusion

Smart beta, in a number of iterations, offers investors an effective and generally low-cost means of seeking outperformance. Good smart beta strategies are based upon sound fundamentals and economic intuition that are confirmed by both in-sample (testing period) and out-of-sample (subsequent to test) data. They also need to be implemented in a way that isn't diminished because of the costs to run it.

Are smart beta strategies failing to survive discovery? It's a good question because other really terrific strategies didn't. Why should smart beta be any different? When massive inflows coincide with periods of underperformance, an objective observer should wonder if a cause and effect is at work. But the same objective observer should not immediately jump to that conclusion. Smart beta strategies, and the factors upon which they are based, are cyclical like just about everything in investing in that they will experience both good times and bad. Just as a manager that ends a ten-year period in the top quartile will likely experience a three-year bottom quartile period along the way, so too will good factors occasionally fall from favor. And, many of the best factors are fundamentally based, meaning that the effect, though powerful, might not be seen until a long period of time has passed.

Smart beta might be repackaged value or other quantitative-based strategies that have been around for years, but that shouldn't diminish one's view. Yes, data mining is an issue to be wary of and yes, asset growth has been substantial, but it remains well below that of traditional stock-picking funds. For an investor with a long-term view, smart beta can serve as an effective means of seeking market outperformance. Given the choice between smart beta and a closet indexer, I'd take smart beta every time.

Notes

1. Arnott, Robert D., Jason Hsu, and Philip Moore. "Fundamental Indexation," Financial Analysts Journal. Vol. 61. No 2. March/April 2005. 83–99.
2. Asness, Clifford. "The Value of Fundamental Indexing." *Institutional Investor*. October 16, 2006.
3. "Understanding Smart Beta," Towers Watson publication. July 2013.
4. Clifford S. Asness Ph.D. and John M. Liew, Ph.D. "Smart Beta Not New, Not Beta, Still Awesome." *Institutional Investor*. September 29, 2014.
5. Ibid.
6. Ron Alquist, Ronen Israel, Tobias J. Maskowitz, "Fact, Fiction and the Size Effect" (May 12, 2018). Available at SSRN: https://ssrn.com/abstract= 3177539 or http://dx.doi.org/10.2139/ssrn.3177539
7. Cliff Asness, Andrea Frazzini, Ronen Israel, Tobias Moskowitz, and Lasse H. Pederson. "Size Matters, if You Control Your Junk," AQR Working Paper. January 2015.
8. Rob Arnott, Noah Beck, and Vitali Kalesnik, PhD. "Timing 'Smart Beta' Strategies? Of Course! Buy Low, Sell High". Research Affiliates Publication. September 2016.
9. "Factor Fight Rages on Between Asness and Arnott" InstitutionalInvestor. com. April 13, 2017.
10. Rob Arnott, Noah Beck, Vitali Kalesnik, PhD, & John West, CFA. "How Can 'Smart Beta' Go Horribly Wrong?" Research Affiliates Publication. February 2016.
11. Attracta Mooney, "Smart beta funds stalked by chaotic 'factor zoo'". *Financial Times*. July 9, 2017.

15

Risk Management

We've covered a lot of ground. In a past, present, and future sort of way, we began with expectations that the future performance of the US stock market may not be as terrific as the past and traditional stock picking based upon old-school fundamental analysis provides little hope to make up the shortfall. Sound asset allocation that aligns your portfolio with your risk and return profile and draws upon differentiated advantages can increase the probability of success. Indexing generally bests active management in the US stock market. Funds that demonstrate conviction through high active share can do even better, as can private equity managers with unique skill and access to information. Smart beta represents a great idea today. How great it will be in years to come is anyone's guess. The future will include investments that harvest and monetize the volatility risk premium—a subject to which we will dedicate more time in subsequent chapters. For now, we should take a brief detour from seeking outperformance and talk about risk.

A penny spar'd is twice got.[1] A 20 percent loss requires a 25 percent gain to just get back to even, to say nothing of the opportunity cost while doing so. Retirees need consistent income and many institutions have stable spending needs. Whatever your goals for whatever investment portfolio for which you are responsible, there are risks and how those risks are managed will play a big part in determining success or failure.

Investment risks are widely varied and go well beyond the variability of returns, but that's a good place to start. Standard deviation, the measure of dispersion about an average, has been a commonly used measure of investment risk for decades. It serves as the measure for risk in commonly used investment models, such as mean-variance optimizations, which we will

© The Author(s) 2018
M. J. Oyster, *Success in a Low-Return World*,
https://doi.org/10.1007/978-3-319-99855-8_15

discuss later in this chapter. A standard measure of risk-adjusted returns is the Sharpe ratio, which is an investment's return less the risk-free rate divided by standard deviation. In this way, investments with different levels of risk can be compared to one another.

Standard deviation has its merits but cannot offer a researcher a complete picture of investment risk, or even a measure that describes what an investor actually cares about. One way to think about it is that the higher an investment's standard deviation, the lower its Sharpe ratio. But what if a great deal of that standard deviation came from massive spikes higher? The Sharpe ratio might be understated leading one to think the investment isn't as strong as it actually is. A solution for this is the Sortino ratio, which is a modification of the Sharpe ratio that uses just downside deviation in the denominator. Downside deviation is the variability of just negative returns or in some modifications, the variability of returns below some target level. Sortino can help paint a clearer picture of the nature of an asset in a way that an investor may care more about than when variability is the only measure of risk.

There exists a massive number of mathematical means by which risk can be measured and described but if we wanted to boil it down to one statement, we could say the following:

Risk in investing is not the variability of short-term returns, or even long term returns for that matter. Risk is the possibility that capital could be permanently impaired.

If I invest some money in a new restaurant and it goes belly up, that money is permanently impaired. The ups and downs it may have experienced along the way might not have told the entire story about risk; risk is the chance that I could lose some or all of the money I invested in it. And not temporarily. Forever.

The restaurant is a good example of how capital can become permanently impaired but not the only one. An investor could commit to a private equity fund. The manager then calls capital from the investor and puts it to work, but loses money. By the end of the fund's life, the manager has distributed some capital back to the investor but it is less than what was called. The difference is permanently impaired. The fund is over and that's it. Another example: an investor could buy a call option or a futures contract with a limited life. If after the contract expires it is worth less than the amount paid, the investor has no recourse. That capital is permanently impaired.

Investors can also permanently impair capital through bad behavior. We know the pain of loss is strong. Imagine the investor who holds a position in a mutual fund that ended a three-year period in the bottom 25 percent of its peer group, trailing its benchmark by a sizable amount. The investor might be tempted to just pull the plug and reallocate those funds to one of the top-performing managers. Unfortunately, many investors do this very thing and Fig. 5.1 in Chap. 5 illustrating the difference between pre and post-hiring/firing performance, shows how such behavior can prove destructive. When the underperforming fund is sold, that relative loss of capital becomes permanent.

It is important that we, as much as possible, understand those emotions that can sometimes lead to self-destructive investment behavior. It is perfectly natural to feel anguish over poor short-term performance and that is OK as long as investment decisions are not made strictly on emotion alone. One question worth asking is, given the poor short-term performance, are my investment goals still attainable? This brings us to another important investment risk, which isn't necessarily about losing money; rather, it is about failing to reach important investment goals. This risk is known as *shortfall risk*.

Here's an extreme example. Imagine a committee that stewards the investable assets for a large not-for-profit institution. Under the guise of prudence and risk control, they invest the entirety of the institution's portfolio in two-year US treasury bonds. These are very low-risk securities. The chances the US government would default on these bonds is virtually nil because they could simply print more dollars to pay whatever was necessary, and because they are relatively short term, they carry only a small amount of duration risk—the risk of price declines when interest rates rise. Sounds rather prudent, doesn't it? Maybe, but probably not.

Most charitable institutions seek to exist into perpetuity and as such require at least intergenerational equity, which is to say the net impact (or utility) of the money they spend in the future will be equally as great as it is today. For that to happen, their net-of-costs return must meet or exceed the amount they spend plus inflation. If they spend 5 percent of their total assets on average each year as most do, and inflation is 3 percent (its long-term average) they need an annualized rate of return of 8 percent. In mid-2018, the two-year treasury bond was yielding just 2.5 percent. That's not good enough to keep up with inflation let alone replenish that which was spent. Even in the absence of any volatility, the institution's total assets would lose over half of their real value in only 13 years and the real spending would be cut by that much as well. Such an event would have a disastrous impact on the institution's ability to fulfill its mission. Not very prudent after all. Managing risk is a critical component of investment success, but the total avoidance of risk can be a recipe for failure.

Risk, the Only Path to Outperformance

Risk is inherent in investing and the greater return required, the greater the risk that must be borne. I am convinced, like many stalwarts of the academic community, that no sustainable outperformance is possible without the acceptance of risk. Sources of outperformance can be identified and in almost all cases, a risk can be assigned that explains them. An investor with a goal to outperform inflation by five percentage points net of fees, for example, can get there but they must accept that they may find themselves down 20 percent in a given year.

I spent years researching and closely following a wide variety of different investment managers and strategies. As a person with a background in derivatives in an investment manager research shop, I always got the first look at managers who employed derivatives as all or part of their process. I remember in 2008 being introduced to a "feeder fund" set up to access something called a split strike conversion strategy managed by a person I'd never heard of, Bernie Madoff. As far as I could tell on the initial glance, split strike conversion was something akin to a buy-write strategy or covered call writing. But then I looked at the historical performance the fund was touting. I knew right away that the magnitude of the returns and the consistency of them was not possible with such a strategy. Something was going on and at the very least, the high returns and amazing consistency were unsustainable. Of course, soon thereafter, the Madoff strategy was discovered to be one of the biggest fraudulent Ponzi schemes in history as he bilked his clients out of billions of dollars and ultimately ended up in jail.

There were other red flags that my colleagues and I noticed giving us a multitude of reasons to take a pass on the Madoff feeder fund, but the point is that strong performance cannot be attained without risk. We would all love to earn 8 percent to 10 percent every single year forever, but we must accept that isn't possible. Good managers may outperform over the long run but nearly all will experience underperformance along the way. Strong performing strategies and techniques will occasionally fall temporarily out of favor. The good news is we can build portfolios that take on only as much risk as necessary to achieve a desired return. At least in theory.

Mean-Variance Optimization

There is a positive correlation between risk and return. A return can be earned on risk-free short-term US government debt but it's miniscule. And theoretically, it is not completely devoid of risk. A graph that shows expected standard deviation (risk) on the x-axis and return on the y-axis can illustrate the positive correlation between risk and return as a line moving upward and to the right—the capital market line (CML). At some point, the line reaches the riskiest asset marking its expected risk and return. Beyond that point, greater return can be achieved but only by employing leverage and the greater risk that comes with it.

Harry Markowitz's Modern Portfolio Theory (MPT) describes how a portfolio can be constructed to maximize expected return for a given risk. The *efficient frontier* plots the best possible portfolio for a given level of risk as illustrated by the top half of the arc shown in Fig. 15.1 below. The portfolio on the efficient frontier that lies tangential to the CML, the tangency portfolio, can be said to be optimal, because given all the portfolios that could be made to maximize return for a unit of risk, it does so more effectively than any other.

With the advent of computers, researchers could easily run simulations known as mean-variance optimizations. When given a group of assets from which to choose, these optimizations would select the specific mix of assets that would be optimal based upon assumptions for return, risk, and covariance relationships between the assets. The problem is that the results were often unacceptable for practical portfolio construction purposes because the simulation would frequently suggest a high concentration in a single-asset category. The solution was to then constrain the model such that allocations to each asset category would be limited to no more than a certain percent, but that of course diminished the value of the model.

Usually when researchers use mean-variance optimizations, they are trying to find the portfolio that will provide them their desired expected return for as little risk as possible as opposed to first understanding the maximum risk that can be endured and then determining how much that would yield in expected return. Ideally, we would start with risk because prospect theory says that

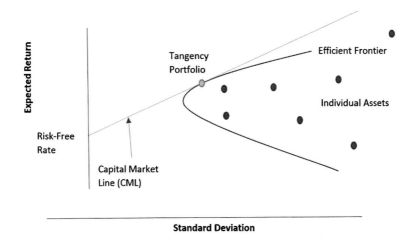

Fig. 15.1 Expected return versus standard deviation

human beings feel more pain from loss than enjoyment from gain, but putting a number on how much loss we are able to lose is more difficult than determining a desired return. This brings us to another issue with mean-variance: the measure of risk is in the form of standard deviation.

Standard deviation is probably not the best measure of investment risk, but it has merit. Imagine an asset-allocation setting exercise where an institution has a long-term return goal of 8 percent, which is comprised of 5 percent spending plus 3 percent to keep pace with inflation. The institution wants to spend 5 percent of its assets per year on average over rolling three-year periods, but it knows that even with averaging, some variation in the actual amount spent will take place. With reasonable confidence in projections for future returns and how widely distributed around the average those returns are expected to be, the institution can more effectively plan for future budgeting variability.

But statistical probability does not provide certainty and there is always the risk that the unforeseen investment drawdown can blow a hole in an institution's cash flow needs. Pensions sometimes solve this problem of return variability by locking in future distribution needs through a process known as duration matching or *liability-driven investing* (LDI). Pensions have a good idea what their cash flow requirements will be even many years into the future. One technique they use is to set aside zero-coupon bonds that mature on the date of a future distribution in the amount that matches the expected distribution. In this way, they have already secured future cash flow requirements, which will not be affected by changes in interest rates or stock market variability.

I once worked with the director of a university endowment attempting to apply the LDI concept to their pool of assets with the thought that locking in future spending amounts could help with budgeting for the university and provide piece of mind. But they never actually went forward with the plan. Given the low interest rate environment, an overwhelming percentage of the endowed assets would have needed to be sequestered to ensure stable spending for just a few years and what was left over was not enough to replenish it when the duration-matched bonds were sold to meet spending needs. Future endowment growth would have been severely inhibited and keeping up with the Joneses is important to many universities. If interest rates one day move to a substantially higher level, perhaps this will be an idea worth revisiting.

It's All About Equity Risk

A portfolio that is designed to achieve more than the most paltry of returns will likely need to include some form of equity. MPT shows how the benefits of diversifying into assets with low or even negative correlations to others already in a portfolio can improve risk-adjusted returns. But even when a portfolio appears well diversified, it might not be. Many investors are surprised to find out how much equity risk their portfolios actually hold. It's not what you own that matters, it's how it behaves.

Consider a portfolio that is allocated 60 percent to equities in the form of the S&P 500 and 40 percent in bonds proxied by the Bloomberg Barclays US Aggregate Bond Index (a 60/40 portfolio). If you imagine just the stock allocation as the starting point and then add the 40 percent bonds, you might expect the portfolio to be fairly well diversified. After all, the correlation between the two from 1975 through 2017 was just 0.21. But the resulting portfolio is not well diversified. It exhibits a massive amount of equity risk. This is illustrated in Fig. 15.2.

The graph plots the monthly returns of the S&P 500 and the 60/40 portfolio. As it turned out, the performance of the S&P 500 had a lot to say about the performance of the 60/40 portfolio. In fact, according to the linear regression line tracking through the scatterplot, over 95 percent of the performance of the 60/40 portfolio is explained by movements in the S&P 500. Even with a full 40 percent of the portfolio in bonds, nearly all the risk it exhibits is due to the stock allocation. How can this be? It's because the equity index has been far more volatile than the bond index over time. In this case, the power of equity volatility overwhelms the much lower volatility of bonds.

Although this is an overly simplistic example, the effect shows up in portfolios that are allocated to a wider variety of asset categories as well. Even institutional portfolios with 20 or more distinct asset categories are often

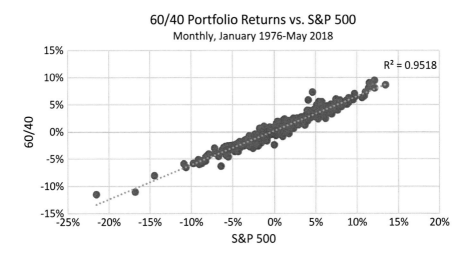

Fig. 15.2 60/40 portfolio returns versus S&P 500

saddled with an enormous amount of equity risk. It's not as though such risk is desired, rather it represents a necessary evil for portfolios that seek returns beyond just a small amount. And it shows up everywhere—private equity, hedged equity, international equity, high-yield fixed income, REITs, and many other places that have different names but a common risk. When the stock market declines, even well-diversified portfolios can feel the pinch.

If Equity Risk Is the Problem, Let's Hedge It Out, Right?

Modern Portfolio Theory is a brilliant concept and diversification is a critical means of long-term risk mitigation. Equity risk is omnipresent in amounts higher than many investors recognize. What if we could hold a portfolio with a large amount of equity risk but then somehow diffuse that risk such that downside moves in the stock market wouldn't sting so much, or even at all. Deliberate and targeted equity risk management, customized to eliminate exactly how much equity risk we want to eliminate for exactly how long we choose, can be done but it requires sacrifice, and it is up to the investor to determine if the equity risk mitigation is justified by the cost that must be levied to have it.

A good way to show how this might work is through an example. Let's say an investor has $10 million in large cap US equity exposure and they would like to be confident that for the next year it won't lose more than 10 percent of its value. If we assume the stock holdings in question look a lot like the S&P 500, the investor can buy S&P 500 Index put options to protect against a desired amount of loss, a strategy commonly known as *protective put* buying. Put options are kind of like insurance policies that protect the owner if something bad happens. In this case, the bad thing would be the stock market falling. To get specific, a put option provides the owner the right to sell the underlying security or index to which it is attached (in this case, the S&P 500) at a specified price (the *strike* price). So if the S&P 500 starts at 2800 and then drops to 2240 (a 20 percent decline) at expiration (the date when the option's limited life ends) but an investor holds the necessary amount of put options with a strike price at 2520, the investor's stock investment will only lose 10 percent.

Taking this example a bit further with real-world numbers, we see that in mid-2018, the S&P 500 Index is at 2801. Consider an investor who at the time wants to hedge (protect) their $10 million equity portfolio against losses beyond 10 percent for the next year or so. We find listed put options set to expire on the third Friday of June 2019 with a strike price of 2525, which is just less than 10 percent lower than the S&P 500's price. Put options with strike prices below the prevailing level of the index are said to be *out of the money*. The question then becomes how many put option contracts to buy? S&P 500 Index options can be purchased in contracts that represent $100 of index exposure each, so to hedge a $10 million equity portfolio, we divide $10 million by the current value of the index, 2801 in this case, then further divide by $100. The resulting quotient is 35.7, so we round up to ensure sufficient coverage, which leads us to 36 contracts needed.

Remaining in mid-2018, S&P 500 Index put options that will expire in June 2019 and have a strike price at 2525 are being offered for sale (ask price) at $72.90 per contract and could be sold at $71.30 per contract (bid price). Let's split the difference and assume we could buy 36 contracts at $72.10 for a total cost of $259,560 ($72.10 × 36 × $100) or about a 2.6 percent hit to expected returns over the course of the next year. Now we can think about what that means in terms of cost.

Like any other item of value, option prices change as a result of demand or the lack thereof. In the early 1970s, Fischer Black, Robert Merton, and Myron Scholes were working on a means by which option prices could be described through a detailed mathematical formula, which would come to be known as the Black-Scholes model. Black and Scholes published a paper[2] in 1973 in which they described the formula and Merton and Scholes received the Nobel Prize in Economics in 1997 for their work (Fischer Black had passed away by the time the award was given but was mentioned by the Swedish Academy as a contributor).

The Black-Scholes model can be daunting but the key point we want to focus on here has to do with arriving at an option's price. When we know the price of the underlying security (sticking with our example, in this case, an index being the underlying instrument), as well as the option's strike price, time until expiration, and the risk-free rate, we only need one more data point to solve for the option's price—the volatility of the underlying index. This is how demand can influence option pricing. If the volatility of the underlying index, for example, never changed, you could just plug in whatever volatility number that was and then calculate the option's price. But of course, stocks and indexes can go through low-volatility periods, have bouts of exceptionally high volatility, and all levels between. The point is this: if you solve the Black-Scholes model using the historical volatility of the underlying index, the resulting option price might not match what that option is trading for in the market. Why? Because the market may be expecting less or more volatile times in the future than had been experienced in the past.

It's the difference between *historical* volatility and *implied* volatility, and the option prices you see in the marketplace are a function of implied volatility.

Understanding the importance of implied volatility can help us frame the protective put example described earlier into period-specific context. A proxy for the prevailing demand for options can be seen in the Cboe Volatility Index or VIX. The VIX is an amalgamation of all the implied volatilities of all S&P 500 Index options and it usually runs counter to the stock market. When markets get choppy, people rush to buy puts to protect against losses in their stock portfolios. This results in increased implied volatility pricing not just in puts but in call options (bets on an ascent) as well due to put-call parity, thus manifesting itself in higher VIX readings. The point of all of this is that in mid-2018 when we looked at the cost to hedge against more than a 10 percent stock market decline, the VIX was at about 12.7, which was among the lowest 18 percent of all VIX readings since 1990. In other words, options were historically cheap so the 2.6 percent cost to enact that protective put was, all else equal, less expensive than at many times in history.

But being cheap doesn't necessarily mean attractively valued. Buying an option may provide a desirable payoff when the subsequent realized volatility of the underlying index exceeds the implied volatility that could have been used in the Black-Scholes model to solve for the market price when the option was purchased. Yet in S&P 500 Index options, implied volatility has exceeded subsequent realized volatility over 86 percent of the time since 1990, meaning that options have been consistently overpriced. This is the *Volatility Risk Premium* (VRP) mentioned previously that we will discuss in subsequent chapters.

Some interesting research backs up the idea that even when the VIX is low, options do not offer attractive value because what really matters is not the absolute price but the difference between implied and then subsequent realized volatility. Roni Israelov and Lars N. Nielsen wrote a paper in 2015 titled, "Still Not Cheap: Portfolio Protection in Calm Markets." In the paper, the authors sorted historical levels of the VIX into deciles and found that regardless of the level of the VIX, implied volatility usually exceeded subsequent realized volatility.

Even in the lowest VIX Index decile, the spread between the VIX Index and realized volatility was a positive 2.5 percent. Option prices may be lower, but they remain expensive in the sense that the long volatility component of one-month options is expected to have negative returns.[3]

So option prices may occasionally appear inexpensive but are usually priced in a way where implied volatility will exceed subsequent realized, which makes them expensive from a valuation point of view.

The question then becomes, is 2.6 percent a reasonable amount to pay for piece of mind or some other practical purpose that an equity portfolio would not lose more than 10 percent over the course of the next year? Certainly different investors with different temperaments, goals, and risk tolerances will have different answers but one can imagine that particular method of risk management having appeal to many. Before we delve into more specifics regarding trade-offs, let's look at another risk-management strategy that could provide an investor with that same protection beyond a 10 percent loss but can be had not for 2.6 percent, but for no out-of-pocket cost at all.

Costless Collar

You may be thinking, how is that even possible? Well, it's not as though there is no cost, just a different choice in how to pay. Here's how it works. Take that same June 2019 S&P 500 Index put with the strike price at 2525 that could be bought for $72.10 and instead of coming up with the cash to buy it outright, fund the purchase by selling out-of-the-money calls. Call options are the opposite of puts. They give the owner the right to buy something (the underlying, in this case, the S&P 500) at a particular price on or before a specific day. Where a put adds value when the index goes down, a call goes up in value when the stock market rises. If I buy the right to buy the S&P 500 Index at 2800 then the index rises to 2900; having the opportunity to buy at 2800 then immediately sell at the prevailing index price of 2900 should be worth at least 100 points times $100 per contract.

When an investor *sells* a call, they hand over the right to buy the index at the strike price level to someone else. If the index goes up, the call seller has to make up the difference. And that may be OK because the seller will accrue some income at the time of sale that may justify the risk of having to pay later.

Let's continue the example from earlier. Around the same time in mid-2018, S&P 500 Index call options that were to expire in June 2019 with a strike price of 2925 were selling for about $86 per contract. To generate the $259,560 needed to buy the put options, 31 call option contracts needed to be sold ($259,560 ÷ $86 ÷ $100). So now the investor owns the 10 percent out-of-the-money put protection and they didn't have to pay anything to get it. What they did give up, however, is opportunity cost. They traded one risk for another in that they hedged equity risk but took on shortfall risk because by selling call options, their equity portfolio's value can only rise by so much until it is offset by liabilities that must be paid to whomever they sold the call options. This strategy is known as a costless collar and a diagram that illustrates the payoff profile is shown in Fig. 15.3.

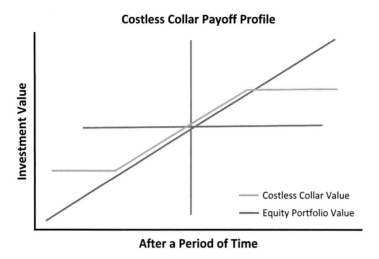

Fig. 15.3 Costless collar strategy payoff profile

If the value of the equity portfolio would decline as shown on the left side of the graph, losses with the costless collar would be limited to a certain point. But also, as stock values ascend to higher levels on the right side of the graph, the costless collar will reach a cap, which will not be exceeded regardless of how high the stock market goes. Is it worth it? In our mid-2018 example, the upside limit would have been about 4.5 percent. Would you trade protection that your stock portfolio would not decline more than 10 percent over the course of the next year for forgoing any equity portfolio ascent beyond just 4.5 percent? Some people might. Loss aversion is very powerful and a person might be willing to accept a 4.5 percent return from their stock investments. After all, we showed in Chap. 1 that future returns from stocks might be only 7 percent or even less if P/E multiples contract from elevated levels. Accepting 4.5 percent from stocks might not be that bad. Unfortunately, that doesn't tell the complete story.

Most investors who own stocks do not have a one-year time horizon. If they did, they would probably own something less risky like US treasury bonds. Equity investors have longer time horizons, so we can't think about stock performance in one-year terms. There is a penalty for volatility that must be endured and that only shows up after multiple periods have taken place. Consider the following Monte Carlo simulation that starts with 10,000 fictional annual stock returns that exhibit a 7 percent average return and 15 percent standard deviation—a reasonable expectation for US equity volatility. Shown in Table 15.1 below are the annualized returns over multi-year periods from a "no constraints" equity portfolio.

Table 15.1 Monte Carlo simulation example: no constraints annualized returns

	No constraints			
	3-year	5-year	10-year	20-year
Annlzd. Ret.	6.30%	6.14%	6.03%	5.97%
Std. Dev.	8.81%	6.74%	4.63%	3.17%

Table 15.2 Monte Carlo simulation example: costless collar annualized returns

	Costless collar			
	3-year	5-year	10-year	20-year
Annlzd. Ret	0.6%	0.6%	0.5%	0.5%
Std. Dev.	3.3%	2.5%	1.7%	1.2%

As you can see, the annualized returns are lower than 7 percent because volatility has taken a bite. Notice also that volatility decreases over longer periods as the returns converge toward the average. Those might be reasonable equity returns for a long-term investor. Now let's run the simulation again, but this time employing the costless collar. The simulation will constrain the 10,000 annual returns such that none will be higher than 4.5 percent and none lower than −10 percent. The results are shown in Table 15.2.

The expected return from this strategy has been essentially wiped out. When the simulated returns were constrained between −10 percent and +4.5 percent, the average (arithmetic) was reduced all the way to 0.7 percent, while the average standard deviation dropped to 5.5 percent from 15 in the unconstrained model. We can say that the resulting equity portfolio, when overlaid with a costless collar, is not actually an equity portfolio at all. It does not exhibit equity-like expected returns and has less equity risk. And maybe that's OK. How much is piece of mind worth?

I wish I could provide you with a magical methodology whereby upside equity returns could be had but downside risk was eliminated. Equity risk can be taken off the table but there's a cost to do so, and by bearing that cost, an investor may transform an equity portfolio into something more fixed-income-like or reflective of another investment category's characteristics. Be wary of packaged products that advertise equity returns without equity risk because if it sounds too good to be true, it probably is. There are risks in there, and probably astronomical costs as well. I saw many of these explode in spectacular fashion in 2008 because of the imbedded leverage that investors couldn't see, as well as counterparty risk, which is the chance that the firm responsible for paying you what you expect on your hedge goes out of business.

Return is not possible without risk. If an investment's risk is not immediately recognizable, a smart investor should either seek it out and understand it or walk away. My colleagues and I didn't know how Madoff was generating the returns he was advertising. We didn't run to the SEC and declare the guy a fraud, we just took a pass. Better to know a risk and make an informed decision about accepting it or not than to be blindsided by a risk that was not known in advance.

Conclusion

Risk is a part of investing and greater risk is required for greater return. Short-term performance variability is not risk, rather true risk is the possibility that capital could be permanently impaired. All-too-human investors make emotional decisions that permanently impair their capital when they give in to the pain of loss and sell what might be a terrific investment after a short period of poor performance.

The most important thing about risk management in investing is ensuring the portfolio aligns with return needs and risk tolerances. An investor should accept all the risk they can bear, but none of the risk they can't. And objectivity is important. If the goal is 8 percent to 10 percent return, that can be achieved, but variability in performance should be expected along the way. If capital preservation, even over short periods of time, is paramount, a lower return must be accepted. Some investors get themselves into trouble when they succumb to unrealistic expectations, usually as a result of short-termism. Times will get shaky and when they do, a stalwart recommitment to the long-term goals should be reinforced.

The derivatives markets are teeming with tools that can be used to manage all kinds of risks, but there is always a cost. Mitigating equity risk is possible, it just requires a choice. Some investors will choose to hedge out some or all of their equity risk and there is nothing wrong with that. There may be a perfectly rational reason to do so and the ability to deliberately callibrate the exact amount of hedging for an exact amount of time can have appeal. Investors should realize, however, that put options are almost always overpriced (relative to what they should be given subsequent realized volatility) and puts are almost always overpriced relative to calls—a concept known as *skew*. That and there is the risk that the hedge doesn't perfectly match the investment it is intended to protect, so called *basis risk*.

Diversification can offer every investor the ultimate in risk management, but portfolios should exhibit true diversification, not just one of each kind of fund in Morningstar's 9 equity style boxes. An analogy for diversification is a table with many legs. Think of a large table that is supported by ten legs. Each leg is wholly independent of the others. If one leg is removed, the table will still stand supported by the remaining nine. Now think about a three-legged stool. If one of its legs is removed, it will topple over. What is the right number for independent investments to be held in a portfolio? That is a matter of opinion, but different investments should keep being added if they are truly different. Investments with different names but a common risk are like table legs connected by a horizontal brace. When one gets knocked out, it will bring down others with it.

Diversification is a great risk-management tool—perhaps the only truly effective one. But it takes time and the recognition of the true risks exhibited by each of the individual investments. There are times when a well-diversified portfolio does not perform well as one that bears a great deal of equity risk. Such times challenge strong investment fundamentals but should not dissuade the prudent, long-term investor. The harsh reality is that to achieve the returns that most investors seek, some equity risk must be accepted. That comes with occasional volatility but should not lead to emotionally-fueled bad decision-making after short-term performance. Diversification can help and should be employed but equity risk cannot be completely eliminated without sacrificing enormous amounts of expected return. If anyone tells you otherwise, watch out, because though hidden, risk is lurking in there somewhere.

Notes

1. Herbert, George (1874). "The Complete Works of George Herbert: Prose". 341.
2. Black, Fischer and Myron Scholes, "The Pricing of Options and Corporate Liabilities," *Journal of Political Economy* 81, no. 3 (May–Jun, 1973): 637–654.
3. Israelov, Roni and Lars N. Nielsen, "Still Not Cheap: Portfolio Protection in Calm Markets," *The Journal of Portfolio Management*, Vol. 41, issue 4, Summer 2015. 108–120.

16

Buy-Write

We've jumped into the options world with both feet and there is no turning back now. As we continue discussing methods for outperformance, we begin to draw upon the *volatility risk premium* (VRP). The VRP represents the premium pricing associated with options relative to their fair value based upon subsequent realized volatility. Figure 16.1 provides an illustration of the VRP.

Stock market volatility can be high; it can be low. Through rattling historical events, most of the time *implied volatility* (IV), as priced in S&P 500 Index options represented in Fig. 16.1 by the VIX, has exceeded *realized volatility* (RV), the actual volatility of the S&P 500 over the subsequent 30 days. I believe that the VRP represents the most significant untapped resource available to investors today. That's not to say it's new. Some strategies that seek to monetize the VRP have been around for decades. Not new, but certainly underutilized. Perhaps the oldest means of monetizing the VRP is the *buy-write strategy* sometimes referred to as *covered call writing*. So as we embark upon seeking outperformance by harvesting volatility, we fittingly start at the beginning.

An Alternative: Buy-Write

The *buy-write strategy* is a derivatives-based method of investing that utilizes *options*. We have touched on options briefly but some history is worth recounting here. Options are derivative securities, meaning they are connected to some other entity such as a stock, index, or futures contract, which is known as the underlying. Among other things, movements in the underlying instrument impact the price of the option.

© The Author(s) 2018
M. J. Oyster, *Success in a Low-Return World*,
https://doi.org/10.1007/978-3-319-99855-8_16

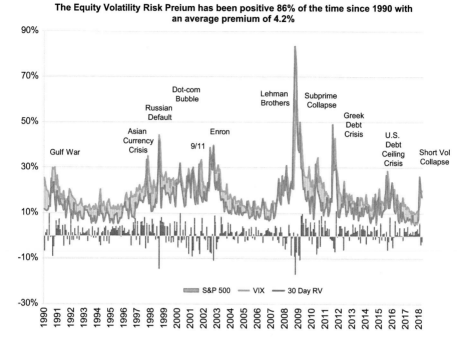

Fig. 16.1 The volatility risk premium (VRP) 1990–2018

Some people believe the first known example of an option can be found in Greek philosopher Aristotle's book titled *Politics*.[1] Aristotle recounted a story about another philosopher, Thales of Miletus, and how he had profited from an olive harvest. Aristotle indicated that philosophers usually don't care much about money, but Thales did so he set out to make some.

Thales deduced through astronomical observations that the coming olive harvest was going to be a bumper crop. He figured demand for olive presses was going to be vast, but he didn't have enough money to buy a bunch of presses. Instead, he took what money he could raise, went to all the press owners in Miletus and Chios and purchased the rights to use their presses at a later date. Turns out he was right; the olive crop that year was indeed large and the presses were in high demand. Thales was able to sell the rights he had purchased at a small price for a substantial profit.

Although Aristotle didn't call it that, Thales had essentially bought a call option on olive press use. He paid for the right, but not necessarily the obligation, to use the olive presses at a fixed price and was then able to exercise his option for a handsome profit.

Something akin to options trading took place in makeshift markets called *bucket shops* in the late 1800s and early 1900s. The name derives from the buckets used to collect trade tickets. Bucket shops afforded investors the opportunity to place a small amount of money to secure control of a security. Modern option investing began when the *Chicago Board Options Exchange*, today known by its more common name Cboe, was founded in 1973 as the first marketplace for listed options. Initially, only call options were traded with put options added in 1977.

The buy-write strategy, which utilizes call options, dates to the beginning of listed option trading and is among the most basic and widely used option strategies employed today. A buy-write position is formed when a core position in an underlying security is purchased, then call options are written (aka, sold short) usually at or just out of the money. The portfolio receives cash from the sale of call options, and if the options are worthless when they expire (when the underlying security's value remains below the call option's strike price), buying them back incurs no liability. Investors often utilize out-of-the-money options, in this case where the call's strike price is above the underlying's price. Out-of-the-money options have a greater chance of expiring worthless than in-the-money options. The further an option is out of the money, the lower its value all else equal, so many buy-write strategies sell the most expensive out-of-the-money calls—those that are just out of the money—to generate the most income.

If, after the call is written, the underlying investment goes up in value, the liability to buy back the call also goes up. The greater liability is directly offset by the increased value of the underlying security, so in a very real sense, the position is *covered* hence the other common name for the strategy—*covered call writing*. If the underlying security goes down, the buy-writer will keep the premium received from the written call with no liability to buy anything back.

In many cases other than a runaway bull market in stocks, a buy-write strategy will outperform an equity index associated with the stock market in which the buy-write strategy operates and does so with less risk. Does that mean that buy-write is better than investing in an index fund? Maybe, but at least different. Additionally, the expected return of a buy-write strategy depends upon how the income is used and where, in terms of moneyness, the call options are written. If a regular cash withdrawal is taken out of the program to facilitate the need for income and the calls are in-the-money (when the underlying security's price is above the call option's strike price), the return may appear bond-like. However, if the proceeds from the sale of calls are reinvested back into the program, like reinvesting dividends, and calls are written out of the money, the return can be stock-like. The first case is designed to provide income, while the second is designed for asset growth. A buy-write strategy can be used as an equity replacement or modified to serve as a fixed-income substitute. We will dig deeper into this idea later.

An Example: One Hundred Shares of Procter & Gamble

Perhaps the best way to illustrate the nuances of buy-writing is through an example. For the purposes of simplicity, the buy-write position illustrated here will be implemented with a stock: specifically, 100 shares of Procter & Gamble stock (PG). Let's say it's mid-October, and PG is trading near 93. For every 100 shares of PG owned, one call option contract can be written as part of a buy-write strategy.

Options are available for trading at a variety of different strike prices and expiration cycles. In this example, the call with a strike price just out of the money with one month until expiration—a November 95 call—is a good choice. Selling one November 95 call contract at the bid price of 2.15 generates $215, less commissions. Between mid–October and the third Friday in November, when this particular option contract expires, one of three things will happen to determine the profitability of the position. Regardless of which way the stock moves, the buy-writer will receive the $215 generated from the sale of the option, but the direction of the stock could affect the value of the total investment. Let's look at each of the three possible scenarios: upward movement, downward movement, and no movement at all.

If the stock stays at 93, the option will expire out of the money—the stock price being less than the strike price; meaning that it will be worthless and nothing will need to be bought back. The value of 100 shares of PG remains the same at $9300, and an additional $215 was added in about a month's time. That works out to over 27 percent per year—nice work if you can get it.

If the stock were to rise, it could be *called away*, meaning that the buy-write investor will be forced to sell the shares of PG at the strike price, in this case $95. So, if PG jumped to $110 per share, the buy-write investor would have $9500 in cash from the sale of the 100 shares at $95 per share, plus the $215 premium generated when the call was written. That's a $415 profit, but if we just owned the shares and didn't write any calls, the $9300 investment would have grown by $1700 to $11,000 on a move from $93 to $110. When stocks or stock markets explode higher, buy-writing tends to lag.

So if the price of PG stays where it is, the buy-write position will make money. The position will also make money if PG advances, but perhaps less than would be made by simply owning PG shares. What if the stock price goes down, in this case to 70? A declining stock price means that the call does not need to be repurchased and the premium will be collected, but the overall investment may lose money on the declining stock price. Although $215 from the written call will be earned, the $2300 loss on the value of PG shares on a decline from 93 to 70 illustrates how the risk of loss in a buy-write position is nearly as great as that of a straight stock purchase. This argues for why a buy-write strategy should be benchmarked against an equity index. Many common buy-write strategies exhibit a high correlation to the stock market.

More to the point, a buy-write position will give up some upside relative to the stock but will lose nearly as much as the stock if the stock price goes down. At first glance, this risk may not seem worth taking. Certainly the risk of loss is one worth considering and we know equity-like risk can be powerful. But the story doesn't have to end here. As long as PG doesn't go out of business, a new buy-write position can be created, generating a new cash flow every month if so desired. Just because the stock dropped nearly 25 percent doesn't mean that the cash flow will dry up.

A decline in the underlying security, whether stock or index, is the principal risk of loss for a buy-write strategy. A drop in stock price will reduce the value of the overall position, but the amount of money that can be generated by selling calls may simultaneously increase offsetting some of that loss. Remember that the price of the PG call with the strike price of 95 written in mid-October was 2.15 when the stock was at $93. Just because the stock dropped 25 percent to $70 doesn't mean that the value of calls just out of the money will go down. They might actually go up because the premium component of option prices tends to increase as the underlying security goes down. It is possible that, even if PG stock declines in value, the amount of income that can be generated by writing PG call options will remain the same or even increase, all else equal.

Unfortunately, this effect could be short-lived. If PG stocks were to drop to $70 by mid-November, the December options—the options that would then be a common choice because they have the least amount of time until they expire—would likely become more expensive, allowing for a similar cash flow as was had in mid-October. But if PG stayed at $70 from mid-November through mid-December, the higher premium might fade, and PG options would decrease in value accordingly. Then there is the risk of underperformance if the stock were to bounce back.

The out-of-the-money option with the highest premium that will generate the most cash when sold when the stock is at $70 could be the one with a $70.50 strike price. If the stock rebounded to $80, for example, all 100 shares would be called away (sold) at $70.50, leaving less cash than necessary to buy another 100 shares and write another call because the stock is now at $80. After a decline in the underlying, it may take longer to get back to even with a buy-write program relative to an investment in the entity to which the calls are attached.

Stock Versus Index Options

Mutual fund managers who pick stocks face a difficult task. They need to know which stocks are more likely to go up than go down to be successful. We spent some of the early parts of this book discussing the challenges that stock pickers have when trying to outperform and it is becoming more difficult all the time. When we consider that, constructing a buy-write strategy through the use of stocks and stock options could prove exceedingly difficult as well. Drawing upon the fact that index funds have generally outperformed active managers, we can consider creating a buy-write strategy through the use of index options.

An index investment offers inexpensive, widely diversified exposure to a market as opposed to an individual stock. Lehman Brothers, Bear Stearns, and others like them illustrated how holding individual stocks places the owner in danger of a total loss if the company blows up. Index investors certainly lost money in the Great Financial Crisis, but distributing the risk across 500 different companies (as in the S&P 500 Index) greatly reduces individual company risk, allowing the investor to take on only the risk for which they have a good chance of being rewarded.

A buy-writing strategy that uses S&P 500 index options isn't quite as simple as buying a stock like PG and then writing PG calls. While S&P 500 Index options track the S&P 500 Index, the price of which is readily available, it isn't possible to invest directly in an index. A whole host of index funds and exchange-traded funds (ETFs) mimic the S&P 500 so closely that the two would be statistically similar to any degree of confidence you like. But nothing says it has to be that way, which is why no products other than cash are deliverable against an S&P 500 Index option. An example will help explain what this means.

In the PG example, a rising stock price might lead to the stock being *called away*, meaning it would be sold from the buy-writer's account at the written call option's strike price. If an S&P 500 Index option was sold to initiate a buy-write position and the index went up, there is no "S&P 500 Index stock" that could be called away. The owner of the call option would receive the amount due in cash, rather than stock, which is why S&P 500 Index options are said to be *cash settled*.

This doesn't mean that a strategy essentially the same as buy-writing can't be implemented with S&P 500 Index options, because it can. Anyone with enough money who chose simply to go into the open market and short sell an S&P 500 Index call option, a *naked position*, could do so with the knowledge that they would have to come up with any necessary cash at expiration. But it might be a lot because the risks associated with naked option selling can be substantial, and with calls the loss is theoretically unlimited.

An index call sold just prior to a stratospheric market advance would result in a tremendous liability to the call seller, who would have to buy it back at an inflated level. With a buy-write position, this risk is mitigated by the fact that the underlying security is owned and can be delivered to the call buyer, who has benefited from the underlying security's advance. More to the point, the liability in a buy-write position is offset by the corresponding increase in the stock price. With S&P 500 Index options, one has nothing to deliver except the cash equivalent of the underlying index, which could be substantial if the index goes up. This is why those who choose to sell S&P 500 Index options need to have a significant amount of money in a margin account to fulfill potential liabilities if needed.

The Vehicles Exist

But, you may ask, what about owning an ETF that seeks to match the S&P 500 and could offset the greater liability to buy back the call when the market advanced? That might do the trick in practicality but not technically. Owning an ETF that tracks the S&P 500, regardless of how well it does so, and then writing an S&P 500 Index call is still considered a naked position. The ETF may *cover* virtually all of the greater liability when the index advances, but it doesn't have to. The lack of an unequivocal connection between the ETFs and the index prevents a buy-write strategy from being implemented with S&P 500 Index options. However, a myriad of other ways exist to employ this valuable concept.

The first possibility is to simply buy S&P 500 ETFs, then write S&P 500 Index calls, which would work, as long as it is understood that the ETFs may not precisely track the index all the time. The structure of ETFs, their policy on reinvesting dividends, and public demand all affect their price relative to that of the index. But some ETFs have options that trade on them, meaning that the ETFs *would* be deliverable in a buy-write strategy because the options are directly connected to the ETF.

One example is the SPDR S&P 500 ETF Trust (SPY). In mid-2018, the SPY was the largest ETF with $259 billion in assets. The SPY also sports the most liquid options market of any ETF or stock. A buy-write strategy could certainly be enacted by buying the SPY then writing SPY options. If necessary, the buy-writer could deliver the shares to the holder of the call. An important distinction about SPY options that differs from S&P 500 Index options is that the SPYs are *American* style, meaning that the owner can exercise the option at any point in time on or prior to expiration. S&P 500 options are *European*—they can only be exercised at expiration. This means that a buy-write strategy could be terminated by the owner of the call any time they wanted to. In most cases, however, the option would not be exercised until very near expiration because with premium still embedded in the price, it is usually not financially advantageous to do so.

A buy-write strategy has the potential to outperform a stock index in the same market. It can be implemented with S&P 500 Index options and ETFs designed to mimic the index; but, in that case, the options would be considered naked. Writing naked options would require a substantial margin account for individuals and may not be permitted for certain institutions. An alternative would be to use ETFs and options against which the ETFs could be delivered—something that can't be done with the S&P 500 Index. That would work, but we also might need to consider the impact of taxes.

Although not a problem for nonprofit institutions, the short-term nature of income from a buy-write strategy can levy a heavy tax burden on an individual. Taxes eat into profits and can be especially painful if the index goes down. Holding ETFs long term but generating income in the short term means that a taxable investor may have to write a big check even after a year when they lost money. If the losses on the ETFs exceed the gains on the written options net of taxes, the buy-write strategy will lose money. If the strategy is employed with ETFs, the options that trade on them would likely produce a short-term taxable gain, which may not be offset by the losses in the underlying securities if the ETFs were held over a long term.

Another way to invest in a buy-write strategy is through an ETF that tracks the *Cboe S&P 500 BuyWrite Index* (BXM). In 2002, Cboe began disseminating the BXM, an index designed to measure the returns of a theoretical portfolio of S&P 500 Index stocks that also systematically sells S&P 500 Index call options against the portfolio. The sold call would be just above the prevailing index level, aka out-of-the-money. The buy-write strategy had been around a long time, but suddenly, the largest options exchange had created a benchmark against which it could be measured. About the same time, professor Robert Whaley wrote an academic paper[2] describing the construction methodology and historical performance of the BXM. Whaley is also known as the creator of the *Cboe Volatility Index* (VIX), which he did about a decade prior to his work on the BXM. Whaley's paper lent a great deal of credibility to buy-writing as investors could see the benefits the strategy could bring. This gave a substantial boost to buy-write programs through greater awareness and understanding and assets began flowing in.

In 2004, researchers from Ibbotson expanded upon Whaley's work with a paper that looked at a longer history and conducted some additional types of analysis on the return data.[3] The Ibbotson Associates research found that the BXM had the best risk-adjusted performance of all equity-based instruments, both before and after controlling for the possible effects of the skew and kurtosis. The compound annual return of the Cboe BXM over its history to that point was 12.4 percent, slightly higher than the 12.2 percent achieved by the S&P 500. The annualized standard deviation of the Cboe BXM, however, had been only 11.0 percent versus 16.5 percent of the S&P 500. This research fueled further inflows into buy-write strategies and acceptance was broadening.

So how has the BXM performed since then? Table 16.1 documents the returns and standard deviations of the BXM and S&P 500 Indexes for trailing periods ending June 2018.

This shows that the BXM trailed over all trailing periods, but that should not necessarily diminish its attractiveness. What we see here is end-point sensitivity due to the stratospheric performance of the US stock market. More recent periods are substantially skewed toward above-average returns for the S&P 500, which influences all the trailing-year comparisons because they all include the same end point.

When we look at calendar year returns in Table 16.2, the relative comparison looks better for the BXM, but the S&P 500 still outperformed most of the time (about 60 percent).

We can also see how frequently the BXM has trailed in recent years. The year 2002, when the BXM was rolled out, was a terrific one for the buy-write index relative to the long-only stock index. Since then, the BXM has trailed the S&P 500 nearly three-quarters of the time. Does the out-of-sample data fail to confirm the original research? Did it not survive discovery? Like so many great ideas, could buy-write strategies have been diluted after a lot of assets flowed in? Maybe, but let's dig a little deeper because we care more about what will happen in the future than what has already taken place.

Table 16.1 Returns and standard deviation of BXM and S&P 500 indexes

	BXM		S&P 500	
	Annualized return	Standard deviation	Annualized return	Standard deviation
1-year	7.3%	3.6%	14.4%	8.6%
3-year	7.7%	5.8%	11.9%	10.7%
5-year	8.1%	5.8%	13.4%	10.1%
10-year	5.7%	11.0%	10.2%	14.8%
Since 2002	9.7%	7.5%	13.3%	11.3%
Inception 1990	8.5%	10.0%	9.7%	14.2%

For periods ending June 2018

Table 16.2 The difference in calendar year returns: BXM versus S&P 500

	Calendar year returns		
	BXM	S&P 500	Difference
1990	4.0%	−3.1%	7.1%
1991	24.4%	30.5%	−6.1%
1992	11.5%	7.6%	3.9%
1993	14.1%	10.1%	4.0%
1994	4.5%	1.3%	3.2%
1995	21.0%	37.6%	−16.6%
1996	15.5%	23.0%	−7.5%
1997	26.6%	33.4%	−6.7%
1998	18.9%	28.6%	−9.6%
1999	21.2%	21.0%	0.1%
2000	7.4%	−9.1%	16.5%
2001	−10.9%	−11.9%	1.0%
2002	−7.6%	−22.1%	14.5%
2003	19.4%	28.7%	−9.3%
2004	8.3%	10.9%	−2.6%
2005	4.2%	4.9%	−0.7%
2006	13.3%	15.8%	−2.5%
2007	6.6%	5.5%	1.1%
2008	−28.7%	−37.0%	8.3%
2009	25.9%	26.5%	−0.5%
2010	5.9%	15.1%	−9.2%
2011	5.7%	2.1%	3.6%
2012	5.2%	16.0%	−10.8%
2013	13.3%	32.4%	−19.1%
2014	5.6%	13.7%	−8.0%
2015	5.2%	1.4%	3.9%
2016	7.1%	12.0%	−4.9%
2017	13.0%	21.8%	−8.8%

Notice that the BXM underperformed by the most when the S&P 500 had its strongest years. That comes as no surprise, and the stock market had been roaring in years leading up to 2017. But the first premise upon which we touched in this book was that future returns of the stock market are not likely to be anywhere near those of the recent past, perhaps seven percent or even lower. But let's say I'm wrong and the future returns will be about average at say, 10 percent. From 1990 through 2017, the S&P 500 failed to top a 10 percent calendar year return on 11 occasions. The BXM outperformed in all but one of those and did so by an average margin of 5.7 percentage points annualized. The year it didn't was 2005 when the S&P 500 was up 4.7 percent while the BXM advanced 4.2 percent. BXM always held up better in years when the S&P 500 declined, providing evidence of equity risk mitigation, which is nice to have. That said, the correlation between the BXM and S&P 500 has been over 87 percent since 1990, so it may not lose as much when the stock market goes down, but it will probably lose something.

Unless the US stock market continues to rip off annual returns of 15 percent or more, a buy-write strategy stands a strong chance of providing outperformance. But whether it outperforms or underperforms, it almost always does so with far less volatility leading to consistently higher risk-adjusted returns. Even if stock market performance is tremendous, a BXM strategy or others like it can serve as a nice addition to a broader investment portfolio. And if market returns fail to meet long-term averages, it could be a terrific one.

A Strategy That's Malleable

Standard buy-write strategies sell calls just out of the money and reinvest the proceeds back into the program. The BXM Index is structured in a similar way as are many buy-write mutual funds. But the concept is expandable and malleable such that it can be modified to reflect different types of risk and reward profiles.

The Impact of Falling Rates

Perhaps the most critical thing to understand when evaluating a potential investment is what that investment is expected to provide. Private equity may make sense for a perpetual institution who can align their ultra-long-term time horizon to access liquidity-constrained investment opportunities. On the other end of the need spectrum is current income. A retiree, or an institution like an endowment or a pension fund, almost always needs an ongoing stream of cash. For those investors, a well-diversified bond portfolio has usually provided for that need. After all, nothing's safer than a US treasury bond. It is backed by the full faith and credit of the US government, which, if needed, could simply print more money to pay back the loan.

If only it were that easy for the rest of us.

Interest rates started high at the beginning of the bull market in the early 1980s, only to drop to the lowest levels ever before bottoming in 2016. In 2011, the ten-year US treasury yield fell below 2 percent for the first time in 70 years and continued to decline all the way to 1.46 percent in July 2016, which was the lowest level in the history of the data since 1900. There is nothing quite like a declining interest rate environment to give stocks a boost. Perpetually declining interest rates allow companies to ever more easily finance expansions, research, and development, and a whole host of other improvements in technology and efficiency. Those factors have driven and will continue to drive capitalism and push stock prices higher over time, but will have a harder go of it in a world potentially devoid of falling rates.

That is not to say, however, that stock prices can't go up in a rising interest rate environment. From December 1959 through December 1969, the ten-year treasury yield rose from 4 percent to 7 percent, while the S&P 500 posted a 7.8 percent annualized return. From December 1959 through December 1982, the same treasury yield rose from 4 to 14 percent, yet the S&P 500 averaged an annualized return of 7.9 percent. Another interesting, and somewhat surprising, point is that despite a positive return from stocks, P/E ratios actually declined along the way. The S&P 500's P/E was 17.7 at the end of 1959 but had dropped to 15.9 by the end of 1969 and to 9.7 by the end of 1982. This is a great illustration of the natural tendency of P/E ratios and interest rates to move in opposite directions, while the stock market posts below average yet positive returns. A similar scenario could be in our future.

Lest we forget, changes in the P/E ratio represent just one of three factors that provide for stock market returns. The other factors, earnings growth and dividends, obviously picked up the slack for a declining P/E ratio in the 1960s and 1970s, because stock market returns were positive. It is perfectly plausible that the subsequent 10 to 20 years following the terrific post-Great Financial Crisis bull market could look a lot like the 1960s and 1970s: dividends may rise due to more favorable tax treatment; the economy could plod along, providing for nominal earnings growth; and, P/E ratios will either stay where they are or even drop a bit, resulting in positive yet below-average stock market returns.

Bonds

But, what about bonds? For investors who are either retired now or an institution with regular spending needs, the amount of money expected from a fixed-income investment is certainly important to know. Far too many retirees who expected a certain amount of money from a fixed-income investment actually received considerably less because interest rates declined. Also, if you sit on the board of an institutional investment plan, you know that providing for ongoing expenses is critically important to achieving your organization's mission. This is where bonds come in, because hoping for positive returns from the sometimes-volatile stock market can adversely inhibit spending amounts during lean stock market years.

So if stocks are expected to post below-average returns, what should be expected from bonds? Current bond yields serve as the best source of information when developing an expectation for future bond returns. Over the long term, bonds don't experience price appreciation as stocks do, so what you see in yield is ultimately what you're likely to get. In mid-2018, for core, investment grade bonds, that number looked a lot like 2.5 percent per year.

I still remember that in my first finance course, the professor quite literally jumped up on the desk and shouted, "When interest rates go up …" then jumped back to the floor and shouted, "…bond prices go down!" He said that if we didn't remember any other thing from the course, we should never forget that connection, and I never have. A rising interest rate environment hurts the returns of fixed-income securities as prices go down. The problem is that the need for cash flow, for a retiree or for an institution, doesn't go away, so a means of providing greater income despite a low yet rising interest rate environment needs to be addressed.

Long-term government bonds didn't fare too well in the rising rate environments of the 1960s and 1970s, returning 1.4 percent annualized during the 1960s and 4.4 percent over the 23 years ending December 1982. In both cases, a long-term government bond investment lost money relative to inflation. If the next 10 to 20 years look like the 10 to 20 starting in 1960, a means of generating income that doesn't lose ground to inflation needs to be found.

Diversification in Bonds

Diversification is not just a good idea at the portfolio level, it has merit within subcategories as well. One good solution to allay some of the risk bond investors endure is to diversify the source of fixed-income exposure. The principal and interest provided by *Treasury Inflation Protected Securities* (TIPS) go up with inflation as measured by the *Consumer Price Index* (CPI). Inflation is a notorious thief of bond returns. Rather than simply buying investment-grade domestic bonds, it may also help to dabble a bit in high-yield or international securities. When compared with domestic investment-grade bonds, these instruments certainly carry a bit more risk, but they actually may lower risk portfolio-wide through diversification.

It also helps if the investment itself is well diversified. Funds that invest with a high-yield or international fixed-income mandate are growing in number, a trend almost certain to continue in the future. Some funds even invest in the sovereign debt of emerging market nations, but as you might imagine, those can be pretty risky. As with stock funds, unique information that can provide a money manager with a competitive advantage in the bond markets is hard to come by. Where it is cheap and common, as in developed countries, everybody has it. Where information is rare, such in emerging economies, it is extraordinarily expensive to cultivate.

Additionally, bond funds are just like stock funds in that they are comprised of individual securities. The same behavioral biases that affect stock pickers can also affect bond pickers. Investing in a bond market other than domestic investment grade can add value and potentially lower risk, but the investment vehicle itself should be widely diversified, have low fees, and make few if any active investment decisions.

Diversification almost always lowers the risk of an investment portfolio, and the higher-risk nature of some of these more exotic fixed-income mandates indicates that a higher return should be expected to compensate for taking greater risk. With the integration of markets worldwide, however, low and potentially rising domestic interest rates may mean lower returns from high-yield and international fixed-income funds. If so, and the other fixed-income mandates still don't provide enough income, obtaining a steady stream of cash whose source doesn't lose value after inflation could be harder to come by than in the past. There is another possibility, which is where the buy-write strategy comes in.

Stock-Like or Bond-Like?

Is buy-write writing stock-like, bond-like, or something in between? The way to answer that question is to treat the investment like each kind and see how it reacts. Before we get to a way we might solve a problem with low expected stock returns, let's first make a buy-write strategy look a bit more stock-like.

Buy-Writing as a Stock-Like Strategy

Looking at buy-writing as a stock-like strategy means plowing all income back into the account to seek long-term asset growth and the benefit of compounding, just like a stock investment. Most stocks don't pay much income—less now than they once did. The role of stocks in a portfolio is to grow assets through reinvestment of dividends or, in the case of a buy-write strategy, income from short-selling calls. In 2002–2003, I conducted a study showing how this might work. I contemplated updating it with more current numbers or not including it here at all, but I believe, though dated, the study has merit and is perfectly applicable today. Table 16.3 evaluates the buy-write strategy when implemented in a stock-like fashion with all the income generated from writing the calls reinvested.

The table shows a fictional buy-write strategy over the course of one year, starting on expiration Friday in August 2002 and continuing through August expiration 2003. Each month, the program would have gone long one S&P 500

Table 16.3 Buy-write strategy example—stock-like

Close on date	Futures price	Call option	Price	Beginning option value	Ending option value	Gain/loss on futures	Account value
August 16, 2002	928.0	September 930	28.4	$7100	—	—	$250,000
September 20, 2002	842.2	September 930	0.0	—	$0	($21,450)	$257,100
	842.2	October 845	32.0	$8000	—	—	
October 18, 2002	883.2	October 845	38.2	—	$9550	$10,250	$243,650
	883.2	November 885	30.0	$7500	—	—	
November 15, 2002	908.9	November 885	23.9	—	$5975	$6425	$251,850
	908.9	December 910	27.0	$6750	—	—	
December 20, 2002	896.7	December 910	0.0	—	$0	($3050)	$259,050
	896.7	January 900	22.8	$5700	—	—	
January 17, 2003	903.1	January 900	3.1	—	$775	$1600	$261,700
	903.1	February 905	24.9	$6225	—	—	
February 21, 2003	847.2	February 905	0.0	—	$0	($13,975)	$268,750
	847.2	March 850	24.9	$6225	—	—	
March 21, 2003	893.2	March 850	43.2	—	$10,800	$11,500	$261,000
	893.2	April 895	25.8	$6450	—	—	
April 17, 2003	891.2	April 895	0.0	—	$0	($500)	$268,150
	891.2	May 895	18.2	$4550	—	—	
May 16, 2003	944.3	May 895	49.3	—	$12,325	$13,275	$272,200
	944.3	June 945	19.6	$4900	—	—	
June 20, 2003	1001.7	June 945	56.7	—	$14,175	$14,350	$278,050
	1001.7	July 1005	12.7	$3175	—	—	
July 18, 2003	990.5	July 1005	0.0	—	$0	($2800)	$281,400
	990.5	August 995	17.2	$4300	—	—	
August 15, 2003	990.5	August 995	0.0	—	$0	$0	$282,900
							$282,900

Index futures contract (a proxy for owning the Index), sold the call that was just out of the money with one month until expiration, and then waited until the option expired. In 2002, the number of different S&P 500 Index options by different strike were not as numerous as they are today; but, there were usually ones available with strike prices divisible by five so the call that was sold was the one with a strike price of the S&P 500 Index futures contract rounded up to the next number divisible by five. Also, front-month options (those with one month or less until expiration) were used, because the decay in time premium is steepest when expiration is the closest. The decline in option premium is the principal source of income from a buy-write strategy, so implementing it when the decline is steepest provides an efficient means of investing.

In this example, a fictional $250,000 is used as the starting balance, because that is approximately the amount of money that would have been needed to have index-like exposure from owning a futures contract. Multiplying the futures contract valued at 992.0 times $250 per point, we get $248,000, the beginning value of the position and approximately $250,000. This is almost direct market exposure, meaning no leverage or excess cash, neither of which is needed for buy-writing.

Three things are worth noting in this example.

1. *The futures price in August 2003 was higher than in August 2002.* An investment in the futures contract alone would have added $15,625, but the value of the buy-write investment would have risen nearly $33,000. This shows the capital appreciation power of reinvested buy-writing income.
2. *The account value declined during the first month, but not as much as would have been experienced if the $250,000 was invested in an S&P 500 Index fund.*
3. *The futures contract moved lower from October 2002 through February 2003 expiration, but the account value would have risen to $261,000, up from $251,850 in October.* This important distinction illustrates the uniqueness of buy writing. In addition to the fact that this buy-write position is long a futures contract, income is being generated and reinvested into the account every month, so it is less risky than an index fund when the market declines. Profitability from buy-writing is not only a function of movements in the market, it is a function of time. The longer the index remains stagnant, the more likely a buy-write strategy will outperform it.

This represents an important fundamental truth of investing—option time premium erodes over time. *Option premium* reflects the understanding that the underlying entity will move in one direction or another during the option's life, and the magnitude of the premium is directly related to size of the expected move. It is what makes an option's price higher than its intrinsic value. *Intrinsic value* is simply the difference between the underlying's price and the strike price. If a call on the S&P 500 Index has a strike price of 2775 while the index is at 2800, its intrinsic value is 25, but chances are good that the price is much higher than that due to premium. The amount of premium in an option depends on the likelihood of the option ending in-the-money at expiration. No one knows for certain what can happen between now and when an option expires and the premium reflects that. As the likelihood of expiring either in or out-of-the-money becomes known, the premium baked into the price goes down until the option price equates its intrinsic value at expiration.

So far we have discussed two important characteristics of options that occur with a high degree of consistency:

- The implied volatility priced into options usually exceeds realized volatility—a phenomenon known as the volatility risk premium.
- Absolute option prices tend to decline over time as the premium fades, steepening in relation to when the location where the option will be at expiration is known with a higher degree of certainty.

Back to our simulation. Let's say we would have initiated the buy-write program just prior to a strong stock market rally. An index fund investment made on February 21, 2003, would have advanced 18 percent by June expiration later that year, but the buy-write strategy would have grown just less than 8 percent. That lag when the index posted mid-teens returns is emblematic of the years when the BXM trailed the S&P 500 as the stock market was rocketing higher. But just as we would expect better performance from buy-write during more tepid stock market times, we see that in this simulation as well. From August 2002 through June 2003, the S&P 500 advanced 8 percent, but the buy-write strategy added nearly 13 percent. Although this is just one example and recognizing the impact that the duration of the return and volatility it might experience along the way would have on performance, a buy-write strategy might be expected to outperform the stock market when equity indexes are posting below-average returns.

Buy-Writing as a Bond-Like Strategy

Now let's look at Table 16.4 to see what would happen if we treated a buy-write strategy like a bond. When an investor buys a bond or a bond fund, they are effectively making a loan to someone who provides them with a return stream over the life of the bond. Buy-writing works in a similar way, but the return

Table 16.4 Buy-write strategy example, all income withdrawn

Close on date	Futures price	Call option	Price	Beginning option value	Ending option value	Gain/loss on futures	Account value
August 16, 2002	928.0	September 930	28.4	$7100	–	–	$250,000
September 20, 2002	842.2	September 930	0.0	–	$0	($21,450)	$250,000
	842.2	October 845	32.0	$8000	–	–	$228,550
October 18, 2002	883.2	October 845	38.2	–	$9550	$10,250	$229,250
	883.2	November 885	30.0	$7500	–	–	
November 15, 2002	908.9	November 885	23.9	–	$5975	$6425	$229,700
	908.9	December 91 0	27.0	$6750	–	–	
December 20, 2002	896.7	December 910	0.0	–	$0	($3050)	$226,650
	896.7	January 900	22.8	$5700	–	–	
January 17, 2003	903.1	January 900	3.1	–	$775	$1600	$227,475
	903.1	February 905	24.9	$6225	–	–	
February 21, 2003	847.2	February 905	0.0	–	$0	($13,975)	$213,500
	847.2	March 850	24.9	$6225	–	–	
March 21, 2003	893.2	March 850	43.2	–	$10,800	$11,500	$214,200
	893.2	April 895	25.8	$6450	–	–	
April 17, 2003	891.2	April 895	0.0	–	$0	($500)	$213,700
	891.2	May 895	18.2	$4550	–	–	
May 16, 2003	944.3	May 895	49.3	–	$12,325	$13,275	$214,650
	944.3	June 945	19.6	$4900	–	–	
June 20, 2003	1001.7	June 945	56.7	–	$14,175	$14,350	$214,825
	1001.7	July 1005	12.7	$3175	–	–	
July 18, 2003	990.5	July 1005	0.0	–	$0	($2800)	$212,025
	990.5	August 995	17.2	$4300	–	–	
August 15, 2003	990.5	August 995	0.0	–	$0	$0	$212,025

stream is generally derived from writing out-of-the-money calls. Let's look at the previous example, but instead of reinvesting all the income generated from selling calls back into the program, let's assume that the income is removed from the account (presumably spent by the investor). In this case, the buy-write strategy is structured as a bond-like rather than a stock-like investment.

Income from this strategy was generated regardless of movements in the stock market, just as it would be from buying a bond. The column titled "Beginning option value" documents the amount of money a buy-writing investor would have generated during this period (a total of $70,875). That equates to 28 percent per year, which if spent, would be far greater than the coupon payments made by most bonds. This income can be generated regardless of stock market performance, *but only to a point.* The problem is that the "principal" is steadily declining, shown in the column titled "Account value." This is because the account loses money when the S&P 500 Index futures contract goes down but doesn't make it back when the futures go up. In August 2002, the futures contract was priced at 928. It dropped to 842 by September expiration and subsequently recovered to 883 by October expiration. The recovery in the value of the futures contract from September to October was muted by the fact that the call, written just out of the money, required an equally great liability at October expiration.

Looking at this another way, notice that the September call, written to provide the income, had a strike price of 930, just higher than the futures value at that time. When the futures contract dropped to 842 by September expiration, the October call had a strike price of 845. Like the prior month's option, it had a strike price just higher than the futures value at that time. If the October call had been written with a strike price of 930, as the September call had been, the overall investment could have benefited from the full recovery in the futures contract. Unfortunately, the October 930 call, when the futures were trading at 842 on expiration Friday in September, was essentially worthless, providing no income; writing it was a waste of time and commission charges.

To get the income, the calls can't be written very far out of the money, which means that strong upward moves in the market will not help this investment strategy. As with every investment, there is a trade-off between risk and reward. There's no free lunch, but a savvy investor who understands these concepts can at least choose what they would like to eat.

Buy-writing can behave similarly to a bond by providing ongoing income to the investor, but it differs in one very important way. A bond will return the principal amount to the investor when it matures (assuming it doesn't default), but unless some of the income generated is reinvested, a buy-write position will eventually deplete its principal completely. It is easy to see how this could happen. Every time the futures contract—or index, stock, or whatever serves as the underlying security—goes down in value, the next call written will have a strike price just above the futures value, capping advances at that new, lower level. If the underlying security then bounces back, the call will go up in value just as much, meaning that the advance in the underlying security will be fully offset by the greater liability to buy back the call.

In short, and considering just the equity component, a buy-write position takes all the pain from declines in the underlying but gets none of the benefits when it advances. The 28 percent coupon would have been nice while it lasted, but the principal on which that coupon was being generated declined steadily and would have eventually dried up completely, disallowing any future income and leaving the investor with a total loss.

Structuring Buy-Write Correctly

That scenario is pretty grim but simply illustrates what can happen if the strategy is not structured properly. What if, instead of a 28 percent coupon, a 10 percent coupon could be had, with the remaining money reinvested into the portfolio so that the principal could remain intact? A 10 percent coupon is higher than most fixed-income investments and the reinvestment of the remaining income might provide for enough asset growth to ensure that 10 percent could be generated in perpetuity. Continuing with the earlier example, let's adjust the strategy in Table 16.5 such that income is spent on a 10 percent-per-year pace, while the remainder is reinvested in the account.

If we spent only a portion of the income generated from selling calls and reinvested the remainder, the strategy might serve as a source of fixed income without completely diminishing the account's total value. So we adjust the simulation such that we remove $2050 per month (approximately 10 percent of $250,000 divided by 12) and reinvest the rest.

Table 16.5 shows that income could be generated without detracting from total return. In this case, only $2050 was taken out of the "Beginning option value" column, and the remainder was reinvested into the "Account value" column. Notice that in this example when the buy-write strategy spent income at a 10 percent annual rate, the account value actually rose. Generally, when the index declines, the strategy loses less because, as when we treated buy-writing like a stock, the reinvested income buffers the position against a market-related loss. So, for this short period at least, we observed a strategy that could have returned 10 percent consistently with no loss of principal.

This was just one example of how buy-write writing could be used in the potentially less-accommodating markets of the future. Remember that inflation

Table 16.5 Buy-write strategy example, 10 percent yield and remainder reinvested

Close on date	Futures price	Call option	Price	Beginning option value	Ending option value	Gain/loss on futures	Account value
							$250,000
August 16, 2002	928.0	September 930	28.4	$7100	–	–	$255,050
September 20, 2002	842.2	September 930	0.0	–	$0	($21,450)	
	842.2	October 845	32.0	$8000	–	–	$239,550
October 18, 2002	883.2	October 845	38.2	–	$9550	$10,250	$245,700
	883.2	November 885	30.0	$7500	–	–	
November 15, 2002	908.9	November 885	23.9	–	$5975	$6425	$250,850
	908.9	December 910	27.0	$6750	–	–	
December 20, 2002	896.7	December 910	0.0	–	$0	($3050)	$251,450
	896.7	January 900	22.8	$5700	–	–	
January 17, 2003	903.1	January 900	3.1	–	$775	$1600	$256,450
	903.1	February 905	24.9	$6225	–	–	
February 21, 2003	847.2	February 905	0.0	–	$0	($13,975)	$246,650
	847.2	March 850	24.9	$6225	–	–	
March 21, 2003	893.2	March 850	43.2	–	$10,800	$11,500	$251,750
	893.2	April 895	25.8	$6450	–	–	
April 17, 2003	891.2	April 895	0.0	–	$0	($500)	$253,750
	891.2	May 895	18.2	$4550	–	–	
May 16, 2003	944.2	May 895	49.3	–	$12,325	$13,275	$257,550
	944.3	June 945	19.6	$4900	–	–	
June 20, 2003	1001.7	June 945	56.7	–	$14,175	$14,350	$258,850
	1001.7	July 1005	12.7	$3175	–	–	
July 18, 2003	990.5	July 1005	0.0	–	$0	($2800)	
	990.5	August 995	17.2	$4300	–	–	$258,300
August 15, 2003	990.5	August 995	0.0	–	$0	$0	$258,300

reduces the value of money over time, a factor that this short-term example did not consider. Obviously, investors should fully understand the risks involved and choose a strategy consistent with their risk tolerances, but if buy-writing could provide a steady 10 percent or even 8 percent income, it would prove a valuable tool and a helpful addition to most investment portfolios.

The Downside

A buy-write strategy can be formed as a fixed-income substitute, but there is the risk that buy-writing will post losses during a bear market in stocks. The larger the coupon amount taken out of the strategy, the bigger the hole that will be dug during stock market declines. Buy-write strategies constructed as equity-like with all the income reinvested tend to exhibit a high correlation to the stock market. The high correlation between buy-write and equities suggests that, although lessened, buy-writing could lose money when the stock market declines. However, the losses will be limited because of the perpetual income generation, which actually becomes more lucrative during market declines. The important point to remember is that bond prices will go down when interest rates go up, so a seemingly low-risk bond could lose money when rates move higher. In mid-2018, interest rates remained low but started creeping up, so providing for consistent income that is not as adversely affected by a rising rate environment may be prudent.

Conclusion

To date, we have discussed a variety of different ways to employ a buy-write strategy. Treating it like a stock and/or investing in an ETF that tracks the BXM, for example, may improve returns relative to a long-only stock index, if that index posts returns near or below long-term averages. If treated like a bond, a double-digit income could potentially be harvested consistently without significant risk to the principal, but it could be adversely affected during stock market declines.

Perhaps more so than other investments, futures contracts and options can be dangerous. It is important to understand the risks and employ the help of a professional advisor qualified to provide sound advice on structuring the strategy so it incurs no more risk than necessary. Finally, there are no guarantees that the future will allow for the same opportunities that were illustrated in this chapter's example. Just because a consistent 10 percent return could be had in the past doesn't mean it will be had in the future. A stock market that declines far enough could still do great damage to a buy-write account. Nonetheless, the strategy's potential makes it compelling relative to the traditional stock and bond strategies. If the future comes to pass as expected or something near to it, stock market returns may disappoint many an investor believing that the astronomical returns will continue unabated forever. In such a future, buy-write strategies may be able to make up the shortfall and limit the bear market in expectations.

Notes

1. Aristotle. Aristotle in 23 Volumes, Vol. 21, translated by H. Rackham. Cambridge, MA, Harvard University Press; London, William Heinemann Ltd. 1944. Book 1. Section 1259b.
2. Whaley, Robert E. [2002]: "Return and Risk of Cboe Buy-Write Monthly Index," *Journal of Derivatives*, Winter issue, pp. 35–42.
3. Barry E. Feldman and Dhruv Roy. *The Journal of Investing* Summer 2005, 14 (2) 66–83.

17

Put Selling

Buy-write strategies have shown an ability to outperform the long-only equity market when stocks post below-average returns. It represents one of the oldest options-based strategies, but it remains a relatively untapped investment resource and is certainly not the only one. The Volatility Risk Premium (VRP) can be monetized in a variety of ways. While buy-writing allows investors to benefit from selling call options, selling put options can serve as a source of investment returns as well.

Just as the Cboe created an index that mimics a common buy-write methodology (which could be used as a benchmark against which such strategies could be measured as well), they also developed an index that is based upon selling puts. They have several actually, with the most prominent being the Cboe S&P PutWrite Index (PUT). The PUT is a benchmark index that measures the performance of a hypothetical portfolio that sells S&P 500 Index put options against collateralized cash reserves held in a money market account.

The PUT was first launched in 2007. It is similar in theory to the BXM, which hypothetically owns all the stocks in the S&P 500 then sells S&P 500 call options against those holdings, where the PUT sells S&P 500 put options against cash that is held in reserve.

Specifically, the PUT is designed to sell a sequence of one-month, *at-the-money*, S&P 500 Index puts and invest cash in one and three-month Treasury Bill rates. The number of puts sold varies from month to month but is limited so that the amount held in cash can finance the maximum possible loss from final settlement of the S&P 500 puts. In the worst-case scenario, the amount at risk for the PUT investor is limited to the amount that was invested.

M. J. Oyster, *Success in a Low-Return World*,
https://doi.org/10.1007/978-3-319-99855-8_17

Said a different way, if the S&P 500 Index fell to zero, a PUT investor would lose all of their mandate but nothing more (no leverage). In this respect, the strategy is fully cash collateralized or *cash secured*.

We noted in the prior chapter that the BXM exhibits a high correlation to the S&P 500. The PUT does as well, so an investor choosing to make an allocation to a PUT strategy or something close to it might consider sourcing it from their equity risk bucket. We looked at how BXM has performed versus the S&P 500; now, let's do the same for PUT. Trailing period performance through June 2018 is shown in Table 17.1 below.

In similar fashion to the BXM, the PUT underperformed the S&P 500 over trailing periods ending June 2017 given the meteoric stock market rise over the years prior. Even out to ten years, which covers the bulk of the post Great Recession rally, PUT lagged the S&P 500. It also trailed since its release in 2007. Should we dismiss it? Certainly not. Let's look at calendar year returns in Table 17.2 for some additional perspective.

A similar pattern exists here relative to that observed with the BXM. Yes, the PUT underperformed in six of the eight years up to and including 2017 but only those when the S&P 500 was posting above-average performance. The story was different when stock market returns were lower. From 1990 through 2017, calendar year returns for the S&P 500 were below 10 percent 11 times. PUT outperformed it in every one and did so by an average of 7.8 percentage points, thus limiting equity risk during times of stress. Though it held up better than the stock market, PUT usually lost money in years when the stock market declined and exhibited an 83 percent correlation to the S&P 500 Index over monthly data from January 1990 through June 2018.

If you are thinking that there sure are a lot of similarities between BXM and PUT, you would be right. In fact, they should theoretically have the exact same return profile. But how could that be? One owns stock and sells calls, the other owns cash and sells puts. We can get there but we should first talk about put-call parity.

Table 17.1 PUT vs S&P 500 trailing performance

	PUT		S&P 500	
	Annualized return	Standard deviation	Annualized return	Standard deviation
1-year	5.7%	4.3%	14.4%	8.6%
3-year	7.8%	5.8%	11.9%	10.7%
5-year	8.0%	5.9%	13.4%	10.1%
10-year	6.8%	11.2%	10.2%	14.8%
Since 2007	4.7%	11.3%	6.4%	15.0%
Inception 1990	9.7%	9.6%	9.7%	14.2%

For periods ending June 2018

Table 17.2 The difference in calendar year returns: PUT versus S&P 500

| | Calendar year returns | | |
	PUT	S&P 500	Difference
1990	8.9%	−3.1%	12.0%
1991	21.3%	30.5%	−9.1%
1992	13.8%	7.6%	6.2%
1993	14.1%	10.1%	4.1%
1994	7.1%	1.3%	5.8%
1995	16.9%	37.6%	−20.7%
1996	16.4%	23.0%	−6.6%
1997	27.7%	33.4%	−5.7%
1998	18.5%	28.6%	−10.0%
1999	21.0%	21.0%	0.0%
2000	13.1%	−9.1%	22.2%
2001	−10.6%	−11.9%	1.3%
2002	−8.6%	−22.1%	13.5%
2003	21.8%	28.7%	−6.9%
2004	9.5%	10.9%	−1.4%
2005	6.7%	4.9%	1.8%
2006	15.2%	15.8%	−0.6%
2007	9.5%	5.5%	4.0%
2008	−26.8%	−37.0%	10.2%
2009	31.5%	26.5%	5.0%
2010	9.0%	15.1%	−6.0%
2011	6.2%	2.1%	4.1%
2012	8.1%	16.0%	−7.9%
2013	12.3%	32.4%	−20.1%
2014	6.4%	13.7%	−7.3%
2015	6.4%	1.4%	5.0%
2016	7.8%	12.0%	−4.2%
2017	10.8%	21.8%	−11.0%

Put-Call Parity

Previously we mentioned that demand for put options when the stock market declines leads to higher implied volatility as part of a put option's price that then manifests in call option pricing as well. That's what makes the VIX go up when the stock market goes down. The price connection between puts and calls is known as *put-call parity*. It seems strange that demand for puts could somehow lead to demand for calls, but here's how it works.

Put-call parity assumes, and it is a good assumption, that if an option becomes displaced from its fair value, investors will either buy it or sell it until they move the price back to fair value through a process known as arbitrage. After all, the Black-Scholes model allows an investor to see what an option should be priced for, and if it is quite different, a buy or sell transaction should take place.

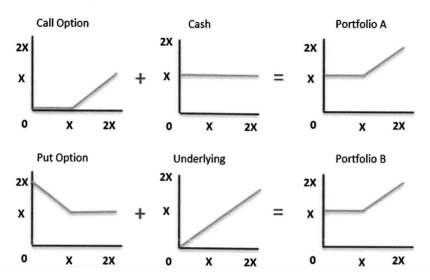

Fig. 17.1 Portfolio examples: payoff profiles

Let's say I own a call option plus some cash, Portfolio A. If whatever the call option's underlying increases in value, I make money, but I don't lose anything more than I've already spent if the underlying goes down. I'm only out the cost of the call option. Now let's say I own a put with the same strike price and expiration date as the call on the same underlying instrument, and I own the underlying as well, Portfolio B. If the underlying goes up, I make money. Yes, the put won't be worth anything, but I will earn from the underlying's ascent. If the underlying goes down, it loses value but is offset by the increasing price of my put so I don't lose anything more than I've already spent. The payoff profiles of both portfolios are illustrated in Fig. 17.1. Even though they hold different things, the behavior of the underlying leads to the same payoff profile for both portfolios. They make money when the underlying increases and break even when it decreases.

This shows that there is a direct connection between the call, put, and the underlying that has to remain intact at all times. If external demand for puts comes in due to an increase in market volatility thus causing the premium (the option's price less its intrinsic value) to rise due to an increase in implied volatility, the linkage will lead to higher premiums in calls as well. If you want to get really wonky, we could look at the mathematical formula that describes the put-call parity relationship.

$$C + X / (1 + r)^t = So + P$$

Where:

C = Call premium
P = Put premium
X = Strike price of both the call and the put
r = Annual interest rate
t = Time, in years; and,
So = Initial price of the underlying.

Without getting into weeds too deeply here, the one thing worth noting is that the call premium and put premium are on the opposite sides of the formula. Therefore, an increase in put premium would lead to an increase in call premium if all the other functions remained the same.

So why should the BXM and the PUT deliver the same returns over time? Let's think about what exactly we have with each. BXM is long equity exposure, short an at the money call. With a call sold at-the-money, the equity exposure is capped so total return during a stock market rise is limited to whatever we received from selling the call. Downside can be as much as the stock market when it falls, plus premium from call selling. PUT is constructed differently but has the exact same payoff profile. Stock market rises and the strategy doesn't participate beyond what was received from selling the put. Stock market declines and the sold put incurs a greater and greater liability in line with the market, so it too will experience a comparable decline when the stock market falls less the premium earned by selling the put.

But we have a funny little problem. PUT has outperformed BXM by a fairly sizable amount since 1990. Please refer to Fig. 17.2 below.

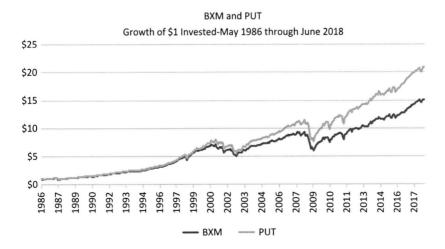

Fig. 17.2 BXM and PUT: growth of $1

When I first thought about this, I thought well, of course puts are more expensive than calls so selling them should provide a greater return versus selling calls. That might explain some of it but probably not all because though puts are indeed more expensive than calls, much of that is manifested in the out-of-the-money variety. Puts and calls at the same at-the-money strike with the same expiration should have the same embedded premium and thus the two strategies with the same payoff profile should perform identically over long periods of time. But they haven't. The reason has to do with a subtle nuance associated with their specific construction methodologies.

In 2014, Catherine Shalen with Cboe dug into the *BXM and PUT Conundrum*[1] and found the answer. She first noticed that though the PUT outperformed the BXM over all periods, the difference between the two began to widen after 1992. Tellingly in November 1992, the final settlement of S&P 500 Index options shifted from the close to the open. Since then, the options have been settled to something called the *special opening quotation* or SOQ of the S&P 500 instead of its closing value. When an option expires, the value of the underlying will determine the option's ending value. For the S&P 500, it isn't the listed closing price or the first printed price the following day, it is the price calculated from the first trade of all S&P 500 stocks the day after options stop trading, in many cases the third Friday of the month. This is the SOQ and should not be confused with the first tick of the S&P 500 Index because the two often vary and can do so by surprisingly wide margins.

Shalen figured at least part of the explanation was there. She also indicated that on an ongoing basis, PUT has slightly higher equity exposure than BXM, describing it as *leverage*. Both BXM and PUT seek at-the-money options to sell, but will go just out of the money if a perfect match isn't available. This means that PUT options will generally exhibit lower strike prices giving them a modestly higher amount of leverage.

In March 2017, Roni Israelov followed up with a paper[2] that also showed that the differences in return between the two indexes could be explained by an expiration day event. He calculated what the performance would have been between BXM and PUT on all but expiration days and found the performance premium of PUT disappeared nearly completely. So what exactly is going on?

The SOQ, the S&P 500 price to which S&P 500 Index options are settled, is usually established early in the trading day just after 9:30 AM ET. New options positions are not then established until a *volume weighted average price* (VWAP) is calculated from trading activity between 11:30 AM and 1:30 PM. Now let's think about what's going on between 9:30 AM and 1:30 PM. The PUT doesn't own anything but the BXM owns the S&P 500.

Said another way, PUT has a beta to the S&P 500 of 0.0 while the BXM has a beta of 1.0. My first thought was then why doesn't BXD outperform PUT? It has more equity exposure and the stock market has gone up over time. That's where another quirk comes in. On expiration days between the SOQ and the end of the VWAP period at 1:30 PM isn't a really great time to have equity exposure. Market participants are reversing hedges and there is often a premium between the SOQ and other intra-day values of the S&P 500 on expiration dates. The BXM is effectively short the SOQ when calls are in the money. It is short a call and wants the SOQ to come in as low as possible, but it is usually elevated temporarily relative to the index itself, which generally does not perform well on expiration mornings. Israelov pointed out that on average, between 2004 and 2015, the S&P 500 Index was down 23 basis points on option expiration mornings. With other minor considerations and taken 12 times per year, this effect almost perfectly explained the difference. So PUT has outperformed BXM, even though it shouldn't, but probably will continue to do so unless the calculation methodology is changed (not likely).

Delta Hedging

Both the BXM and PUT offer a solid opportunity to outperform the S&P 500 in the future, particularly if the stock market performance fails to exceed long-term averages. Both BXM and PUT are terrific strategies, but both have a high correlation to stock market. That equity exposure, however, can be removed through a process called *delta hedging*. *Delta* describes the expected change in an option's price based upon a change in price experienced by the option's underlying instrument. An example can show how it might work.

The easiest way to think about delta is with a stock and an option that trades on that stock. Let's say an investor believes that put options are over-priced and wants to short sell some into the marketplace. They short a put option on XYZ stock, which has a delta of -0.5 but by shorting they incur the liability to buy it back at some later date. Put options increase in value when the underlying security (XYZ stock in this case) loses value, thus increasing the shorter's liability. They lose when the underlying loses, so the sign of their delta exposure is positive. They are delta 0.5. That means that for an instantaneous $1 decline in XYZ stock, the option will move up in value by 50 cents. An investor who is short that option (having sold it) incurs a liability to pay the holder whatever it is worth at expiration. With a 0.5 delta, the option seller is half exposed to the risk of XYZ declining, a risk that can be mitigated by shorting S&P 500 Index futures in an amount that is 50 percent as large as the notional amount (mandate size) of the short option position. Now the investor, at least for an instant, has limited their downside equity risk. Sounds good and simple, but not so easy to implement.

With markets constantly in motion while they are open, the delta of an option, particularly one near the money, doesn't stay stable for long. An investor can delta hedge equity risk, but then may quickly find themselves either under- or over-hedged after a move in the underlying. After this occurs, the position will need to be reweighted and configured to reflect the proper amount of hedging. Depending upon how frequently the reconfiguring takes place, doing so can prove costly from both a financial and time point of view. Less frequent reconfiguring can leave a position exposed to unwanted risks between rehedging events.

Of course, there is another problem. What if XYZ stock declines faster than the S&P 500. The liability to compensate the put option's owner will increase greater than the offsetting short in S&P 500 Index futures. This is known as *basis risk*, where a hedge isn't perfectly matched with whatever risk it is trying to protect against. Shorting XYZ stock could take away basis risk but shorting stocks comes with some additional costs. The owner of a stock may provide you the opportunity to borrow it and then sell it into the marketplace but will require compensation for the time over which the shorting occurs. Additionally, an investor who is short a stock is responsible for paying the dividend if the stock issues one. That is a mistake I made early in my career and one I will never forget.

Then what happens if the stock market and/or XYZ goes up? The hedged position is short the S&P 500 Index futures so it will lose money on that part of the investment during market ascents, which is offset only by the premium received when the put option was sold. As part of a larger portfolio with additional equity risk exposure, that might be OK but could inhibit the strategy when viewed in isolation.

Delta hedging is employed by many and it can help dial in a particular risk/reward exposure, but the trade-offs between cost and time on one side and the potential for unwanted risks on the other should be considered.

Selling Puts for Rebalancing Purposes

To date we talked about how put selling can be employed to enhance returns. PUT can offer the potential for outperformance relative to the S&P 500 and can prove particularly effective during below-average stock market periods. Put selling can also serve other portfolio needs, one in particular is rebalancing.

Another paper by Roni Israelov, in collaboration with Harsha Tummala,[3] looked at how, instead of using traditional techniques, portfolio rebalancing could be aided through the use of option selling. The thought is that investors, particularly institutional investors, are deliberate in their choices regarding subcategory asset allocation. As markets move, allocations deviate from original targets thus exposing the investment portfolio to unintended and undesirable risks. Selling options can not only reduce the impact of such risks, the process can enhance return as it monetizes the volatility risk premium.

Israelov and Tummala included an example of an investor managing a $10 billion portfolio with a 60 percent allocation to stocks and 40 percent to bonds. In this case, it was a single stock trading at $100. Then call and put options (that they assumed were European meaning they could be exercised only at expiration) were sold at strike prices near the stock's current value. Movement in the stock would then lead to either a purchase or a sale of the underlying stock.

They considered a scenario where the stock rose 4 percent to $104 while the value of the bond side of the portfolio remained unchanged. Now the investor holds $6.24 billion in stocks (60 million shares of a $104 stock) and $4 billion in bonds having moved the percentage allocations to 61/39. The traditional rebalancing solution would require a simultaneous sale of $96 million of stock and purchase of $96 million in bonds to get back to 60/40. But the investor sold calls that ended in-the-money requiring the sale of stock at the $100 strike price, the revenue from which could be used to buy the necessary amount of bonds to bring the portfolio back to 60/40.

Had the stock gone down, a similar process would be enacted. A 4 percent decline in the stock value would bring that side of the portfolio down to $5.76 billion and again, assuming no change in the bonds' value, results in a 59/61 allocation. But the puts sold at the beginning would require the purchase of stock, which could be funded by selling some of the bonds to bring the portfolio back to 60/40.

The point of all this is twofold. First, the moves that would have been made (selling stock after it had gone up, buying stock after a decline) would have been conducted with traditional rebalancing anyway, but unlike more commonly used methods, premium is being generated every time an option is sold. Options tend to be overpriced relative to fair value, so selling them over time (monetizing the Volatility Risk Premium) can provide a return enhancement. Second, an option-selling overlay can provide necessary discipline to help avoid behavioral errors that can inhibit returns. Think about a portfolio that just holds stocks and bonds—no option-selling overlay. If the stock drops by some percentage amount, and perhaps remains there for an extended period of time, the investor may be tempted to sell it thus locking in a loss and permanently impairing that investment capital. If the analysis that led to the initial allocation was sound and hasn't changed, a decline in the stock's price should prompt a purchase not a sale, which is exactly what the overlay forces the investor to do.

Conclusion

We started the discussion of the Volatility Risk Premium with the buy-write strategy in Chap. 16, moving to put selling in this chapter as well as delta hedging and an options overlay strategy that can assist in portfolio rebalancing. The BXM and the PUT, as well as similar indexes and strategies, offer the potential for outperformance, particularly if stock market performance is soft. Delta hedging can offer protection against equity risk, but comes with added costs, complexity, and different kinds of risks. Risk is like energy—it cannot be completely eliminated, but it can be changed into something different that we may prefer more. The Volatility Risk Premium is perhaps the most significant, untapped investment resource available to investors today. Monetizing it with common buy-write and cash-secured put-selling strategies provides a good opportunity for stock market outperformance but requires the acceptance of a high degree of stock market correlation. Perhaps there is another way.

Notes

1. Shalen, Catherine, "The BXM and PUT Conundrum," Cboe Paper. 2014.
2. Israelov, Roni, "PutWrite versus BuyWrite: Yes, Put-Call Parity Holds Here Too," AQR Capital Management, LLC. March, 2017.
3. Israelov, Roni and Tummala, Harsha, "An Alternative Option to Portfolio Rebalancing," (October 30, 2017). Available at SSRN: https://ssrn.com/abstract=3061975 or https://doi.org/10.2139/ssrn.3061975.

18

The Options Income Index

Introduction

On several occasions, we have mentioned the Volatility Risk Premium (VRP), which is the difference between the implied volatility priced into options and the subsequent realized volatility thereafter. If options were priced at exactly their fair value, implied volatility would equal realized volatility, but it doesn't. Implied frequently exceeds the realized. The persistent overpricing of options provides an opportunity to monetize the disparity into a viable investment strategy. I have said it before that I firmly believe the VRP represents the most significant untapped investment resource available to investors today.

Unfortunately, it is not perfectly simple to monetize the VRP and when attempting to do so, other risks may be incurred. If it was possible to directly sell implied volatility while simultaneously buying realized, the returns would be astronomical. Look at it this way—measured monthly from January 1990 through June 2018, the average difference between implied volatility and the realized volatility one month thereafter was 4.1 percent. Over that same time period, the average monthly return posted by the S&P 500 was 0.9 percent. And many people incorrectly assume that the VRP is just amplified equity risk. It isn't. The correlation between the difference between implied and realized volatility and the S&P 500 has been just 16 percent.

But volatility isn't an asset. The VRP exists because of option demand—investors want to buy options, particularly puts, and they are willing to pay a premium to do so. Option prices can be thought of the sum of two things—intrinsic value and premium value. When options are overpriced, and they almost always are, they trade at a premium, which is due to inflated implied

© The Author(s) 2018
M. J. Oyster, *Success in a Low-Return World*,
https://doi.org/10.1007/978-3-319-99855-8_18

volatility pricing in the option. When you buy or sell an option, you do so to both parts—you can't sell just the implied volatility component, you have to sell intrinsic value as well.

Selling options can serve as a means of monetizing the VRP but it isn't a pure one. Buy-write and put-write strategies monetize the VRP but only in part, and they incur equity risk as exhibited by their high correlation to the stock market over time. From January 1990 through June 2018, the PUT was 83 percent correlated to the S&P 500 and the BXM was 87 percent correlated to the stock index over that same period.

Let's look at it in a slightly different way. Is the VRP a *factor*? Is it an *alternative risk premia*? Recall from Chap. 14 how AQR frames this question. To be considered a viable factor, it must demonstrate positive characteristics when tested according to these three things:

- Economic Intuition
- Evidence
- Implementation

There is certainly economic intuition to support the VRP. Drawing from a behavioral desire to avoid the pain of loss, investors willingly overpay for the protection that put options provide and put-call parity keeps the premium priced into calls generally on par with puts. Given that the primary driver of this characteristic is rooted in human behavior, it can be expected to remain structural.

Evidence? Certainly. Implied volatility has exceeded realized volatility 86 percent of the time since 1990 and remains highly consistent. This characteristic has been known for many years, yet it persists unabated almost irrespective of whether absolute volatility is high or low.

The VRP shows well according to the first two characteristics of being a factor. The third is not so easy. Given that an opportunity to directly access the VRP in its purest sense is elusive, we might have to concede, with full intellectual honesty, that it falls just short of being called a factor. But that doesn't mean it shouldn't or can't be monetized into a viable investment strategy.

In 2010, I was observing all the interesting and high Sharpe ratio VRP-monetizing indexes the Cboe was creating and releasing. At the time, I was helping institutional clients allocate investment capital and I was continuously reviewing various types of strategies across the entire spectrum of the investment universe. Gaining equity exposure was easy and straightforward and clients understood it. If I was going to dedicate some of my limited time with clients explaining a strategy they didn't understand well, it would need to be truly differentiated and provide a clear benefit to their portfolio if added. Although my firm's clients held a great deal of exposure in a prominent buy-write strategy, other VRP-focused solutions weren't, at the time, gaining much traction. Although I don't personally believe this, many were dismissed as simply more complicated ways of gaining equity exposure.

With that in mind, I set out to create my own VRP-monetizing strategy—one that had equity-like returns but a lower correlation to the stock market than that which was exhibited by the BXM or PUT and most importantly, strong protection against a catastrophic loss.

Questions Lead to Answers

The modern options market provides the opportunity to construct a wide variety of different strategies. With options, we can form strategies that are malleable, in that their characteristics can be molded in just about any risk/reward direction as we saw with the buy-write strategy in Chap. 16. When seeking a differentiated means of harvesting the VRP, I sought to narrow the focus in hopes of arriving at a viable strategy without testing every possible strategy. When developing what I call the *Options Income Index* (OICX), I asked a series of questions, the answers to which helped guide the development process. The questions I asked and the subsequent answers I concluded are as follows:

1. Should options be used in an investment strategy?

Options are dynamic instruments that can be utilized to increase return, reduce risk, or generate income. The options market has evolved to the point where virtually any return-seeking or hedging position can be constructed through their use. The listed options market is supported by the Options Clearing Corporation (OCC), which acts as a guarantor between clearing parties, ensuring that the obligations of the contracts it clears are fulfilled, thus virtually eliminating all counterparty risk.

2. Should options be bought or sold?

The VRP provides clear and persistent evidence that options, particularly S&P 500 Index options, have been overpriced relative to fair value over time. The most likely cause for the disparity is rooted in human behavior, which suggests that the phenomenon is structural and likely to remain in the future.

3. Why use S&P 500 Index options?

In 2016, average daily volume on S&P 500 Index (SPX) options grew to in excess of one million contracts per day continuing the upward trend that had been in place for many years. Given the massive depth of the market, S&P 500 Index options are generally less likely to be affected by short-term supply/demand imbalances than equity or other index option series making them more effective at providing the desired risk/return position. SPX options are also available at a variety of strike prices, in many cases moving upward and downward away from the underlying index in increments of just 0.2 percent away from the next closest strike. This provides the opportunity to dial in the exposure very precisely to the desired location.

Additionally, S&P 500 Index options are *European* meaning that the owner of these options is not able to exercise them until they expire. In this way, a seller of the options knows that the position they have enacted will remain in place for the life of the option. Most equity options are *American*, making them less favorable for option selling in that they can be exercised at any time up to and including expiration.

SPX options might also provide some tax-friendliness for those investors beholden to the IRS. Under Section 1256 of the US Tax Code, profit and loss on transactions in Cboe's SPX options are entitled to be taxed at a rate equal to 60 percent long-term and 40 percent short-term capital gain or loss, provided that the investor involved and the strategy employed satisfy the criteria of the Tax Code.[1]

4. Should the options sold be in-the-money or out-of-the-money and why?

In the previous chapter, we talked about *delta* where delta is the first derivative of its price with respect to a change in the price of the underlying. For index options, delta measures the sensitivity of an option's price relative to changing index prices.[2] Delta is also often used as an estimate for the probability that an option will, at expiration, end in-the-money. It makes sense then, that in-the-money options usually have higher deltas than out-of-the-money options and the further out-of-the-money they are, the lower the delta. Therefore, the prices of in-the-money options are more affected by market movements than out-of-the-money options. The goal of this strategy is to capture as much of the option price premium as possible while avoiding unwanted market-based volatility, so out-of-the-money options should be used.

5. How far out-of-the-money should the options be sold and why?

Far out-of-the-money options exhibit lower deltas than those closer to the money or in-the-money. The probability of a successful option-selling transaction (when the option expires worthless) is greater the further out-of-the-money the option is sold. With this in mind, options should be sold as far out-of-the-money as possible. However, the furthest out-of-the-money options usually exhibit very low absolute prices with little-to-no premium, so selling them would not allow much of the option price premium to be harvested. These also tend to be thinly traded and their prices can be affected by supply/demand imbalances. So, a compromise must be struck such that options are sold as far out-of-the-money as possible to avoid unwanted delta and to enjoy a high probability of success, but not so far out that virtually no premium would be collected from the sale.

But the devil is in the details. Years ago, I ran an options-selling strategy that placed positions a static percentage out-of-the-money. It worked great, until it didn't. The return profile over long periods of time was very attractive but the strategy experienced a great deal of stress when the stock market was enduring its inevitable bouts with volatility. A far better solution is to allow the prevailing volatility environment to help guide position placement. Unlike other VRP indexes, I chose to incorporate a dynamically adaptive component for the OICX that would be expected to smooth the return stream and limit the correlation to the stock market. It starts with a look at the VIX.

The Cboe Volatility Index (VIX) serves as a proxy for future volatility expectations, and although normally overpriced, it does provide a continuously changing view of the prevailing volatility experienced by the S&P 500 Index. Selling options, regardless of where they are placed, can generate income. Selling options that have a high probability of expiring worthless should lead to consistent income and a reasonably low correlation to the stock market.

The 95 percent confidence interval is often considered the minimum threshold at which a high level of confidence is established. Adding and subtracting two standard deviations both above and below the mean of a normally distributed data set captures 95 percent of the data. Applying this line of thinking to stock market performance where monthly returns on the S&P 500 represent the sample set and the VIX is a proxy for expected volatility, we can mathematically determine the distance out-of-the-money at which the options should be sold such that a 95 percent probability of success can be expected.

The VIX represents the market's expectation for volatility over the next 30 days, but is denoted in annual standard deviation. To estimate what 30-day volatility (v_m) might be, we need to divide the VIX by the square root of 12.

$$v_m = \frac{VIX}{\sqrt{12}} \tag{18.1}$$

We then establish a range with upper and lower bounds in which the S&P 500 Index is expected to end 30 days hence (with 95 percent confidence) by adding and subtracting two-times v_m to the current value of the S&P 500 Index.

$$R_u = S + 2 \cdot v_m \tag{18.2}$$

$$R_1 = S - 2 \cdot v_m \tag{18.3}$$

Where R_u is the upper bound of the range, R_1 is the lower bound of the range, and S is the current value of the S&P 500 Index. This provides us with a range in which the S&P 500 Index is expected to remain for the next 30 days with 95 percent confidence and as such, serves as the point at which options should be sold in hopes of maximizing the collection of the option price premium with as little volatility and stock market influence as possible. When volatility is high, positions are systematically placed further out-of-the-money than when volatility is low. The goal is to generate returns as consistently as possible regardless of the prevailing volatility environment. Now let's move forward with some additional questions.

6. How much time until expiration should be left when the options are sold?

The implied volatility component of an option's price decays until all that remains of an option's value at expiration is its intrinsic value. Early in an option's life, this time decay is gradual, but its pace accelerates as expiration nears. The time decay property of options is also known as *theta*. The closer an option gets to expiration, the less valuable it becomes, other factors being equal. And for many options, the closer it nears expiration, the more quickly its time value decays. This is illustrated in the theta curve shown in Fig. 18.1.

Research from Ibbotson Associates[3] indicates that the expected total premium from writing 12 consecutive at-the-money, one-month calls, is approximately twice the expected premium from writing four consecutive at-the-money, three-month calls, all else being equal. Selling 12 one-month calls generates more premium than selling four three-month calls because doing so means spending more time in the steepest part of the theta curve.

Out-of-the-money options, however, experience time decay more linearly than at-the-money options. Research from Williams and Hoffman[4] indicated that the more out-of-the-money an option gets, the closer its premium decays

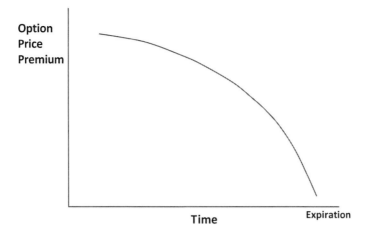

Fig. 18.1 The theta curve: option price premium through time

in straight-line fashion. Since we seek to sell options as far out of the money as possible, does it really matter how much time the option has until expiration? If an option's theta curve was a perfectly straight line, no time until expiration would be superior to any other, but all options experience time decay more quickly as expiration approaches, so they should be sold in advance of the steepest part of that curve to maximize the rate of decay. That means as close to expiration as possible. But always selling options with only a very short period of time until expiration has its drawbacks.

What About Weeklys?

Writing options with the shortest amount of time until expiration maximizes the benefit of selling premium when it is decaying the fastest, but there are issues that arise in actual implementation. Let's look at options that, when sold, are the ultimate collectors of theta curve steepness. As of mid-2018, the Cboe offered listed index options with only one week until expiration called S&P 500 Index weekly settlement options, or *weeklys*.

Selling weeklys have some appeal because with a limited amount of time until expiration, the harvest rate of time decay is greater than those with longer lives. Said another way, weeklys take advantage of the steepest part of the theta curve—the sharp downward slope just prior to expiration. The impact of this is observable in another index—the Cboe One-Week PutWrite Index (WPUT). The WPUT, launched in 2015, is similar to the PUT in that it sells

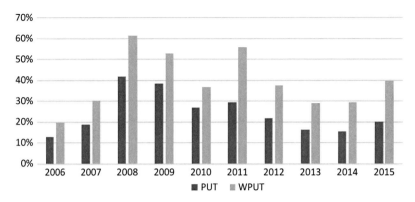

Fig. 18.2 PUT and WPUT aggregate gross premiums received for calendar years 2006–2015

at-the-money puts and is cash collateralized while doing so, but collects option premium *weekly* while the PUT utilizes the sale of the more traditional monthly options.

In 2016, Oleg Bondarenko conducted an analysis of both PUT and WPUT and found that the gross premiums collected from selling a year of weekly options exceeded that of selling a year of monthly options,[5] a result similar to that which was found in the Ibbotson study mentioned previously and is illustrated in Fig. 18.2.

This shouldn't be confused with actual performance of the indexes, it's just the gross premium received on options that were sold. Although premium collected always provided a positive influence on returns, the actual performance of the indexes can certainly be negative at times because they also incur equity risk. What this shows is that all else being equal, greater premium can be received from weeklys versus monthly options. But the Bondarenko paper also included a performance comparison between the two indexes finding the PUT posted a 6.6 percent annual compound return versus 5.6 percent for the WPUT over the course of the study. Why would a put-selling index that receives greater gross premiums underperform one that operates a very similar strategy collecting less gross premiums? I hope you're sitting down because here comes another Greek letter. It has to do with gamma.

In Chap. 17 we pointed out that, among other reasons, delta-hedging out an index option's equity risk can be challenging because the delta can change frequently. The rate at which delta changes per movement in the underlying is known as *gamma*. Gamma can impact options with short times until expiration in important ways. Consider the most extreme example where an option is issued at-the-money with one day until expiration. The theta curve will be exceptionally steep as the price reflects pure premium and that premium will be gone by the end of the trading session. At the same time, gamma will be quite high, meaning that the delta could see massive moves throughout the day. Recall delta is a proxy for the probability that an option will expire in-the-money. Our fictional daily option might start the day with a 50/50 chance of being in-the-money but might quickly move to a much higher probability on a relatively small move in the underlying security. One could imagine how this might eat into a strategy's returns when the prices of high gamma options are whipping around constantly when they are close to expiration as their final value is being determined. Over time, it may even out because the standard deviation of long-term returns is actually lower for WPUT than PUT but masks more performance-eating volatility over shorter periods of time.

Out-of-the-money put options generally see the beginnings of meaningful theta curve steepening at about three months until expiration. Though the steepness is greatest close to expiration, a program of selling options with a severely limited time until expiration brings about other issues that can overwhelm the benefits of such a steep theta curve. In the end, the choice of time until expiration needs to split the difference between three months and one week. I chose one month, which has the added benefit of limited complexity in that a new position could be opened immediately after old positions expire.

7. Should puts, calls, or both be used?

We have talked about how demand for puts has led to higher premium pricing but it isn't just anecdotal. There is solid academic research to back it up. In an important work on the subject, Nicolas Bollen and Robert Whaley (yes, the same professor who created the VIX) considered whether demand, or as they termed it, *buying pressure* affected the shape of implied volatility functions[6] and found that changes in implied volatility are directly related to net buying pressure from public order flow. They also found that changes in implied volatility of S&P 500 options are most strongly affected by buying pressure for index puts. The authors mentioned that institutional investors buy index puts as portfolio insurance and the deep out-of-the-money puts exhibit the highest premium.

Bollen and Whaley grouped options into five categories by delta and found that the difference between implied volatility and realized volatility for deep out-of-the-money puts (those with lower deltas) was 9.58 percentage points, more than any other category. They also found that demand influenced the implied volatility function of both out-of-the-money calls and puts on stocks, but demand for out-of-the-money index calls was far less. One could rationalize this by suggesting that investors will buy insurance contracts (puts) on both stocks and indexes but only lottery tickets (calls) on stocks. The S&P 500 isn't likely to be instantaneously bought out at a substantially higher price like some stock-issuing companies can be.

This strongly suggests that puts should be targeted for sale when seeking to benefit from the option price premium because when attempting to monetize the VRP, we should look where the difference between implied and realized volatility is greatest: in out-of-the-money puts.

8. Should the option position be implemented through a spread or as a naked sale and why?

The seller of an option incurs a liability to buy it back either at or before it expires. Although a substantial move in the index would be required, simply selling a put with no other offsetting positions (naked) could result in a significant loss if the underlying index cascaded lower. The PUT Index sells naked puts but is collateralized in the sense that the cash can finance the maximum possible loss from final settlement of the options. In other words, potential losses from an investment in the PUT would be limited to the total amount invested, even if the S&P 500 fell to zero.

The amount of potential loss from the sale of naked puts necessitates a significant amount of collateral such that the maximum loss can be contained to no more than the invested amount. This limitation requires that most viable, cash-collateralized put-selling strategies sell near-the-money options because those will generate more income than out-of-the-money options. Selling puts can result in losses when the stock market goes down, but generating a substantial amount of income from selling high-priced at-the-money puts can mitigate a portion of that. When selling out-of-the-money puts naked, the delta can start small but grow substantially leading to high potential losses when the stock market declines, and in order to generate a decent return, many out-of-the-money naked put sellers do so without being fully collateralized—aka levered. And that can get messy. So, we want to sell out-of-the-money puts because that is where the VRP is the greatest, but we don't want the stratospheric risk of selling them naked. We can mitigate that conundrum through the use of a spread.

A *spread position* limits losses relative to a *naked sale* of an option where the profits on one side offset losses on the other. Certain kinds of spreads can be enacted such that the largest potential loss is limited to a predetermined, finite amount, regardless of how significantly the underlying index moves. A spread can be constructed so the maximum loss is lower than selling naked options, and out-of-the-money options can be used in a way that generates comparable returns as at-the-money options and do so with a lower correlation to the stock market.

A wide variety of spreads can be initiated to facilitate a certain view, far too numerous to fully explore here. We focus on a bull spread with puts (or a bullish put spread), which provides the desired exposure for the OICX's construction. A bullish put spread is constructed by simultaneously buying one out-of-the money put and selling another out-of-the-money put, where the sold option is closer to the money than the purchased one.

9. How much of the available capital should be allocated?

PUT and BXM are constructed such that 100 percent of the mandate's capital is placed at risk. They aren't levered but they utilize all that is available to them. By contrast, a spread structure can provide for comparable returns while placing far less capital at risk. Additionally, the instantaneous potential maximum loss can be known with absolute certainty at all points in time. There aren't many investments that can say that.

When forming the spread, the distance between the two strikes can be based upon convenience and practicality because the number of contracts used can be tailored to arrive at the desired exposure, almost regardless of how far apart the strikes are. For example, using 30 contracts to initiate a spread that is five points between the sold and owned options will result in a maximum potential loss of $15,000. The same amount of exposure can be achieved by initiating a spread using 15 contracts where the strike prices of the options are ten points apart. In constructing the OICX, I chose 30 percent as the maximum potential loss at any given time. This was based upon my experience advising institutional clients recognizing common limits on what level of loss could be reasonably accepted. Many institutional portfolios are constructed such that the maximum theoretical loss would be between 20 and 25 percent. With the OICX, as an investment that targets equity-like returns, I chose to allow its maximum loss to be slightly greater than the 20 to 25 percent maximum of the total portfolio, but only marginally so.

In this way, the sold put is the one that falls closest to the bottom of the 95 percent probability range. The put that is simultaneously purchased is the one that is the next lowest strike price at that time, and the number of contracts used to form the spread is the amount necessary to deploy 30 percent of available capital such that no more than a 30 percent loss would be experienced regardless of how far the S&P 500 fell until the options expired.

Questions Answered, Now Construction

With answers to nine important questions, we can now construct the index. In doing so, a bull spread with puts is placed out-of-the-money at the bottom of the 95 percent confidence range described earlier and built from options with one month remaining until expiration. The specific spread is enacted such that the maximum possible loss is no more than 30 percent of available capital.

What Can Go Wrong? A Case Study from 2008

Placing the initial spread will result in income as the sold put being closer to the money will almost always be more expensive than the put that is purchased, but a liability remains until the options expire. If the index ended below the sold put at expiration, the seller would be required to settle that transaction for its fair value in cash. Certainly the distance away described by the expected range and the offsetting purchased puts limit the probability and amount of losses, but losses are certainly possible. Here's an example.

At the beginning of a new monthly options cycle on September 19, 2008, the S&P 500 Index closed at 1255.08, with the VIX at 32.07. The bottom of the probability range for a new position added on that day would have been 1025 so a put would have been sold there with an offsetting put purchased at 1000. A few days later on October 7, 2008, the S&P 500 had dropped to 996.23. Had this been an expiration day and with no other action, the loss would have been equal to the total exposure resulting from the spread. If the exposure and resulting loss was 30 percent, many years of more consistent performance would be necessary just to return to pre-loss asset values. Such occurrences, although rare, are significant enough that minimizing the probability that they could occur is critical to the long-term viability of the OICX. Another critical point is this—although the maximum possible loss is always just 30 percent, that is only for one month. Additional risk management is necessary to meaningfully limit the probability that multi-period losses would be endured. The good news is that the index can be constructed to include such risk-reducing tools.

I wanted to create an index that systematically incorporates actions that a disciplined investor might take during periods of stress. An automatically triggered contingency can serve as an important risk-mitigation tool where an all-too-human investor might make a behaviorally influenced error when market intensity shoots up. To stem the catastrophic losses that would be incurred during these rare but inevitable market declines, the OICX is constructed with a contingency plan that will immediately and automatically generate income that can offset losses. The specific means of accomplishing this is described below.

If the S&P 500 ends a day below the top strike of the bullish put spread, that spread will be closed and a new spread will be simultaneously opened based upon the same criteria for construction of a new position described previously. I refer to this contingency as a *reset*.

The first and most important reason a reset is enacted immediately upon the S&P 500 Index closing below the top strike of the spread is to stem the losses and keep a bad situation from becoming abysmal. Continuing the previous example can help illustrate this point.

The spread created by selling a put at 1025 and purchasing a put at 1000 on September 19, 2008, would have netted an approximate credit of $0.68 per contract. This assumes that the sold option was priced 20 percent below the midpoint of the end of day bid/ask spread and the purchased option was priced at 20 percent above the midpoint of the end of day bid/ask spread. Assuming a fictional account of $100,000 with 30 percent of that deployed, this transaction would have generated approximately $813 and is summarized in Table 18.1.

On October 7, 2008, the S&P 500 Index declined precipitously and closed not only below the top strike at 1025 but also below the bottom strike at 1000. Closing the position at the end of the day on October 7 would have resulted in a loss of $15,264, net of the initial $813, which sums to a realized loss of $14,451 or 14.5 percent. Offsetting that entire loss would have been impossible without severely compromising one or more of the OICX's stated construction rules. Describing how the loss could have been fully offset can clarify the point.

The first possibility would have been to enact a new position based upon the standard distance out-of-the-money, but with more than just one month until expiration. Faced with such a significant loss, the required amount of

Table 18.1 Example of fictional account with 30% deployed

	(a)	(b)	(c)			
	Account assets	Sold put strike price	Purchased put strike price	Strike different	Desired exposure	Contracts [(a * 0.3)/ (b − c)]/100
September 19, 2008	$100,000	1025	1000	25	30%	12

time would be significant. The increase in the VIX that occurred while the stock market declined placed the bottom of the expected range all the way down at 690. The only listed options around 690 at that time were at 700 and didn't expire until December 2010. The next lowest strike was 600, so keeping the desired exposure at 30 percent would have allowed only three contracts to be used to create the spread. The resulting income from this spread would have been only $3600—nowhere near enough to cover the nearly $15,000 loss. But then adding insult to injury, that transaction would have prevented any additional income to be generated for nearly 15 months thereafter if deployed capital was limited to 30 percent. To offset the loss completely would have required using 12 contracts but that risk exposure would have been 120 percent of available capital, which would require leverage—something to be avoided in this kind of strategy.

The reality is that whenever the S&P 500 moves outside the probability range, a loss will have to be accepted, but not one so large as to completely destroy the program. We have to live to fight another day. Effective monetization of the VRP is like farming, which is why we sometimes refer to it as *harvesting*. It is a slow and steady process. There aren't any big paydays, and the avoidance of catastrophic loss is critical. Rather than attempting to eliminate all possible losses, the construction methodology of the OICX should trim losses as much as possible then provide for the opportunity to recover. This can be accomplished by prudently, and without behavioral bias, enacting a new position based upon the established rules as soon as the S&P 500 Index ends a day outside of the expected range.

Now back to what the OICX actually did. On October 7, 2008, a new put spread was constructed based upon the established rules placing the top strike at 725 and the bottom strike at 700 with November 2008 expiration options and deploying 30 percent of available capital. This generated $995 of income, which dropped the total loss modestly from $14,451 to $13,456. But that's not the most important thing it did. Enacting that new position provided safety; it increased distance away from the money lowering the probability that a subsequent loss would follow. An opportunity to live to fight another day. Even though the S&P 500 Index continued to decline in the fall of 2008, it did not close below 725 before November expiration. Placing the new spread at the bottom of the expected range based upon the rules described previously provided the opportunity to generate income while allowing the stock market to eventually settle.

In order to effectively harvest the VRP, a balance must be struck between generating income and avoiding losses. Placing spreads close to the money will generate significant income but will result in losses more frequently than positions placed further out-of-the-money. Losses must be accepted, but enduring multiple losses consecutively would be disastrous, so mitigating that risk is critical.

Performance of the OICX

I love the phrase, "you'll never see a bad backtest." It highlights the issues associated with data mining discussed with regard to smart beta strategies in Chap. 14. Reviewing the past performance of a passive, rules-based index is fraught with fewer issues than trying to determine what decisions a human might have made in past situations, but even the construction of an index could potentially be influenced by what had been working up to that point with future returns failing to match the historical ones. I originally developed the OICX in 2010 and measured the returns it would have provided based upon the construction criteria described previously, for an investor from the beginning of 1990 through the end of 2010. The backtested performance was good. But importantly, the out-of-sample data collected since then, without changing anything about the index's construction methodology from its original 2010 form, also showed favorable results, which supports the viability of the index. Let's look at some specifics.

Although the VRP isn't necessarily a factor like those discussed in Chap. 14, it can be instructive to consider how the OICX's performance compares with some of the factors that are commonly drawn upon when forming smart beta portfolios. AQR offers historical data on a variety of factors that form an actual return stream. They do this by sorting stocks that exhibit positively according to a certain factor characteristic from those that exhibit negatively according to that characteristic. They build a portfolio that is long the positive ones and short the negative ones such that the factor is isolated. The performance of that portfolio can be considered the performance of that factor.

The performance of each AQR factor portfolios is net of the risk-free rate. Since the risk-free rate can, of course, provide a risk-free rate of return, they subtract it from the factor's return to better gauge its viability. Figure 18.3 shows the performance of a number of factors along with the BXM, PUT, and the OICX. All three VRP-harvesting indexes are net of the risk-free rate as well.

First we need definitions of each of the factors:

MKT: The US stock market return, net of the risk-free rate.
SMB: *Small minus big*, the factor that suggests small cap stocks will outperform large cap stocks.

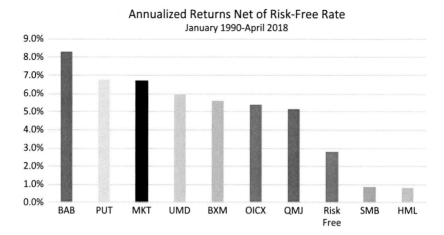

Fig. 18.3 BXM, PUT, and OICX performance

HML: *High minus low*, the factor that suggests high book-to-market stocks (less expensively priced) will outperform low book-to-market stocks (the more expensively priced names).

UMD: *Up minus down*, the momentum factor that suggests stocks with strong recent performance will outperform those with poor recent performance.

BAB: *Betting against beta*, the factor that suggests that due to constraints on leverage, higher beta stocks are more sought after than they otherwise should be, resulting in inflated prices, which allows lower beta stocks to outperform.

QMJ: *Quality minus junk*, the factor that quality companies (those that are profitable, growing, and well managed), outperform their lower quality, junkier counterparts.

Even though this data covers a long period of time, we must always be considerate of end-point sensitivity. BXM, for example, has outperformed the S&P 500 for much of its history but trails over even long-term periods ending mid-2018 because of the uncharacteristically strong period of stock market performance. Conducting an analysis like this at different times may lead to different results. Factors like markets and styles, swing in and out of favor. Even though Rob Arnott and Cliff Asness do not agree on whether trying to time factors is a good idea, they both recognize that factor performance (both absolute and relative) is cyclical.

So what do we see here? Since 1990, betting on beta has been a terrific factor. Some investors who don't have access to leverage seek out ways to juice their stock market exposure by buying high beta stocks. This results in a systematic overpricing relative to lower-beta names that when reverting to fair value over time results in outperformance from those with less equity risk (beta). By contrast, the value (HML) and small cap (SMB) factors have been abysmal.

The OICX is in the middle of the pack with a solid equity-like return. Equity-type investments should be expected to return in excess of 5 percent above the risk-free rate over the long term and the OICX has. But the OICX was designed explicitly for consistency of performance and to limit stock market risk. This means it may trail the S&P 500 during exceptionally favorable stock market times and may be expected to outperform when returns are less favorable. In calendar years since 1990 when the S&P 500 underperformed its average of 11 percent, the OICX outperformed it every year except two and did so by a whopping 9.4 percentage points on average.

So what about risk? Figure 18.4 illustrates the standard deviations of the factors and VRP indexes since 1990.

When viewed together, Figs. 18.3 and 18.4 illustrate the tradeoff between risk and reward. Of all the factors/indexes that exhibited better performance than the OICX since 1990, all but one, PUT, did so through greater variability. Standard deviation is important but investors care about losses more than variability. Figure 18.5 shows the percentage of losing months for each group since 1990.

The OICX lost money less frequently than any other group, making it the most consistent performer. That was one of the primary features upon which its construction was based. What you may be surmising is that with fewer losses but comparable standard deviation to others, it must lose more when it

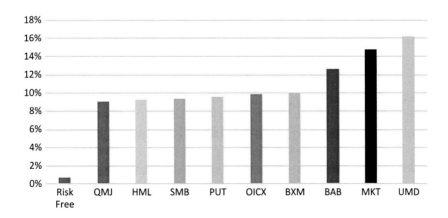

Fig. 18.4 Standard deviation of monthly returns, January 1990–April 2018

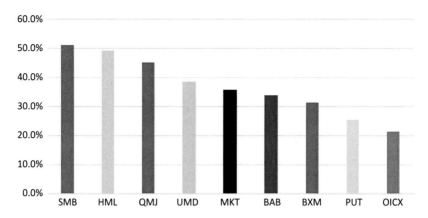

Fig. 18.5 Percentage of losing months, January 1990–April 2018

does happen to lose. That can be true at times. The OICX exhibits a slightly more negative skew than the others, but that is also part of its design. It is a conscious tradeoff. The risk inherent in any return-seeking investment cannot be eliminated, but it can be reconfigured by choice. Which is worse, one 15 percent decline or five 3 percent declines? Some may figure that a single loss can be overcome if it isn't astronomically large because an investor can absorb it and move on thereafter. By contrast, an investment that experiences losses more frequently might lead to frustration and ultimately abandonment of what might otherwise be a good strategy.

The OICX was designed for consistency not perfection. It is not built to never lose money; that is unrealistic. It is built to limit losses to manageable amounts then live to fight another day. Looking at single-month return streams is instructive and skew is an important consideration, but what about losses strung across multiple months?

Maximum or *max drawdown* measures the distance between an investment's peak and its subsequent drawdown. It serves as an effective measure of absolute loss, something most investors consider critically important. Figure 18.6 illustrates the max drawdown of each factor and index from January 1990 to April 2018.

This shows that of all the categories, the OICX experienced the shallowest peak-to-trough decline over the entirety of the data series. The dynamically adaptive strike placement, which is dependent upon volatility regime, as well as the risk-mitigating reset provision (allowing it to fight another day), helped the OICX avoid catastrophic declines that befell the other types of investments—particularly those with a high correlation to the stock market.

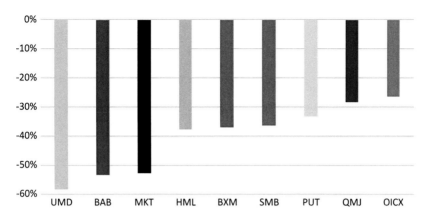

Fig. 18.6 Maximum drawdown, January 1990–April 2018

The S&P 500 experienced two separate declines of over 50 percent (daily data) just since the start of the twenty-first century, but the OICX avoided similarly sized meltdowns as it limited its largest drawdown since 1990 to about half that amount. In 2002 when the S&P 500 was more than 44 percent below its peak (monthly data), the OICX was down just 7.6 percent. In 2008 when the S&P 500 had dropped over 50 percent below its all-time high, the OICX was down just 8.9 percent. As an investor, what do you really care about? The skew statistic calculated from a month-to-month return stream or the actual depth of loss experienced over any period? I suspect most would care more about the latter, and the OICX exhibits strong risk-mitigating properties in that respect.

Conclusion

One of the most prominent themes I hope to convey with this work is to help investors find viable solutions for potential stock market outperformance such that the shortfall could be recovered if the market returns less in the future than it has in the past. A diversified mix of factors in a smart beta strategy stands a good chance of doing so, as does a top quartile private equity fund. But I am exceptionally optimistic about the future for VRP-harvesting strategies such as the BXM and PUT. I also believe the OICX will outperform the S&P 500 in a lower-return world and do so while limiting stock-market risk as well as the risk of a catastrophic loss.

Notes

1. Sourced from Cboe SPX options fact sheet. Investors should consult with their tax advisors to determine how the profit and loss on any particular option strategy will be taxed. Tax laws and regulations change from time to time and may be subject to varying interpretations.
2. Kolb, Robert W., *Futures, Options, & Swaps, Third edition*, Blackwell Publishers Inc., 1999, p. 425.
3. Feldman, Barry and Roy, Dhruv, "Passive Options-based Investment Strategies: The Case of the CBOE S&P 500 BuyWrite Index," Ibbotson Associates, July 28, 2004, p. 20.
4. Williams, Michael and Hoffman, Amy, *Fundamentals of the Options Market*, McGraw-Hill, 2000.
5. Bondarenko, Oleg. "Analysis of Index Option Writing with Monthly and Weekly Rollover," University of Chicago. 2016. 5.
6. Bollen, Nicolas P.B, Whaley Robert E, "Does Net Buying Pressure Affect the Shape of Implied Volatility Functions?" *The Journal of Finance* Vol LIX, No. 2. April 2004.

19

Portable Alpha

As we wrap up the discussion of strategies for potential stock market outperformance, one final concept remains—*portable alpha*.

Many investors are comfortable with the traditional idea where $1 of cash can buy $1 of an investment. Fortunately, opportunities to outperform exist for such investors. But for those with the ability to view the $1 of cash as a tool that can be used to tailor and enhance an investment's risk/return profile, a broader opportunity set for potential outperformance exists.

When many investors hear the word "derivatives" they shift in their seat with discomfort as their brain flashes terrifying images of volatile swings in price fueled by massive leverage that makes casino gambling seem tame by comparison. One problem that many of us who deal in derivatives face, regarding the way our subset of investing is viewed, is that those frightening images are not necessarily fictional. Just about anyone can take a small amount of money and if allocated with *leveraged* exposure when using futures or options, control a much larger amount. If I have $50,000 in cash, I can control $500,000 or more in stock market exposure such that a relatively common 10 percent market move against me can wipe out my entire investment.

But derivatives shouldn't be painted solely with a negative brush. You can think of derivatives like electricity. Yes, you can shock yourself if you aren't careful but when utilized responsibly, an investor can be privy to an entire new world of possibilities. Derivatives can help create highly malleable risk/return profiles, the likes of which will be necessary if simply buying and holding a traditional allocation to long-only equities will leave an investor short of their goals. Portable alpha offers one method for drawing upon derivatives to tap into the greater potential that certain investment resources can provide.

© The Author(s) 2018
M. J. Oyster, *Success in a Low-Return World*,
https://doi.org/10.1007/978-3-319-99855-8_19

Portable alpha describes the idea of using a derivative instrument to secure a core allocation, then deploying excess cash to a different area, the profits from which can then be brought back and added to the original investment. *Alpha* is a term loosely used to mean outperformance, and *portable* just means that the alpha can be made in one investment then brought over to another.

A derivative security can be used to gain an allocation to a certain kind of market exposure in a desired amount. In this case, we will be talking about an equity position, the most common of which is large cap domestic equities, which can be replicated with S&P 500 Index futures. An example can help clarify.

If I have $700,000 that needs to be put to work in a stock market mandate, I could buy the necessary number of shares in an actively managed large-cap mutual fund, a smart beta fund, an index fund, or a bunch of individual stocks. But I could also use a futures contract. Investors don't really *buy* futures contracts. Instead, they go long hoping the price goes up or short expecting a decline. One S&P 500 Index futures contract provides the holder with S&P 500 Index exposure in the amount of $250 times the index. In mid-2018 with the S&P 500 at around 2800, that worked out to controlling a $700,000 position in the index per contract (2800 × $250).

Investors who utilize futures contracts are required to maintain margin accounts, which act as a buffer against potential losses. But the amount that must be held on margin can be a small fraction of the total mandate size. For example, in mid-2018 to maintain control of $700,000 of stock market exposure, an S&P 500 Index futures investor's margin account would need to hold only $28,000—just 4 percent of the total mandate size. For practical reasons, however, a larger amount would be needed because an adverse move in the index, even if it was small, would require additional money to be added to the margin account, topping it back up to at least the minimum. When this happens, it is known as a *margin call*. So to avoid constant margin calls, let's imagine a margin account that held not 4 percent but a larger buffer of 10 percent of the mandate size, in this case, $70,000.

The theory that forms the foundation portable alpha is as follows—if I only need to hold $70,000 in a margin account to secure my full equity mandate size of $700,000, I can use the remaining $630,000 to invest in something else. If the something else earns a profit, I can *port* it back to be included with the futures contract as part of the broader equity mandate. The combination of the futures contract that matches the market with something that posts a positive return results in market outperformance. It is a terrific concept, but a few important things are worth watching out for.

Leverage

Many investors find the concept of leverage, controlling more market exposure than mandate size, nothing short of revolting. They surmise that it has no place in investing in any form. That is puzzling because if human society shunned leverage in the physical sense (levers, pullies, etc.), we would not have any of the infrastructure we have today. It is like saying, "No, we can't build that building because I can't lift the steel I-beam by hand." Why then the aversion to leverage in investing? If we could get to the heart of some people's aversion to leverage, we would probably find that it isn't the concept itself that is revolting, it is what is being levered and how much, and rather than ask hard questions or learn new concepts, it is easier to dismiss the idea out of hand and move on.

Leverage isn't necessarily a dangerous thing, but it can be, and portable alpha offers a fertile ground for bad behavior with leverage. Prior to the Great Financial Crisis (GFC), many portable alpha strategies were designed with a futures or swap contract (more on this later) representing 100 percent of the mandate size then a substantial allocation to a hedge fund, the returns of which were ported back for a combined allocation. A question worth asking is, "Does that represent a levered portfolio?" On the one hand, the answer is an obvious yes. When $100 worth of investment assets control more than $100 of investment exposure, that's leverage. "But on the other hand," the pre-crisis portable alpha proponents might say, "an investor shouldn't care about leverage in that sense because historically, the hedge fund used as the source of alpha has had virtually no correlation to the stock market." Therein lies the risk. Leverage in this case isn't the problem; the problem is what is being levered. By suggesting that this obviously levered position has no more risk than the stock market itself is simply not true and many investors learned that the hard way.

Portable alpha can be thought of as a mini portfolio, which should be comprised of different kinds of investments, each with their own unique risks. This is what *Modern Portfolio Theory* is all about—a portfolio's risk-adjusted returns can be improved by the addition of something different and in some cases, even if that something different is riskier than the portfolio itself. The key word here is *different* because it needs to be truly different. Siloed. Idiosyncratic. A leg supporting a broader table with no connection to any other legs. And correlation of past performance can't always help determine differences. In either a portfolio sense or in a portable alpha strategy, diversification, that is, the components behaving differently from one another, only really matters during periods of stress. Long periods of low correlation can often mask hidden connections between asset categories that show up when times get tough. And unfortunately, that is exactly when the components *need* to behave differently. All of this is to say that the alpha portion of a portable alpha strategy should look very different from the core component to which the alpha is being ported. *Leverage* might not mean *outsized risk* if the over-100 percent exposures are held in truly different things, but an allocation of more than 100 percent equity risk is dangerous.

So, what's the one investment that is truly different than the stock market? The risk-free rate, which has provided a return of about 2.8 percent annualized from 1990 through June 2018. It exhibits virtually no correlation to the stock market even during stressful times and almost always provides a positive return. If an investor could get 100 percent of their equity exposure with only 10 percent of their mandate size and then invest the remaining 90 percent in the risk-free rate, they could have outperformed the stock market by about 2.5 percentage points annualized since 1990. Alas, if it were only so easy.

The Costs

As you might have guessed, this strategy is not as simple as it seems. Replicating a stock market index with futures isn't free. Making the trades cost money, but it usually constitutes a small percentage of the total investment. The bigger cost is the cost of carry.

The Cost of Carry

A *cost of carry* is imbedded in a futures contract. One way to think about it is considering what it might cost to store a commodity like grain. If I go long a grain futures contract, I agree to buy a certain amount of grain at some point in the future. Until I take delivery of that grain when the contract expires, it has to be stored somewhere, which costs money—a cost that I bear in the inherent pricing of the grain futures contract. In many cases, the futures contract will be higher priced than the underlying spot because it includes a kind of a convenience fee for being able to accrue price changes of a commodity without actually having to bother with the commodity itself.

It is the same thing with S&P 500 futures contracts, only the cost of carry is less, because storing electronic money doesn't require a warehouse or a silo. The cost is an opportunity cost, which comes in the form of a lower return on investment because the money could otherwise be loaned out. In the case of S&P 500 Index futures, the cost is often proxied by the Intercontinental Exchange London Interbank Offered Rate (ICE LIBOR). LIBOR is a short-term interest rate on money that banks loan each other so it represents a good estimate of the opportunity cost. At its essence, a stock index futures contract should be priced at what it would cost to buy and carry an equity portfolio that reflects the value of the index itself. To build such a portfolio, money must be used, which could be making a return on investment elsewhere.

On the other side, the owner of a futures contract does not gain the benefit of dividends that the holder of the stock portfolio would, so the price has to be adjusted for that as well. In the end, the fair value of a futures contract starts with the price of the spot index, is adjusted higher for the opportunity cost that would be sacrificed if the money was used to buy stocks, and then adjusted downward for the fact that the futures contract holder won't receive any dividends. The formula below spells it out.

$$FV\,futures = Spot + Financing - Dividends$$
$$= Spot \times \left[1 + R\left(days / 360\right)\right] - Dividends$$

Where R is the prevailing short-term rate such as ICE LIBOR. Notice that the R is on the opposite side of the equation from the futures contract's fair value (FV). LIBOR is usually higher than the risk-free rate (short-term US government debt) because although low, there is a risk that one bank might not pay back another while the US government could just print more dollars to satisfy a loan. At the end of a futures contract's life, it will equal the spot price but will frequently exceed the spot prior to that point. If that is the case, a loss will be incurred every month as an investment rolls from one month to the next. It's like a water bucket with a hole in the bottom. Even when accounting for dividends, a portable alpha strategy constructed with S&P 500 Index futures and the risk-free rate would likely underperform the stock market over time.

But that's certainly not the end of the story. Portable alpha can serve as a highly viable investment strategy, we just have to get a little creative and maybe make some compromises. Risk can't be eliminated, but it can be changed, redirected, or molded into something different that can provide an alternate risk/return profile that offers the potential for stock market outperformance. One example is this—how might a portable alpha strategy derived from US equity futures and core fixed income have fared over time?

Creative Portable Alpha

Let's start with the S&P 500 replicated with futures plus a porting of the risk-free rate. Since we know such a strategy will lose money relative to the index, let's look at taking a bit more risk, first by staying within fixed income but moving modestly out the risk spectrum. Although not risk free, the *Bloomberg Barclays US Aggregate Bond Index* (AGG) has historically exhibited a low correlation to the US stock market and limited maximum drawdowns. As such, it might serve as a reasonable source of alpha for a portable alpha strategy.

We begin by combining S&P 500 futures, through a continuous contract,[1] with an investment in the AGG. If we assume we will hold 10 percent of the mandate size in a margin account, we add the futures contract's return to 0.9 times the AGG's return. Looking at data since April 1982, Table 19.1 shows performance and risk of this portable alpha solution as compared to the S&P 500 Index.

Although transaction costs and fees are not included, we can still claim that a portable alpha solution created this way could have provided a terrific source of outperformance. But it did so while taking greater risk as shown in the higher standard deviation. Although the AGG isn't very risky, this portable alpha combination is a levered creation and as such, potentially subject to greater-than-unlevered stock market risk. The correlation between the S&P 500 futures and the AGG was only 18 percent so the AGG's addition, in a very *Modern Portfolio Theory* sort of way, improved risk-adjusted returns relative to the stock index futures alone.

But it is riskier in an absolute sense. Perhaps a more important measure of risk, however, is maximum drawdown. Over the period in question, the maximum drawdown of the portable alpha solution and the S&P 500 was virtually the same. So you might say this portable alpha solution offers the potential for market outperformance for a comparable maximum, "worst case" risk, but might prove more volatile along the way. We should keep in mind that interest rates experienced a steady decline during the period in question, which supported the performance of the AGG. How such a strategy might perform in a rising rate environment remains to be seen.

Table 19.1 Performance and risk: portable alpha solution versus S&P 500 index

Monthly data	Portable alpha	
April 1982–May 2018	With AGG	S&P 500
Return	16.4%	11.9%
Standard Deviation	16.1%	14.7%
Correlation with SPX	96.5%	–
Maximum Drawdown	−50.3%	−50.9%

Portable Alpha with Less Liquid Alphas

Prior to 2008, quite a few portable alpha solutions were created by combining equity exposure with hedge funds. Up to that point, the better hedge funds almost never lost money, which made them great candidates for the alpha in a portable alpha strategy. But after portable alpha investors felt the pinch of both the equity and hedge fund positions declining at the same time, the concept faded from favor. Which is why the point is worth making again—portable alpha is a terrific strategy, but the alpha *absolutely* has to be different than what it is being ported back to, and the risk that it could lose money during periods of stress for the core position (like a stock market decline) needs to be nothing more than *de minimis*.

Not all hedge funds lost money in 2008 and some have strung together amazingly consistent track records through the years. The best ones charge high fees and are either impossible to access, are unflinching in the face of the fee compression that has spread across the whole of the hedge fund universe, or both. By 2018, hedge funds had come under intense pressure as the performance of many failed to live up to expectations. But beyond tepid performance, perhaps a less obvious reason hedge funds fell out of favor is the growth of factor-based strategies that have cut into hedge fund turf. Smart investors recognized that much of the differentiated performance that hedge funds had provided (for 2 percent management fee and 20 percent incentive) could be had by investing in factors for a fraction of the price. There is a saying for this—alpha is just beta that someone hasn't discovered yet. So can we use a factor or some combination of factors as the source of alpha in a portable alpha strategy? Yes, but before we illustrate how, let's first talk about *swaps*.

Swaps

Futures contracts are liquid, and being so can have its merits but drawbacks as well. When an S&P 500 futures contract moves up or down, the margin account increases or decreases. Given a loss of large enough size, the margin account will fall below its maintenance margin resulting in a margin call requiring new cash to be added before the holder can again begin accruing moves in the contract's value. To date we have talked about liquid sources of alpha that could be quickly sold to provide funds for the margin account as needed. But what if the alpha has liquidity constraints like most hedge funds? Theoretically the funds could be sourced from another location in a broader portfolio, but that might result in a misalignment where risk exposures are moved outside their intended targets. Swaps can help solve this problem.

In an equity swap contract, two parties swap the return of an index in exchange for some fixed rate of return like ICE LIBOR plus a spread and/or fee. This can achieve the rate of return from the index, just like a futures contract, but without daily marking to market. Conceivably, a swap agreement could be made in which the party receiving the index's rate of return wouldn't need to put up anything out of pocket and could invest the entire investment in an alpha source. Because the swap contract isn't marked to market every day like a futures contract, the alpha investment wouldn't need to be withdrawn until the swap agreement matured.

The problem? An investor needs a substantial amount of capital to enter into an agreement with a swaps dealer. And then there's the *counterparty risk*, that the holder of one side of the swap isn't able to pay. Any investor entering into the long-stock-market side of a swap would almost certainly require an immense amount of assets and a high level of sophistication for another party to take the other side. It might be tough to come up with the equity side of a swap after a substantial stock market decline that has priced down an investment portfolio as a whole. A counterparty would need great confidence that the equity side's holder could pay if they had to.

Factor Portable Alpha

In Chap. 18 we looked at the performance of several factors that were constructed from long and short stock positions based upon a particular characteristic. They exhibited various levels of return and risk, and they all behaved at least somewhat differently. Figure 19.1 shows the various correlations of these factors relative to the US stock market.

Four of the five factors here exhibited negative correlation to the stock market. That guarantees nothing but hints strongly at the potential for a viable source of alpha in a portable alpha strategy—particularly if the inverse correlation occurred with a positive absolute return. *Quality minus junk* (QMJ) showed the most negative correlation with the S&P 500. Let's look at how combining it with an S&P 500 Index futures contract to form a portable alpha strategy might have performed relative to the stock market itself in Table 19.2.

These results are encouraging. Again, no fees or transaction costs are included here but the relative performance of a portable alpha strategy combined with the QMJ factor could have outperformed the S&P 500 by over three percentage points annualized since the beginning of 1990 and did so with substantially lower standard deviation. Notice also the maximum drawdown—nearly half that of the S&P 500 at just 28.2 percent.

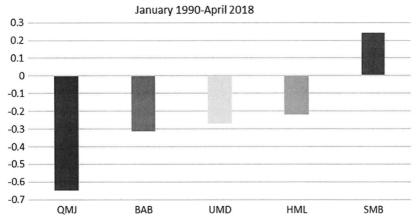

Fig. 19.1 Correlation with the S&P 500 index

Table 19.2 Portable alpha strategy in combination with QMJ factor

Monthly data	Portable Alpha	
January 1990–May 2018	With QMJ	S&P 500
Return	13.1%	9.7%
Standard Deviation	11.9%	14.2%
Correlation w/SPX	81.9%	–
Maximum Drawdown	−28.2%	−50.9%

Can these results be achieved in the future? No one knows for certain, but QMJ as the alpha source in a portable alpha strategy shows potential. Usually during periods of market stress, the quality names hold up better than those less stable companies. In 2008 when the S&P 500 Index was down 37 percent, QMJ was up 33 percent. In 2002 when the S&P 500 Index was down 22 percent, QMJ was up 22 percent. And even though it was more than 64 percent negatively correlated to the rising stock market since 1990, it posted positive absolute returns of more than five percentage points in excess of the risk-free rate.

One final but critical point here—this only works if the factor is constructed from going long high-quality stocks and short low-quality stocks. Some investible "quality" factor portfolios are simply a conglomeration of high-quality names, no shorting of the lower-quality companies. The factor may outperform the market over time but will exhibit a high correlation to the market itself, which would make it a poor alpha choice in a portable alpha strategy.

Almost every stock, even the high-quality ones, can be affected by movements in the market as a whole. QMJ may not produce positive returns all the time, and in fact it was in the red about 45 percent of the time since 1990. But it, along with several other uncorrelated factors, shows the potential to add value over time and more importantly, do so during periods of market stress making it a terrific candidate for a portable alpha strategy.

Volatility-Based Strategies

Certain factors can provide alpha for a portable alpha strategy. So too can strategies that draw upon volatility as their source of return.

There is a great deal of misunderstanding surrounding volatility-based strategies and many investors choose to bike shed them all into one big group. This is not just short-sighted, it is potentially dangerous given the highly varied risks that different volatility strategies take on, and certainly the magnitude as well. But it is not surprising. Years ago, and despite vast differences in strategy and risk, many investors lumped all hedge funds into the same bucket. And let's face it, many still do, but database and index provider HFR helped provide clarity by parsing hedge funds into relative value, event-driven, global macro, and other categories, which are now more commonly understood and accepted subcategory delineations. I expect volatility-based investment strategies will experience a similar evolution, and if it comes to pass, the Cboe and Eurekahedge should garner much of the praise.

Eurekahedge stakes claim to the world's largest hedge fund database. They teamed up with the Cboe to form four volatility-oriented indexes that can serve as classifications, each comprised of equal weightings to hedge funds that can be considered aligned with one of the four volatility styles. The four benchmarks, and a definition of each, are as follows[2]:

- *Cboe Eurekahedge Short Volatility Index*: The *short volatility index* is an equally weighted index of constituent funds designed to provide a broad measure of the performance of underlying hedge fund managers who take a net short view on implied volatility with a goal of positive absolute return. The strategy often involves the selling of options to take advantage of the discrepancies in current implied volatility versus expectations of subsequent implied or realized volatility.
- *Cboe Eurekahedge Long Volatility Index*: The *long volatility index* is an equally weighted index of constituent funds designed to provide a broad measure of the performance of underlying hedge fund managers who take a net long view on implied volatility with a goal of positive absolute return.

- *Cboe Eurekahedge Relative Value Volatility Index*: The *relative value volatility index* is an equally weighted index of constituent funds designed to provide a broad measure of the performance of underlying hedge fund managers that trade relative value or opportunistic volatility strategies. Managers utilizing the strategy can pursue long, short, or neutral views on volatility with a goal of positive absolute return.
- *Cboe Eurekahedge Tail Risk Index*: The *tail risk index* is an equally weighted index of constituent funds designed to provide a broad measure of the performance of underlying hedge fund managers that specifically seek to achieve capital appreciation during periods of extreme market stress.

With these indexes in place, and performance data readily available, researchers can be more thoughtful about how they position volatility-based strategies in their investment portfolios. Let's look at historical performance to get a sense of each in Table 19.3.

Data here is from January 2005 through May 2018, except for the Tail Risk Index, which began in January 2008. What stands out right away is the poor performance of tail risk strategies, which makes sense. Many tail risk funds buy out-of-the-money puts, which we know stand to lose money over time because those puts are consistently and vastly overpriced. But volatility strategies come in a variety of flavors. Leading up to mid-2018, volatility had been mostly low save a spike in February 2018, so the positive absolute return posted by the Long Volatility Index, with considerably lower standard deviation than the S&P 500, is worth noting.

Over the period in question, the Relative Value Index outperformed the S&P 500 Index with a fraction of the variability. These include strategies managed by some very smart people who can unlock value from volatility and do so with very little stock market risk. Additionally, the Short Volatility Index too had posted equity-like returns with far less volatility. What you may be thinking is, "Hey wait a minute, didn't short volatility strategies blow up in February 2018?" The Cboe Eurekahedge Indexes are comprised of hedge

Table 19.3 Historical performance Cboe Eurekahedge indexes

Cboe Eurekahedge Volatility Indexes	Return	Standard Deviation	Correlation to S&P 500
Long volatility	4.3%	6.3%	−28.3%
Relative value	8.8%	3.7%	19.2%
Short volatility	7.8%	8.3%	49.6%
Tail risk	−5.3%	12.0%	−43.8%
S&P 500 index	8.4%	13.7%	100.0%

funds, not ETFs or mutual funds. The short volatility ETFs that lost upwards of 90 percent of their value in early 2018 represent one of the most ignorant investments in history, and there have been plenty. I can only surmise that investors in those products never actually looked at a graph of the VIX before they chose to short it. Such unbridled stupidity can cast all volatility strategies in a poor light, which is unfortunate. And sadly, news organizations and many investors incorrectly co-classified vastly different volatility-based strategies together following the February 2018 meltdown, an event that was limited to only a small number of bad actors. Much work remains before an awareness of differences in volatility-based strategies is common among the investing public. But we'll get there.

Portable Alpha Using Volatility

QMJ's positive absolute return combined with a negative correlation to the stock market makes it a tremendous candidate for the alpha in a portable alpha strategy. The Cboe Eurekahedge Long Volatility Index exhibits a similar profile. Let's look at how it could have fared in a similar role in Table 19.4.

These results are encouraging as well. A portable alpha strategy derived from an investment in S&P 500 Index futures and the Cboe Eurekahedge Long Volatility Index (LV) would have outperformed the S&P 500 with less variability. Although the LV had a negative correlation with the stock market, the portable alpha combination exhibited a high correlation to the S&P 500, emblematic of the dominance of equity risk observed in other situations we have discussed previously. But notice also the maximum drawdown—just 30.9 percent when the S&P 500 was down over 50 percent from its all-time high. When the stock index was down 37 percent in 2008, the portable alpha with LV dropped just 13 percent. LV's tempering of downside risk while providing a source of positive alpha over time makes it a tremendous candidate for alpha in a portable alpha strategy. Of course, a direct investment in the

Table 19.4 Portable alpha with long volatility index versus S&P 500 index

Monthly data	Portable Alpha	
January 2005–May 2018	With LV[a]	S&P 500
Return	10.5%	8.4%
Standard Deviation	13.3%	13.7%
Correlation w/SPX	91.1%	–
Maximum Drawdown	−30.9%	−50.9%

[a]Cboe Eurekahedge Relative Value Index

Cboe Eurekahedge Long Volatility Index, or any index for that matter, is not possible, but seeking a manager (or multiple managers) that has those characteristics and can fill that role may provide the solution.

The advent of well-defined volatility indexes can help raise the awareness of some highly viable strategies and make them easier to use as they find their proper place in a broader portfolio. They represent an important first step, but they aren't perfect. The PUT, which is clearly a short-volatility strategy, has only a 58 percent correlation to the Short Volatility Index. And not all strategies will fit neatly into one of the four boxes. The OICX, for example, is a strategy constructed with characteristics that make it part short volatility and part relative value. Its correlation to the Short Volatility Index is 54 percent and 32 percent to Relative Value, so positively correlated but not highly so. The OICX is negatively correlated to Long Volatility and Tail Risk.

Not all volatility-based strategies are created equal. Investors who know the difference and can utilize their attributes provide themselves with an additional tool to potentially help them achieve outperformance.

Conclusion

In a low-return world, anything that consistently enhances return can help investors reach their goals. The chances of gaining this outperformance through the use of active managers are slim and getting slimmer. In the future, market participants will need to rely on new ideas that provide return as efficiently as possible. The tools that can do so exist today and will prove invaluable to those who know how to use them. Portable alpha investments made in the years prior to 2008 had, in some cases, disastrous results that soured many on the concept, but the idea is solid if implemented properly. Portable alpha offers one of the most opportune means by which stock market outperformance can be achieved—a critical goal in a low-return world.

Notes

1. S&P 500 Futures, Continuous Contract #1 (SP1) (Front Month) Data source: Quandl.com. Nonadjusted price based on spot-month continuous contract calculations. Raw data from CME.
2. Cboe.com.

20

Epilogue

I love the phrase attributed to Mark Twain: "It ain't what you don't know that gets you into trouble. It's what you know for sure that just ain't so." *The New Republic* points out[1] that this quote, which was used at the opening of the movie *The Big Short*, was never actually said or written by Twain. Michael Lewis' book of the same name starts out with a similar quote; this one can be ascribed to an actual individual, in this case, Leo Tolstoy in *The Kingdom of God is Within You*.

> *The most difficult subjects can be explained to the most slow-witted man if he has not formed any idea of them already; but the simplest thing cannot be made clear to the most intelligent man if he is firmly persuaded that he knows already, without a shadow of a doubt, what is laid before him.*

Anchoring is a strong cognitive bias. But perhaps no other concept is more important in investing today than recognizing that old ways of thinking may need to be disgarded in favor of new and different ideas in order to achieve investment goals in the years to come.

Doubtless, many investors "know for sure" that the stock market ascent enjoyed since early 2009 will continue unabated. Such sentiment would not be without historical precedent. The 1920s, the 1990s, the first few years of the twenty-first century were all periods of tremendous returns sweeping investors up in waves of optimistic enthusiasm that were then followed by abysmal stock market performance in the years thereafter punctuated by disastrous crashes along the way. I hope I'm wrong. I hope technology, demographic demand from emerging markets, and fiscal and monetary policy all work together to keep the stock market booming.

© The Author(s) 2018
M. J. Oyster, *Success in a Low-Return World*,
https://doi.org/10.1007/978-3-319-99855-8_20

What will be missing regardless is the protracted decline in interest rates that started in the early 1980s and supported one of the most favorable environments for stocks in the history of investing. After cresting in 1981 when short-term interest rates were in the upper teens, rates fell for the next 37 years accelerated by the unconventional bond-buying program known as *quantitative easing* (QE) that squashed rates to zero and rocketed stock indexes well into all-time-high rarefied air. Five-year stock market returns in the 37 years that followed the 1981 peak in rates were five percentage points more likely to post double-digit returns than the 37 years preceding the high mark in rates.

If interest rates rose quickly from mid-2018 levels, stock performance would almost certainly suffer. Even if rates remained stagnant (and there is good reason to believe this will be the case) the absence of a *duration tailwind* should further limit expectations for stock market returns. Over really long periods of time, stocks should earn about five percentage points above the risk-free rate, but they don't have to. And they frequently haven't after starting at elevated price multiples, which in mid-2018, they were.

So a shortfall in returns may need to be made up, but traditional means might prove insufficient. An investor who believes that a stock-picking mutual fund will outperform year after year because it has done so in the past may find that investment falling short. This is not to say that the professionals who select stocks in hopes of outperforming the market should not do what they do or none of them will ever outperform. It is just to point out how challenging their world has become so realistic expectations are in order.

The large cap US stock market exhibits as much or more efficiency than any market in the world, meaning that information is quickly, completely, and equally disseminated into the hands of any market participant who wants it. After regulations leveled the playing field for everyone, professionals saw many of their trusted tools for outperformance taken away. And although the Benjamin Graham method of fundamental analysis remains brilliant decades after it was first described, it became diluted due to overuse. If an idea is great enough, it will eventually see its impact diminished if an overwhelming amount of assets flow to it. History is replete with examples of tremendous concepts failing to survive discovery.

Until machines armed with artificial intelligence are making all the investment decisions, human behavior will play a role, which can be a blessing or a curse. Common cognitive biases can inhibit our performance when emotions overwhelm rational thought, while intuition can serve as a complement to strictly data-driven decision making. If something feels wrong, it very well may be.

Even if the stock market performance of the future fails to match the rosy returns of the recent past, investment goals can still be achieved. A passive allocation to a low-cost index fund can be a great idea. Even a few basis points saved is money earned and every penny will count in a low-return world. That and indexing the large cap domestic equity market has outperformed most active managers over time. An index fund can serve as a core position for even the most sophisticated investor. But we don't have to stop there. Active managers that demonstrate substantial conviction by building high active share portfolios with long holding periods may deliver better after-fee returns than their closet-indexing counterparts. And although the massive amount of money that needs to be put to work is unsettling, pockets of private equity may serve an investment portfolio well. Manager selection is more important in private equity than almost any other area because the difference between the top performers and the bottom dwellers has been vast and there is no reason that won't be the case in the future as well. Smart beta strategies too can improve performance relative to a passive, cap-weighted index alone, but they are cyclical and could be diluted by overwhelming asset inflows.

At the portfolio level, asset allocation can drive performance and make the difference between success and failure. Smart investors draw upon the advantages they hold. For those with the wherewithal to do so, forgoing some liquidity to access investments with better potential performance than their public market equivalents can meaningfully enhance performance. Diversification is critical and doing so by spreading risk across multiple types can lead to more stability in performance and limited maximum drawdowns relative to portfolios more highly concentrated in a single risk (like equities). If value can't be added through subcategory asset allocation, focus all the attention on manager selection. For those who do engage in active asset allocation, tracking each categories' recent performance to help distinguish between those with strong or poor momentum can enhance performance.

Finally, the Volatility Risk Premium offers a tremendous untapped basis for investment performance and can be accessed in a variety of different ways including buy-write, cash-secured put selling or through a spread such as that utilized by the OCIX. The derivatives markets can appear daunting and navigating them should be done with care, but the potential to craft specifically defined risk/return profiles and maximize the ability of investment resources, such as with portable alpha, creates a fertile ground on which outperforming strategies can grow.

I'm optimistic about the future. If stock market returns fall short of long-term averages and most stock pickers still fail to keep up, many investors may fail to reach their goals. But they don't have to. What's required is some healthy objectivity regarding the stock market and for those seeking to outperform it, an understanding of how our behavior can inhibit decision making, and a willingness to think differently by letting go of preconceived notions. The tools for outperformance are there, and opportunities abound, even in a low-return world.

Note

1. Alex Shephard, "Minutes, News and Notes," TheNewRepublic.com. 2015.

Index[1]

---

[1] Note: Page numbers followed by 'n' refer to notes.